NAOMI...

WHEN I SAW HER FOR THE FIRST TIME I WAS IMPRESSED NOT ONLY BY HER BEAUTY AND ELEGANCE, BUT ALSO BY HER DETERMINATION TO CONQUER THE WORLD. EACH TIME I WORK WITH HER SHE CONQUERS MY HEART AND CAMERA. SHE IS ONE OF A KIND.

ELLEN VON UNWERTH

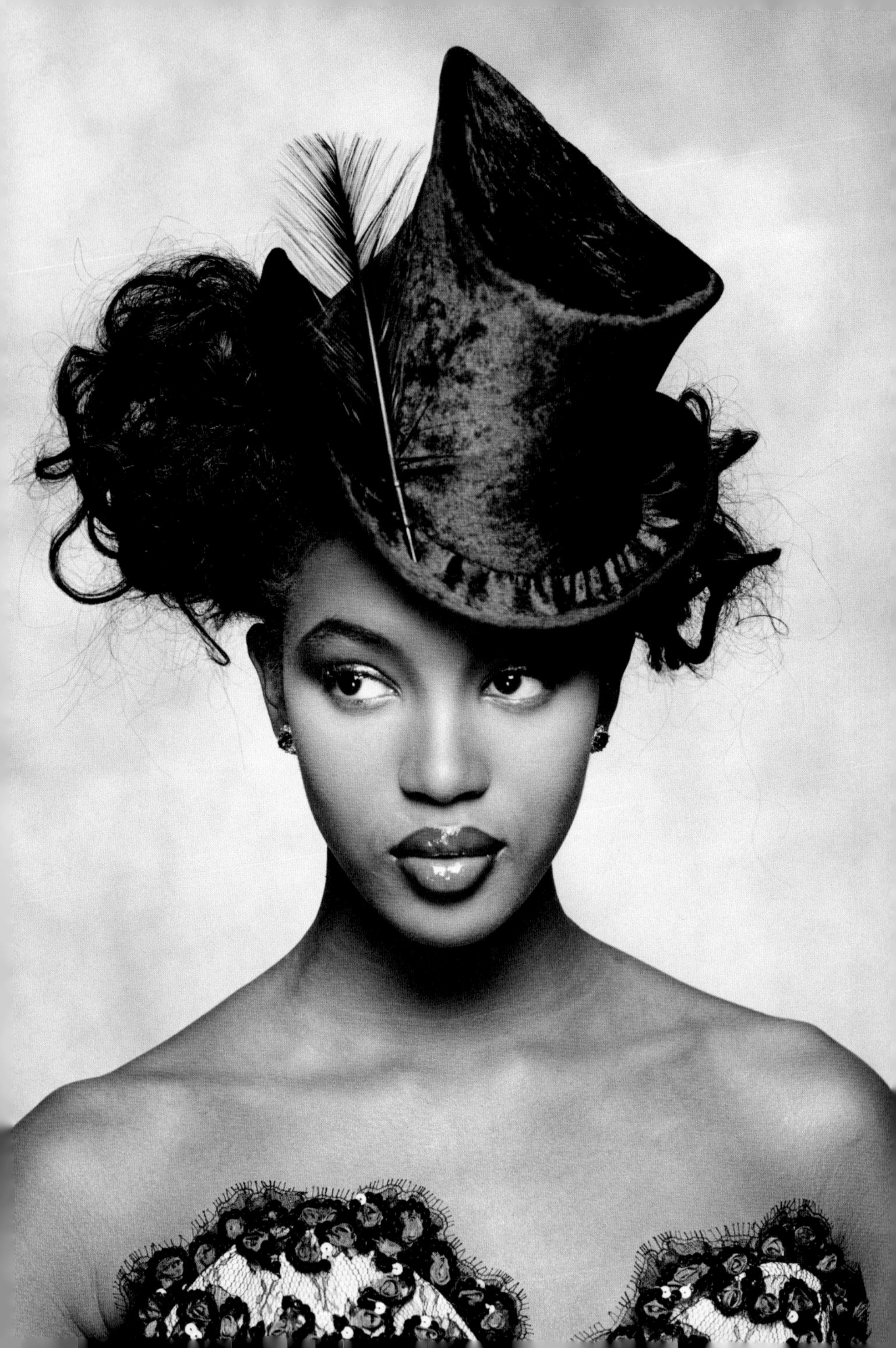

NAOMI

TASCHEN

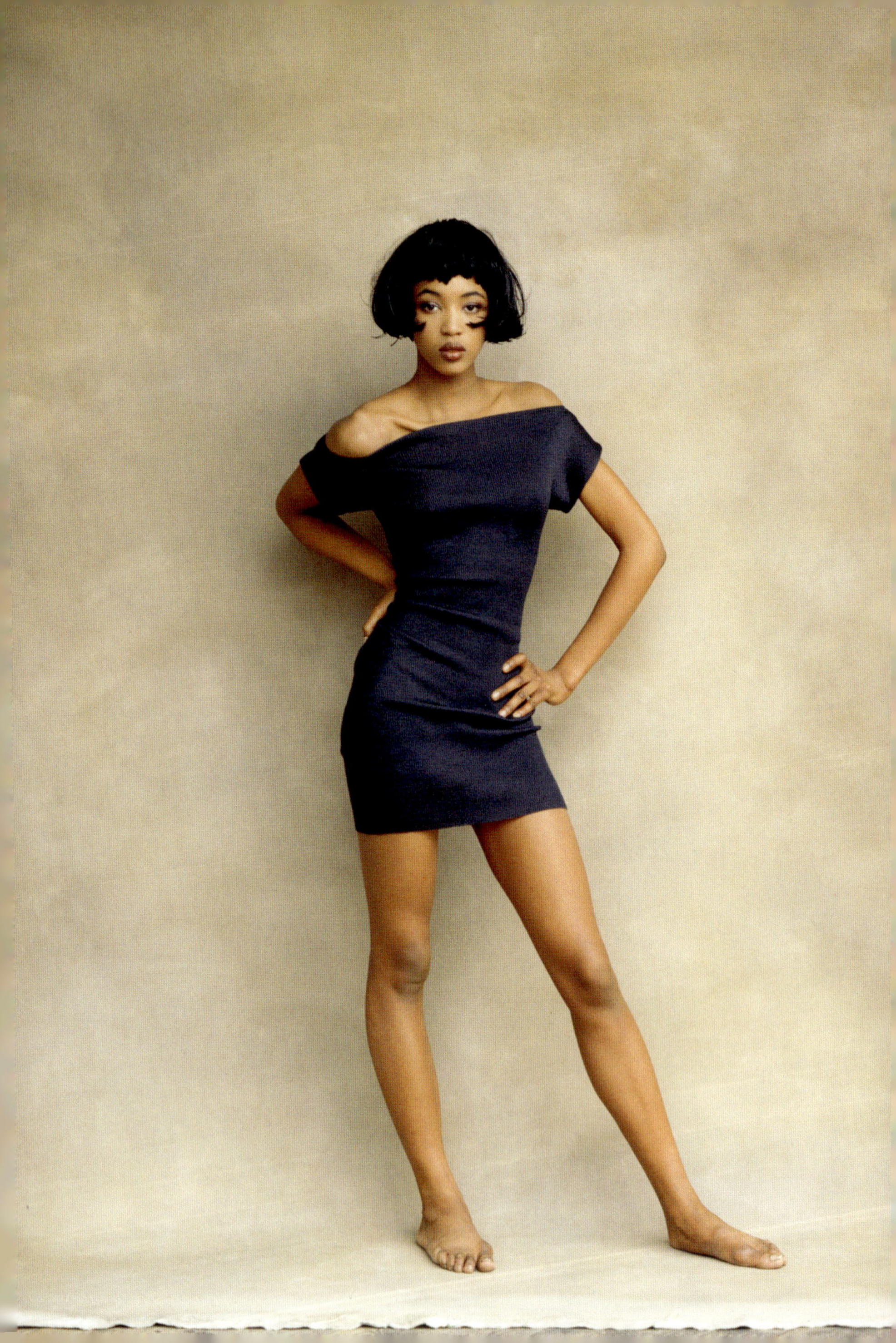

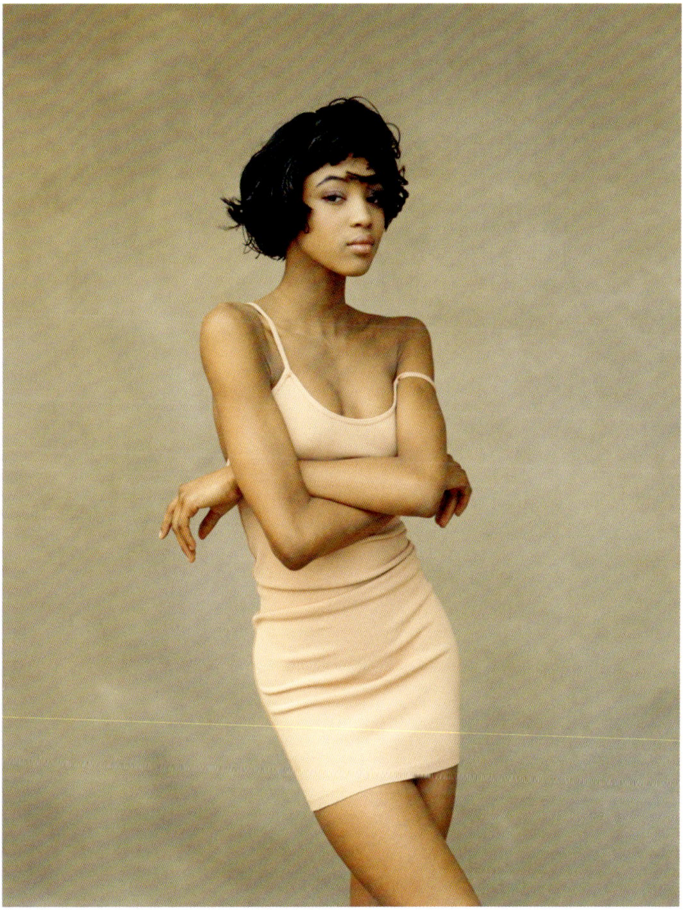

(Previous Spread) **Terence Donovan, 1988 • Martin Brading, 1987**

I DIDN'T REALLY KNOW HOW TO MOVE LIKE A MODEL. I WAS JUST DANCING AROUND WITH THE PHOTOGRAPHER BILL KING.

NAOMI CAMPBELL

Arthur Elgort, 1988

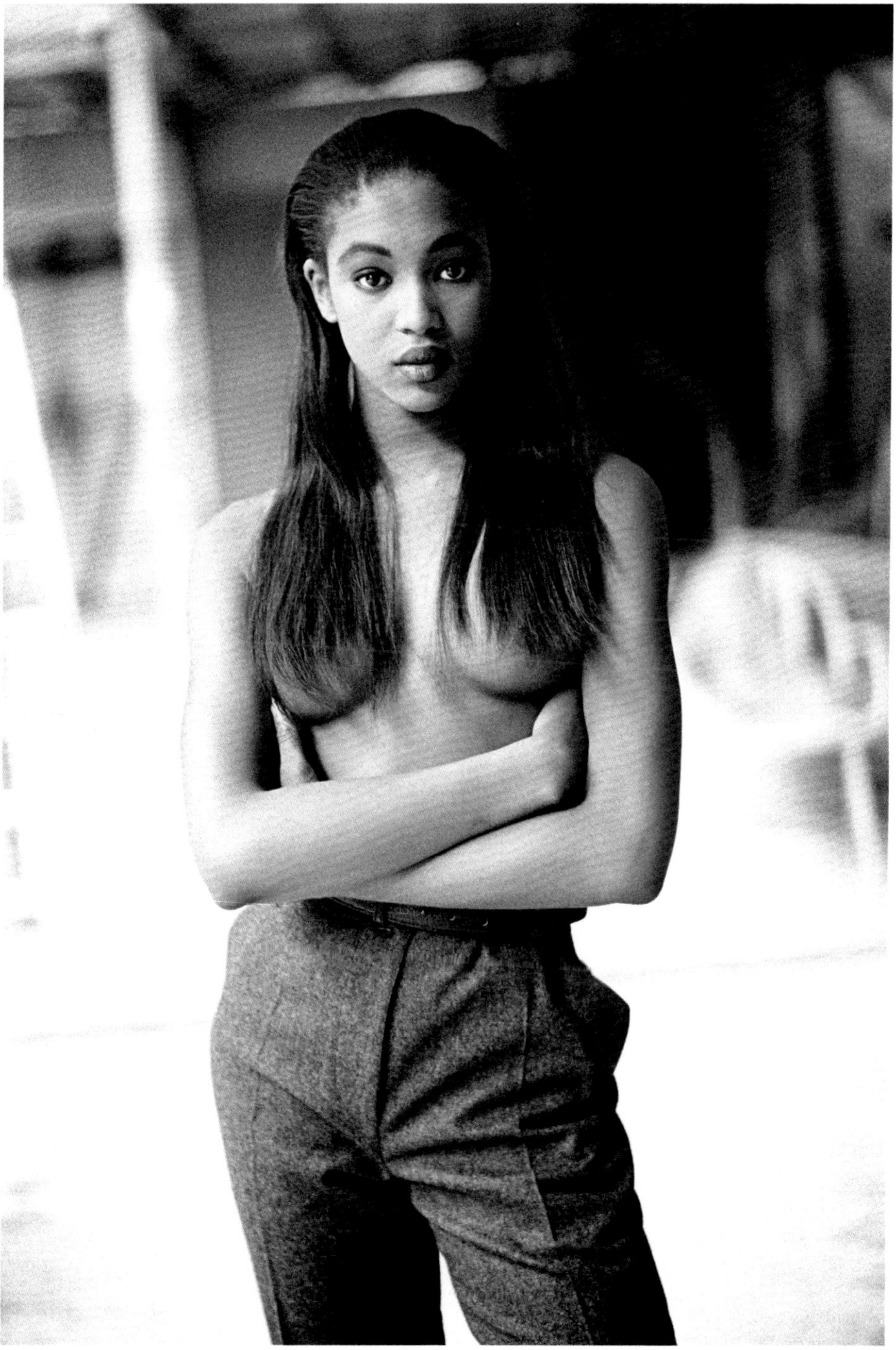

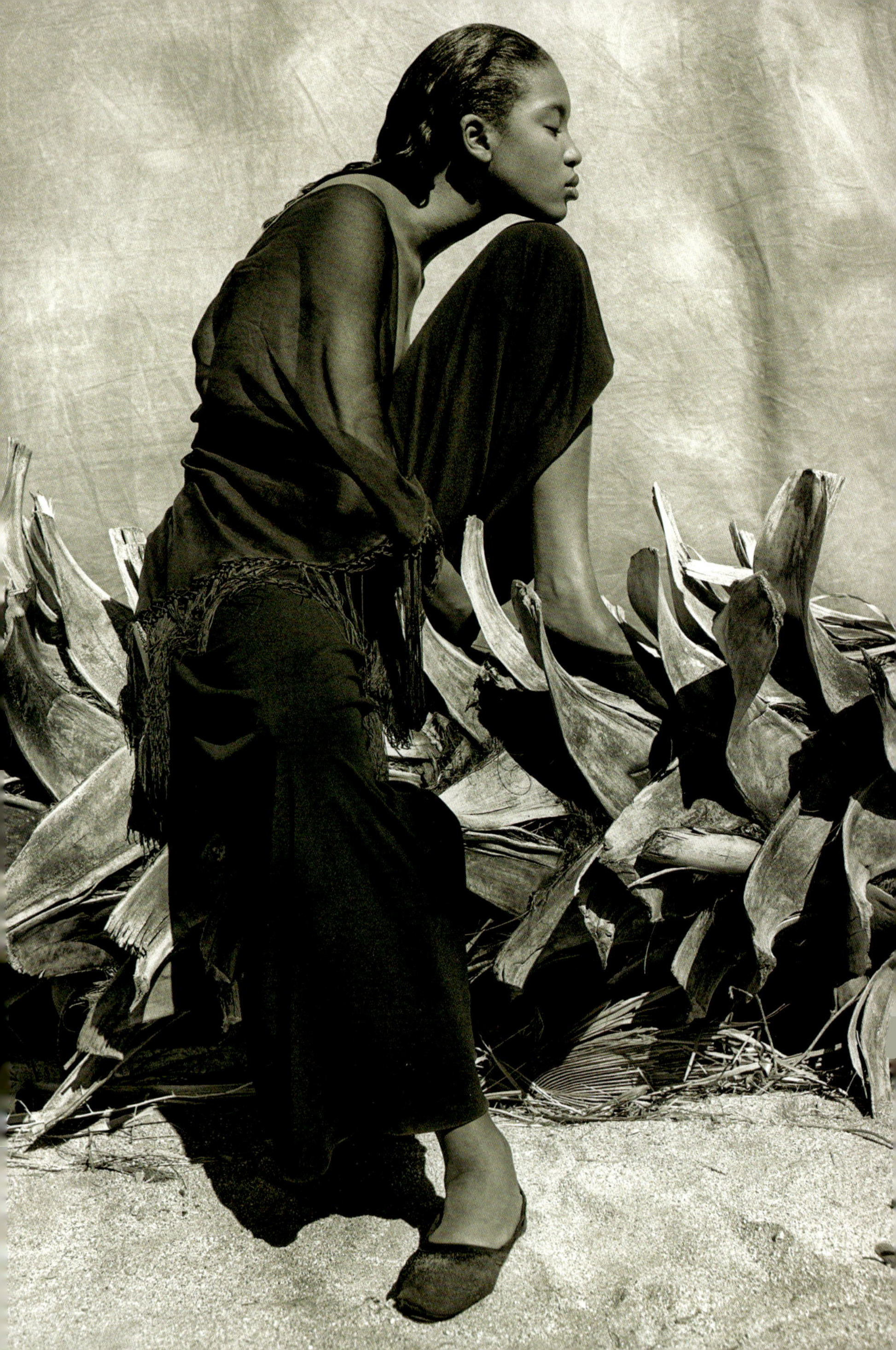

I ALWAYS FELT THERE WAS SOMETHING VERY SPECIAL AND PARTICULAR ABOUT HER. SHE'S LIKE A RACEHORSE. VERY ELITE.

AZZEDINE ALAÏA

Albert Watson, 1989

I BROUGHT HER FROM
ENGLAND TO AMERICA . . .
. . . FOR A SESSION BASED ON
DANCE. AFTERWARD SHE
MET STEVEN MEISEL,
AND THE REST IS HISTORY.

GRACE CODDINGTON

Peter Lindbergh, 1988

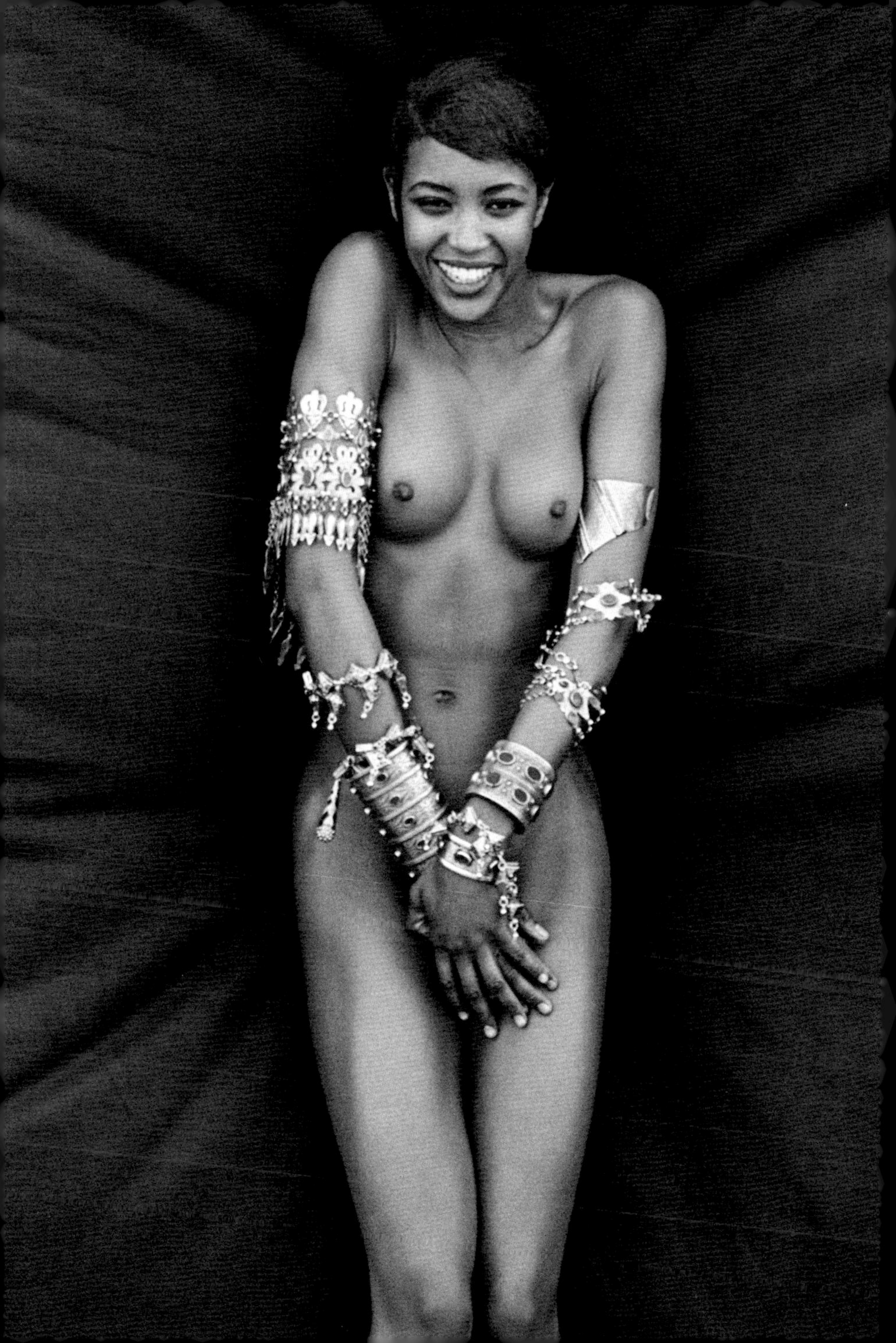

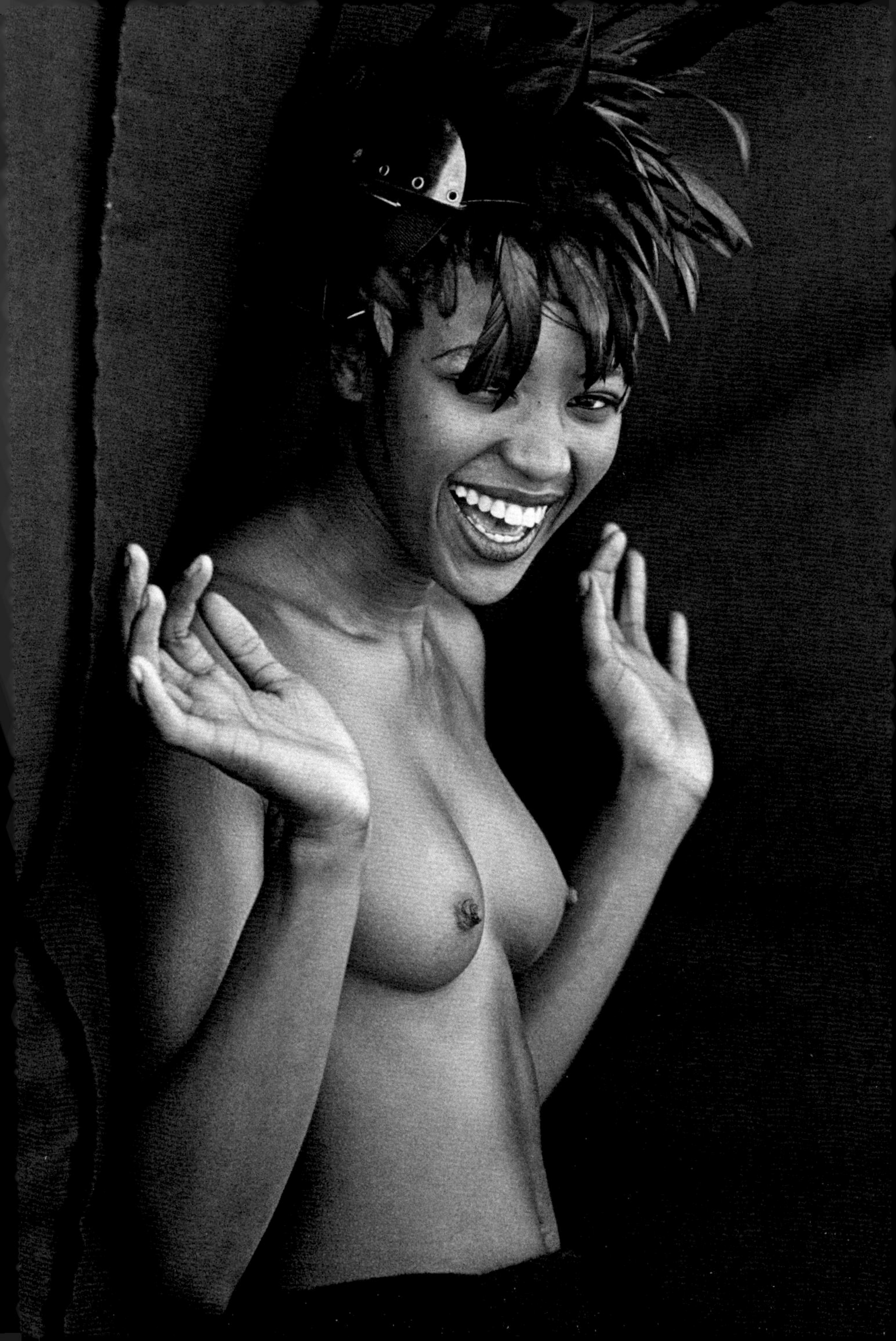

I LOVE TO TAKE PICTURES
OF WOMEN WITH PERSONALITY,
CHARACTER AND STYLE. THIS
IS FOR ME THE REAL BEAUTY.
NAOMI IS ONE.

PETER LINDBERGH

(Opposite & Following Spread) **Peter Lindbergh, 1988**

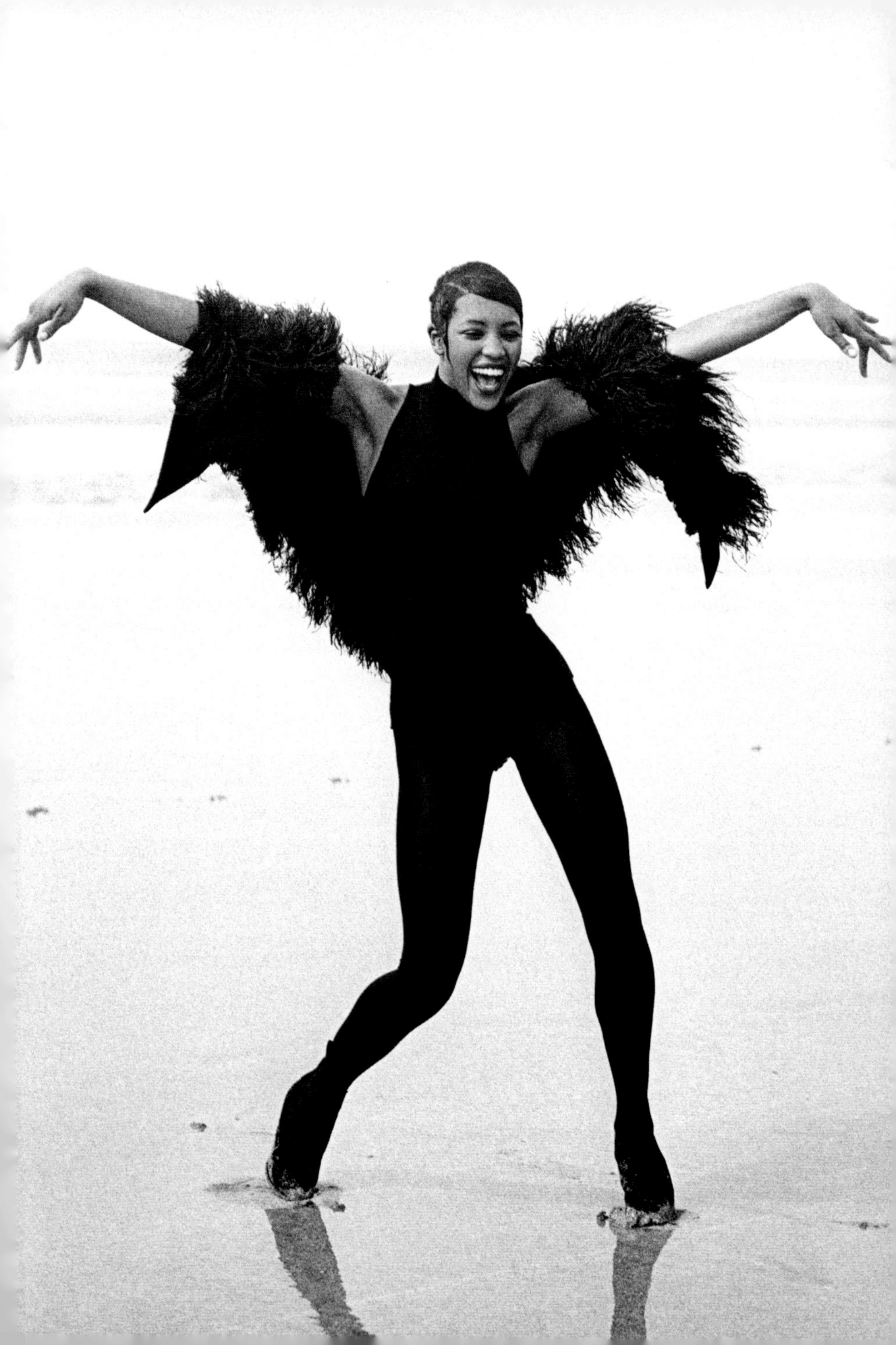

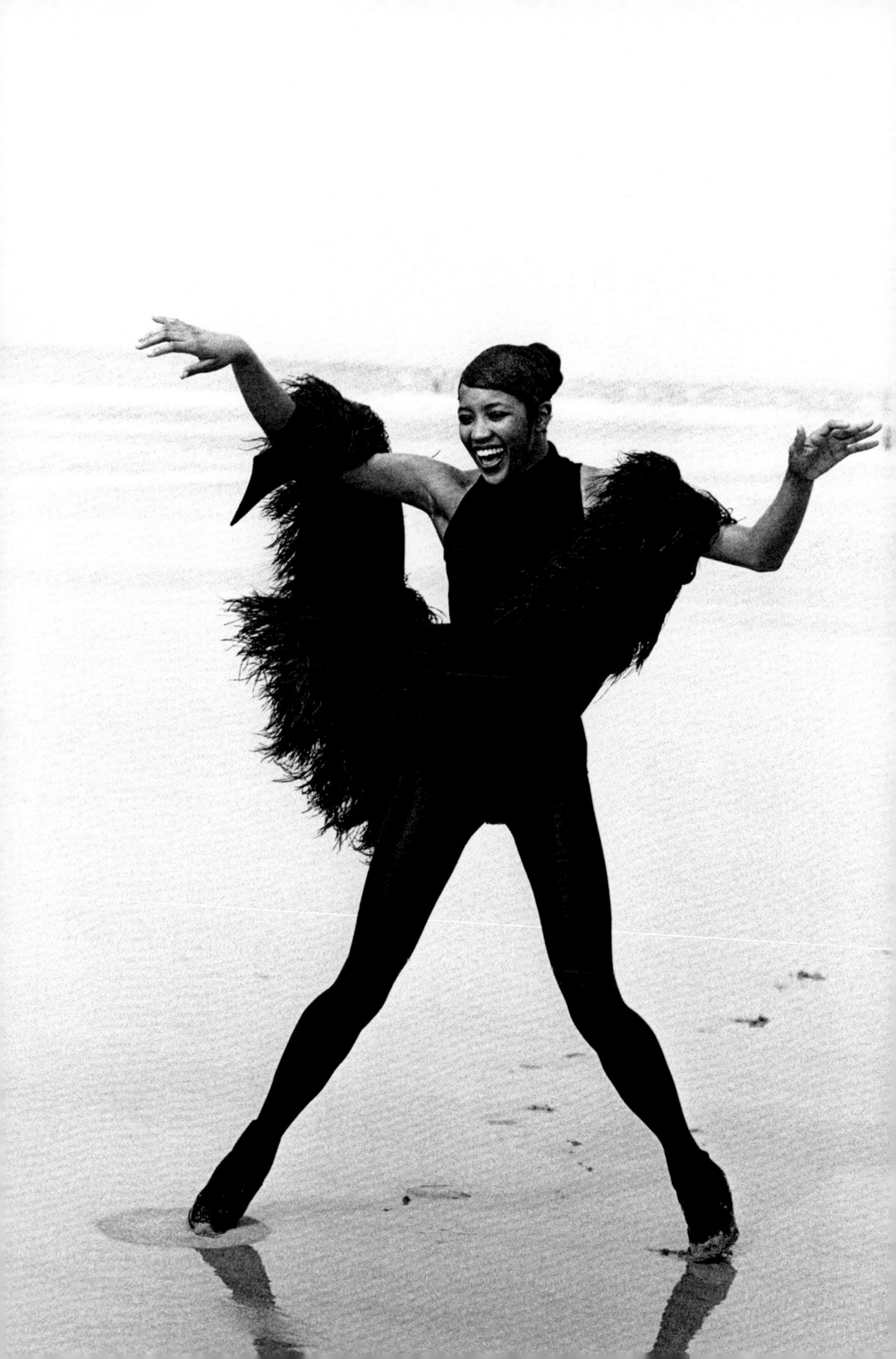

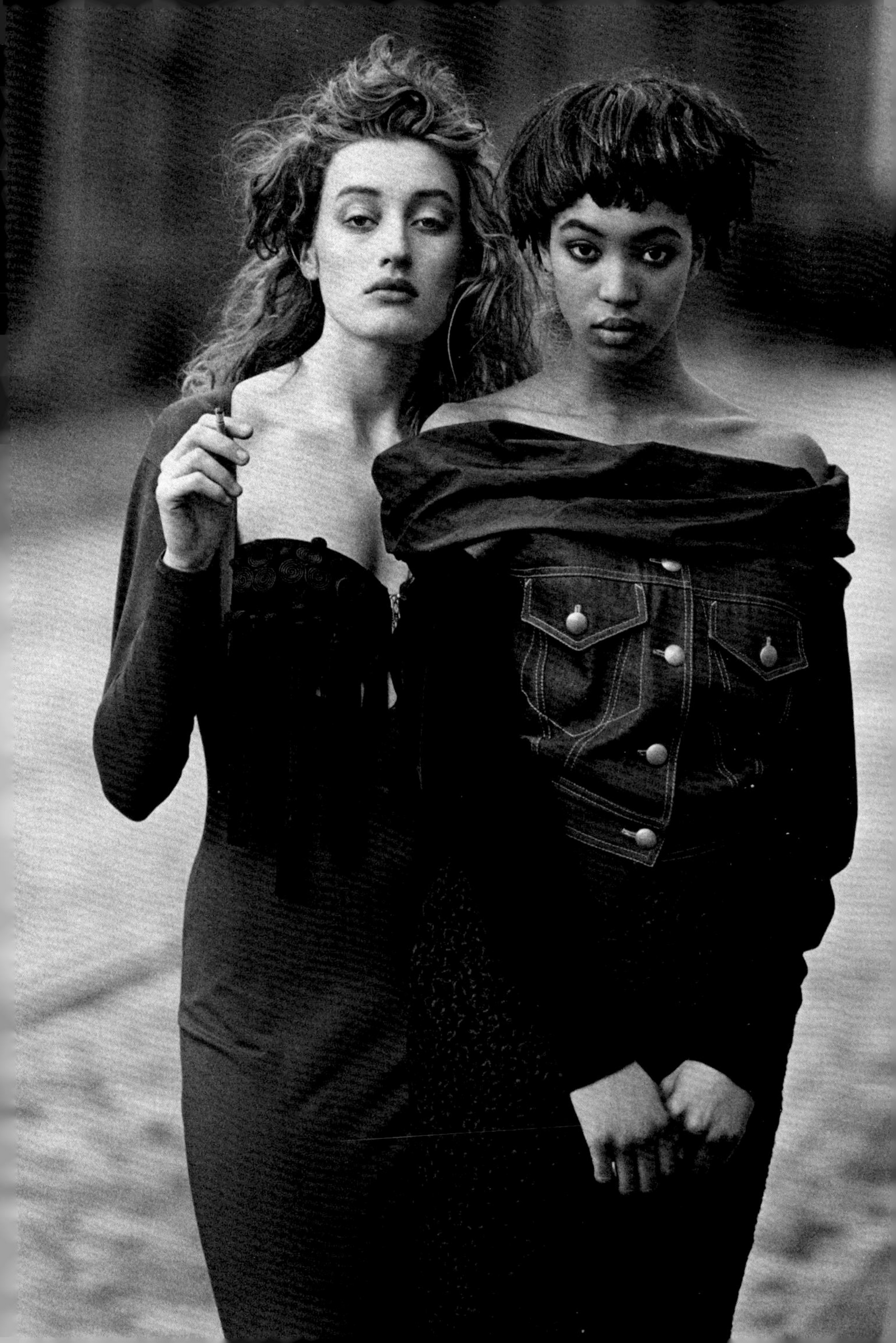

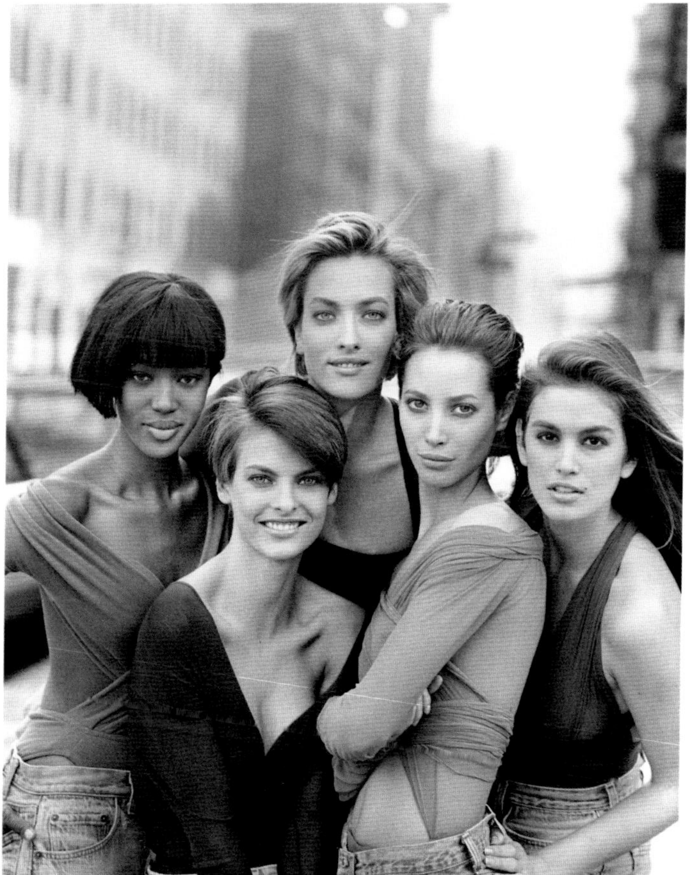

Peter Lindbergh, 1987 • Peter Lindbergh, 1989

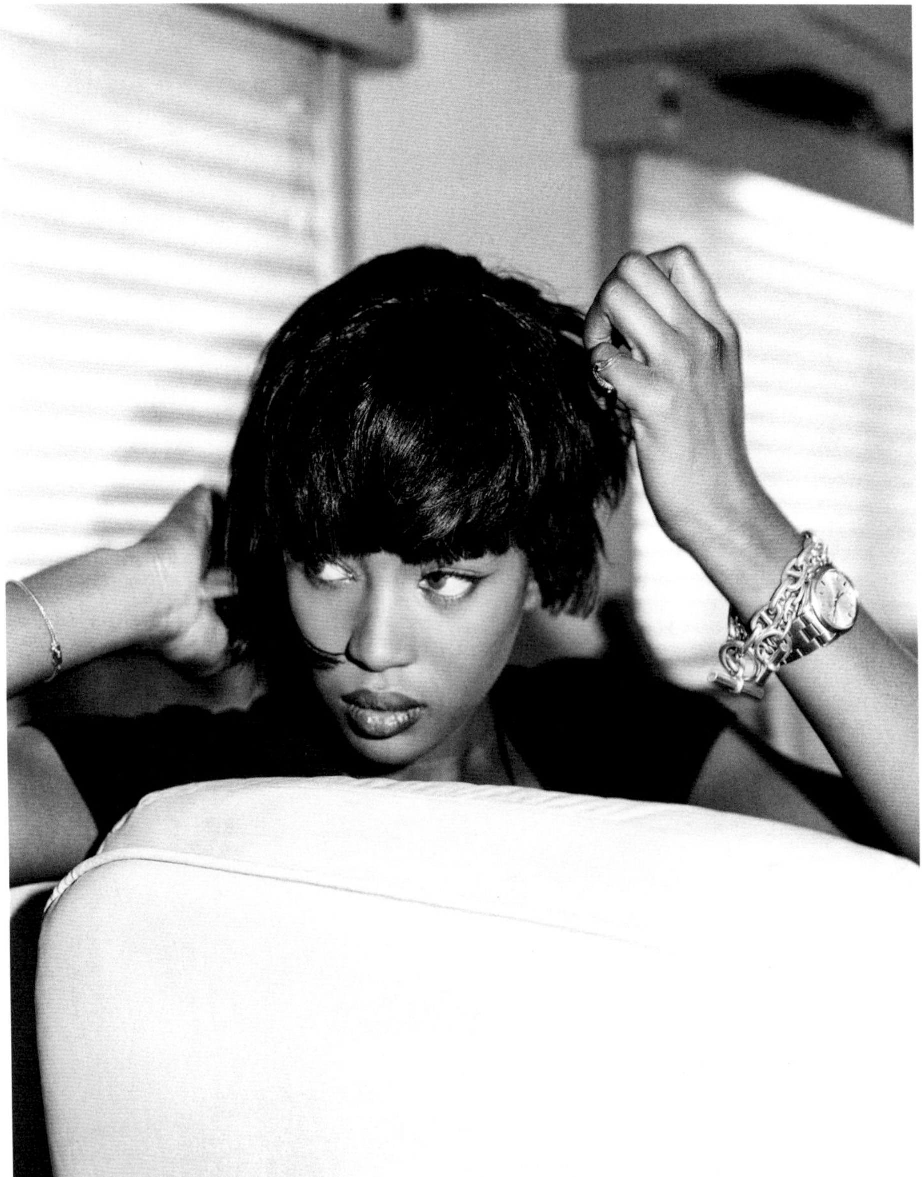

THERE'S NO ONE LIKE
NAOMI . . . SHE'S AN ICON,
A STAR, A ROLE MODEL –
HER BEAUTY, GRACE, HUMOUR
AND INCREDIBLE UNIQUE
ENERGY TAKE EVERYTHING
TO THE NEXT LEVEL.

KARL TEMPLER

Bruce Weber, 1989

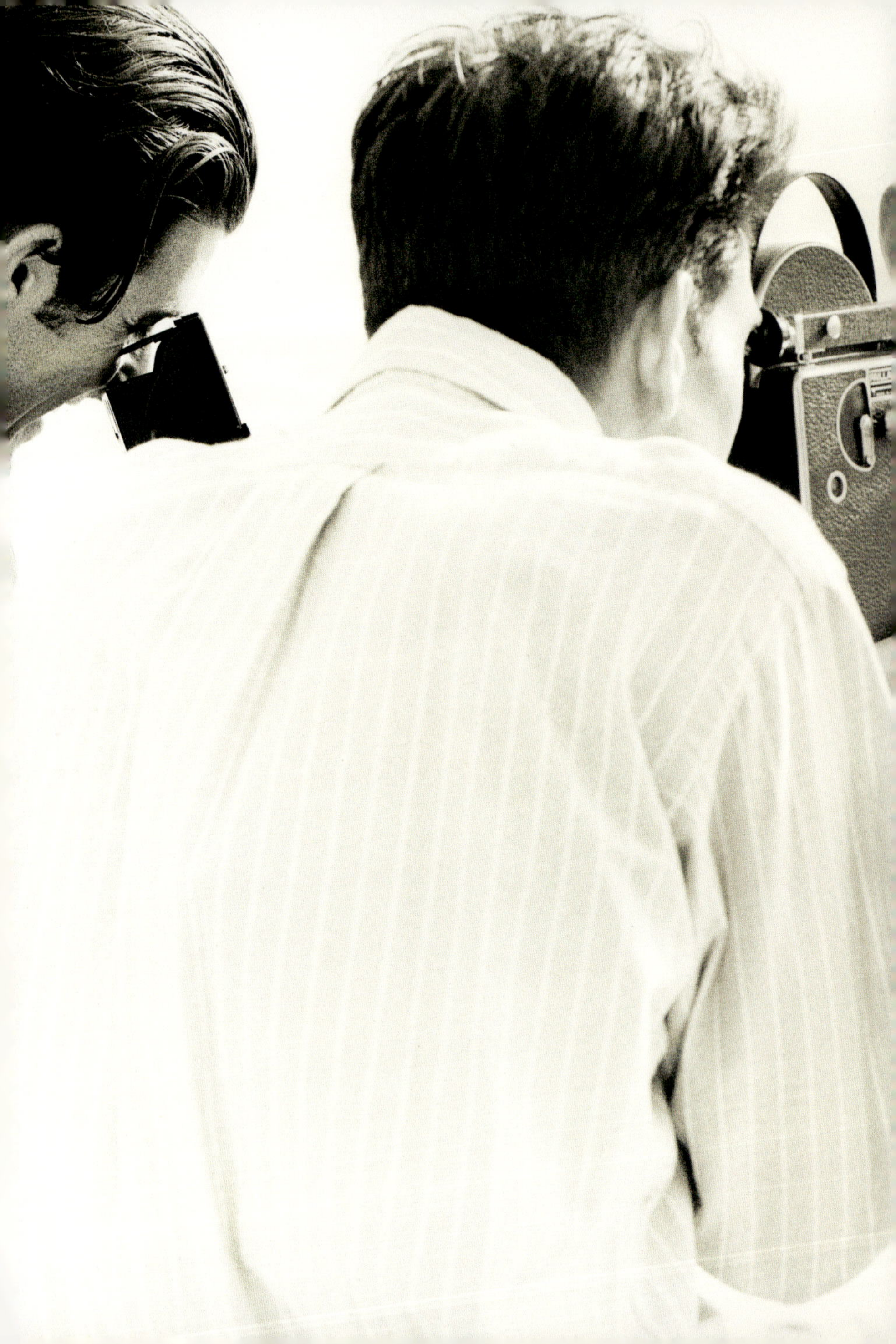

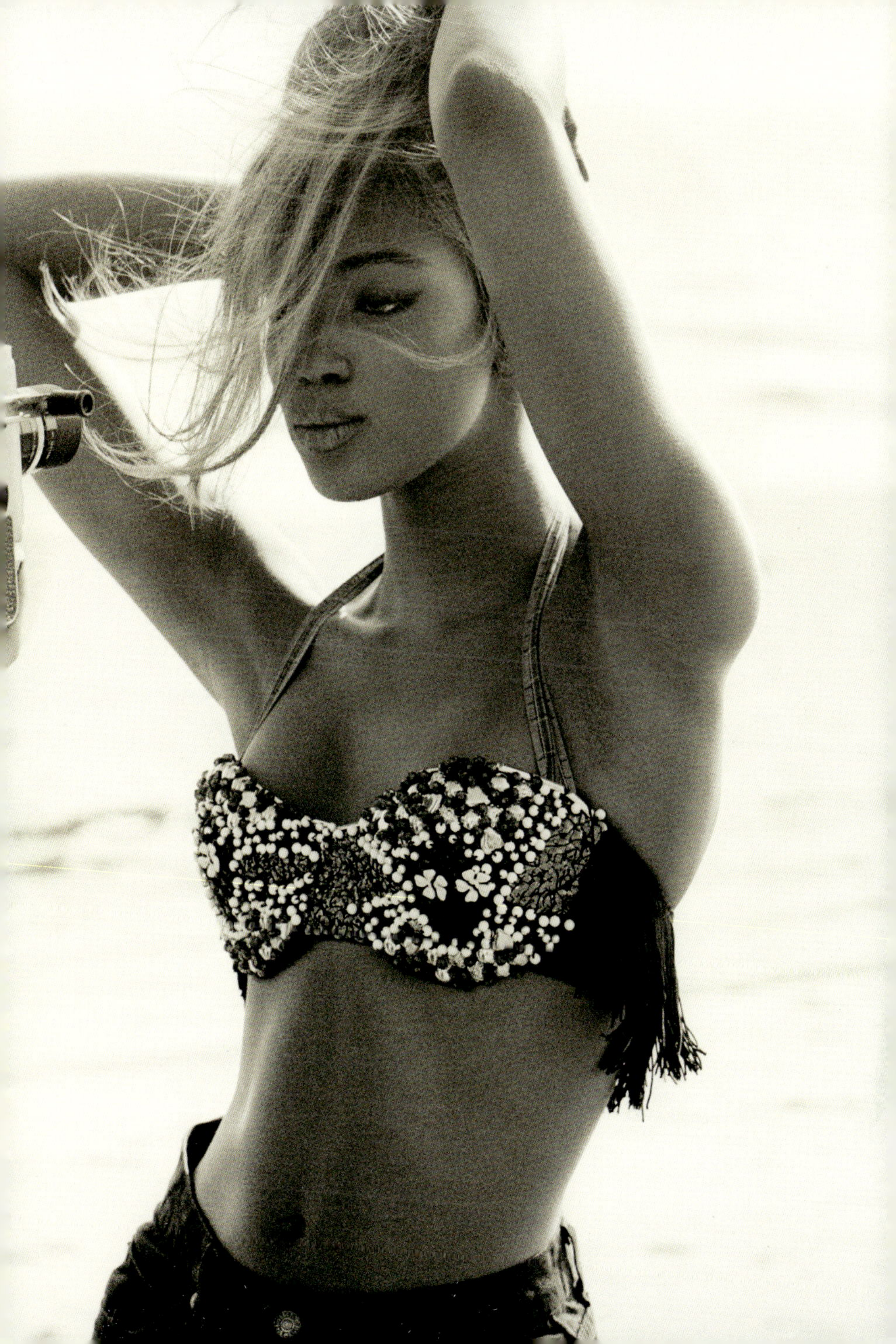

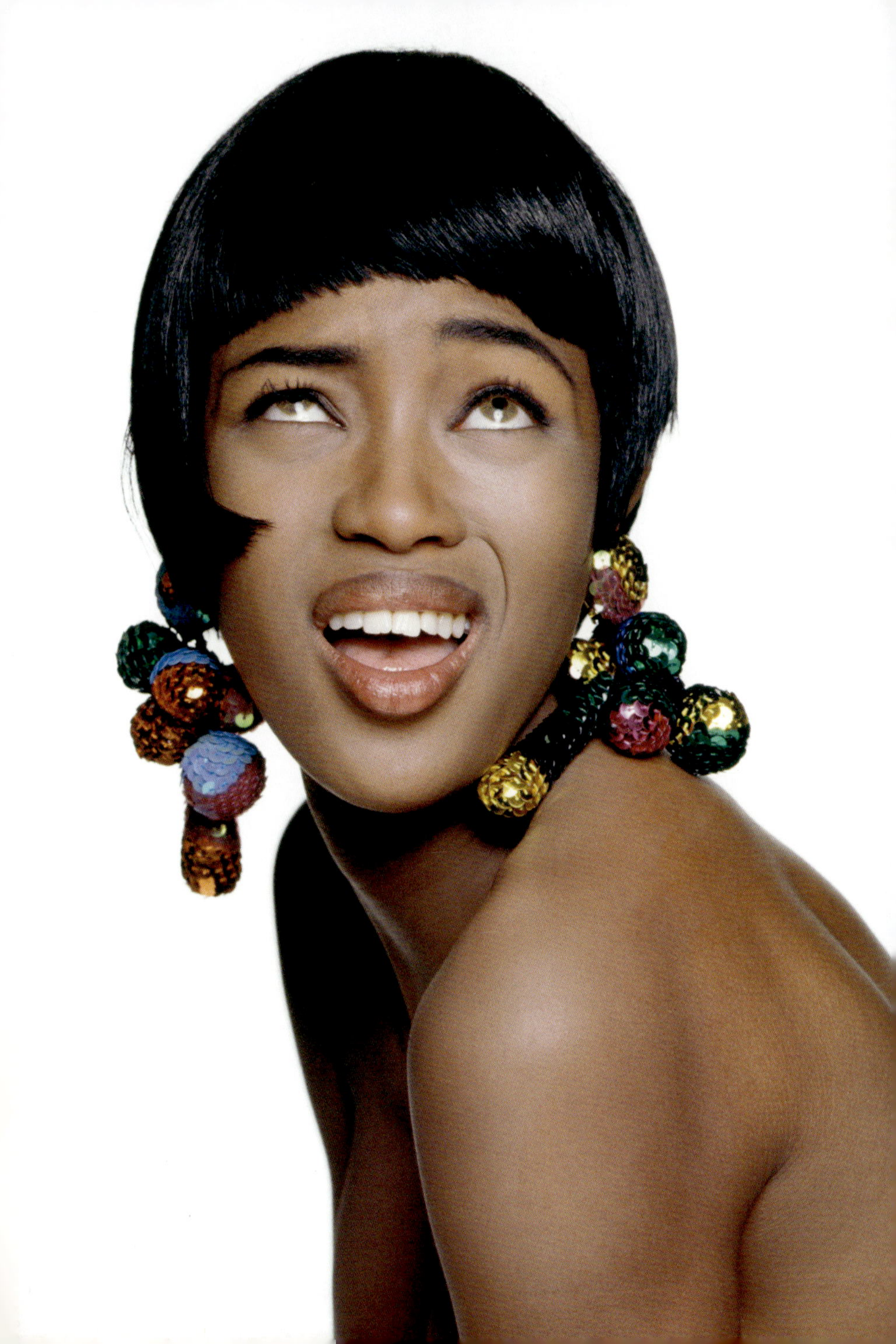

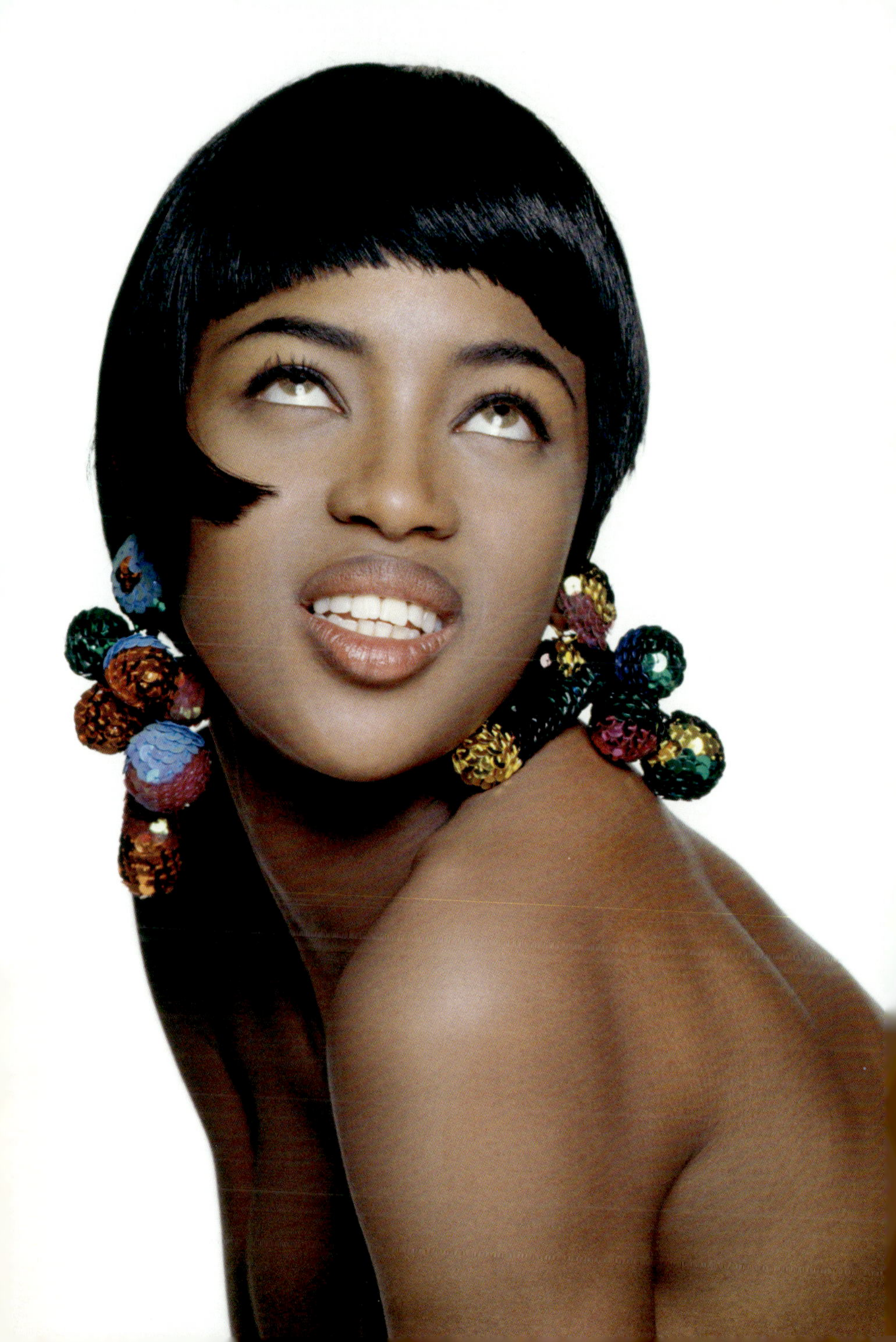

WE HAVE NEVER SEEN ANYTHING LIKE IT. ONE THING IS TO SEE A PICTURE OF NAOMI. ANOTHER THING IS TO SEE HER IN MOTION, WHICH IS JUST JAW-DROPPING.

VIVIENNE WESTWOOD

(Previous Spreads) **Steven Meisel, 1989 • Bruce Weber, 1989**

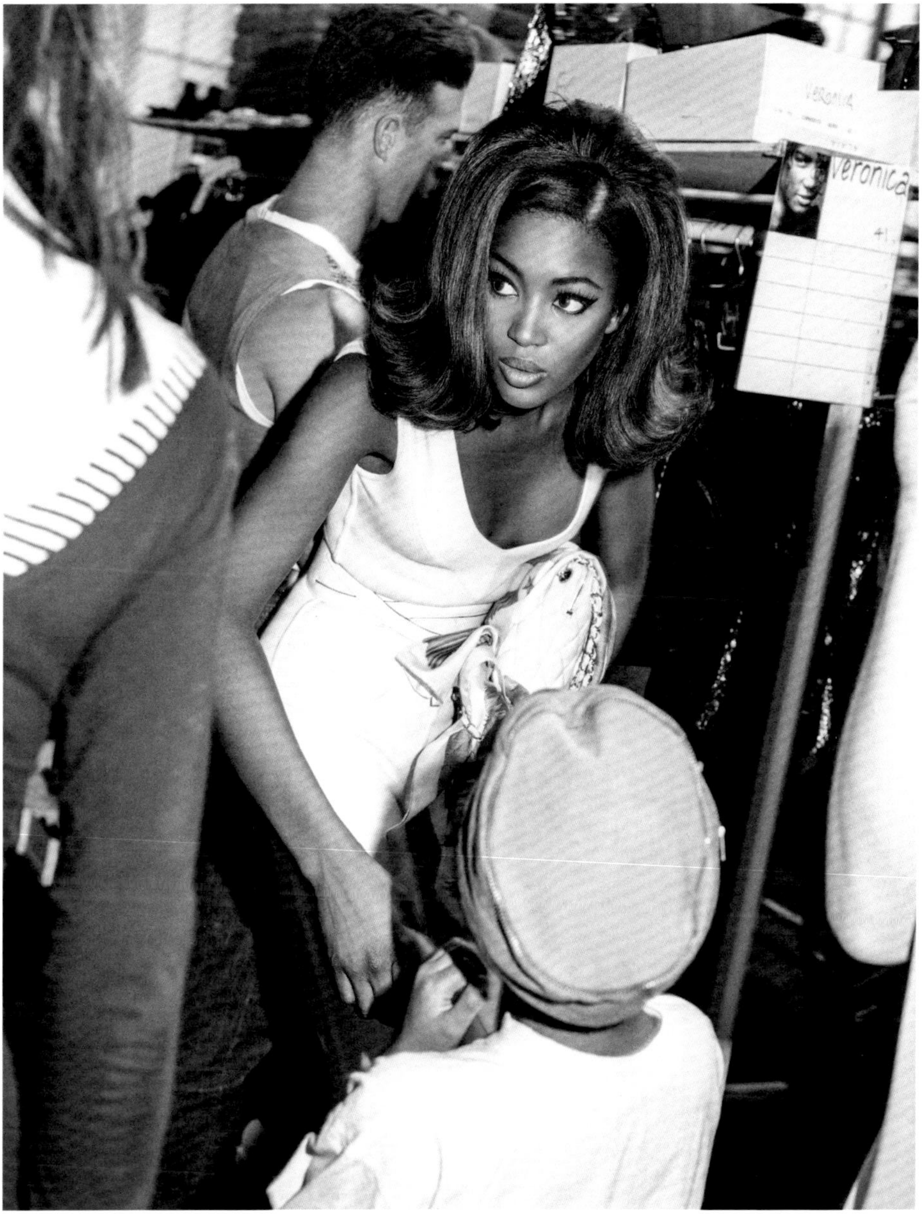
VERONICA
Veronica
41

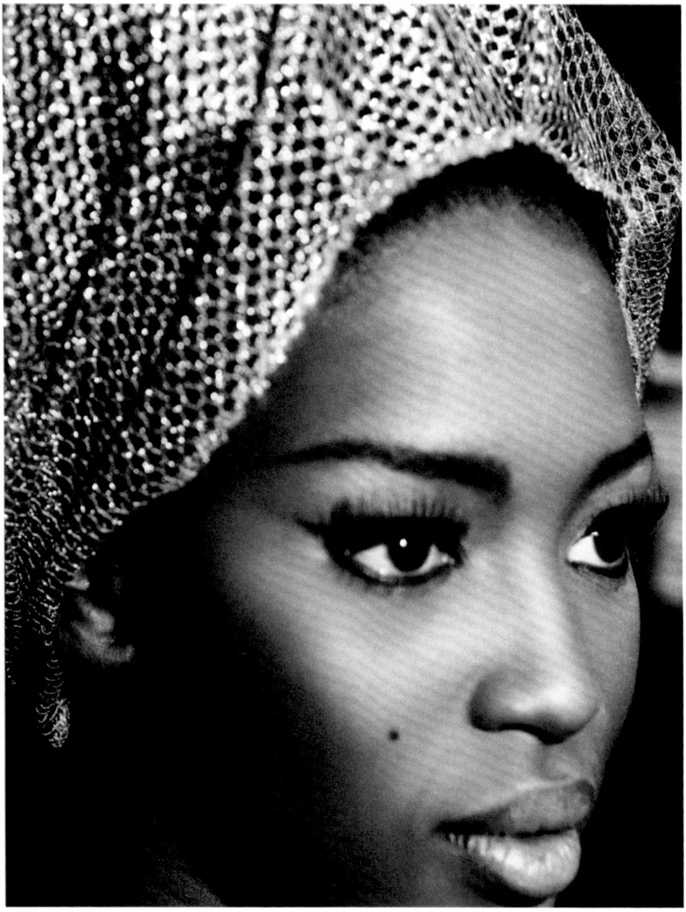

Bruce Weber, 1989

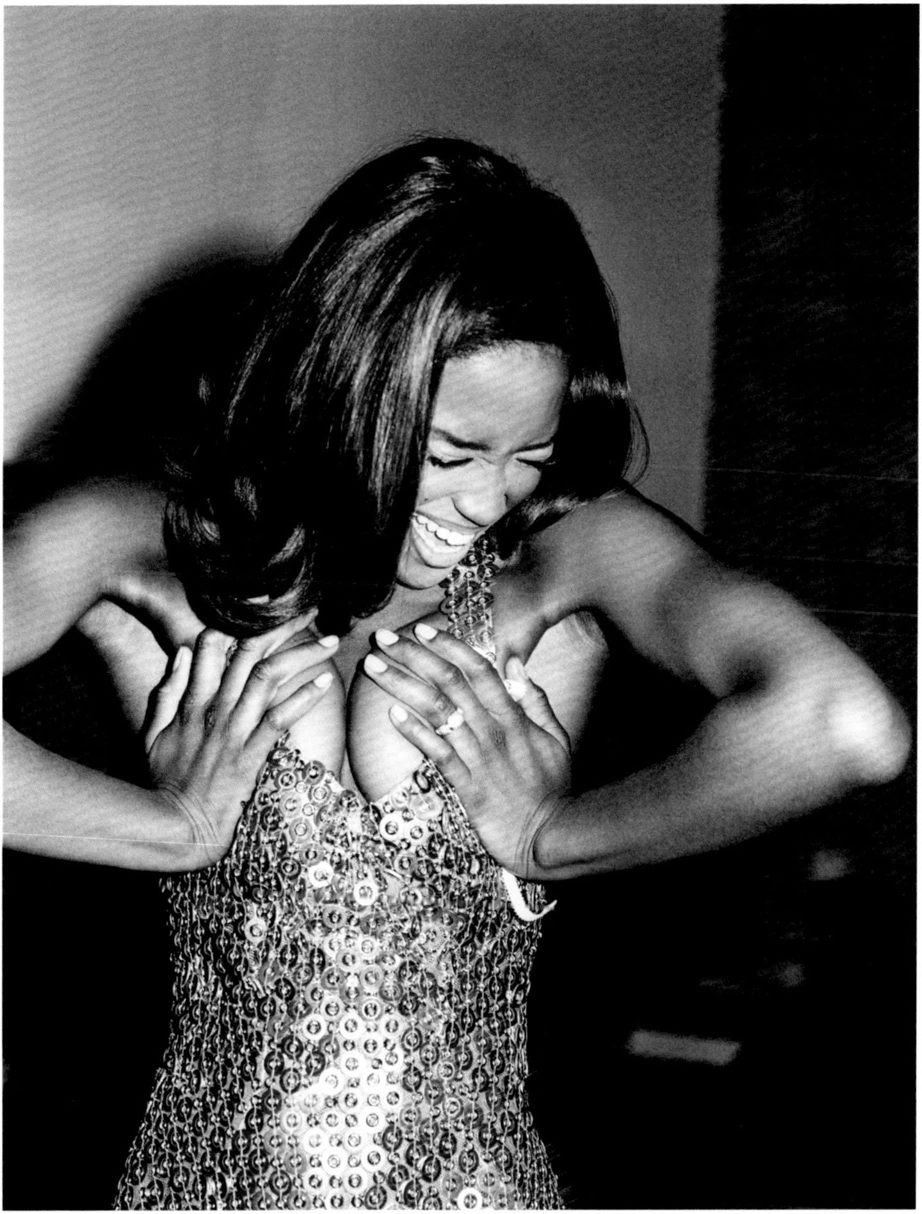

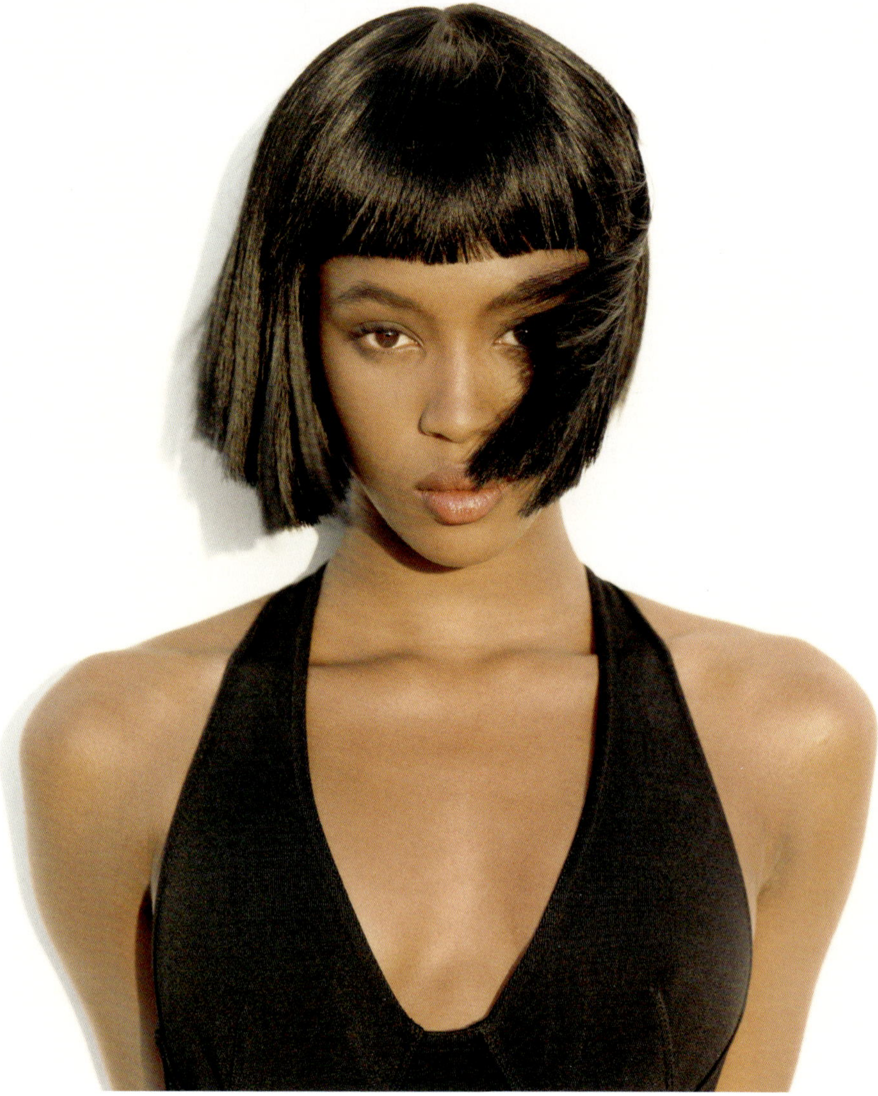

I DON'T THINK I WAS BORN BEAUTIFUL. I JUST THINK I WAS BORN ME.

NAOMI CAMPBELL

Herb Ritts, 1988

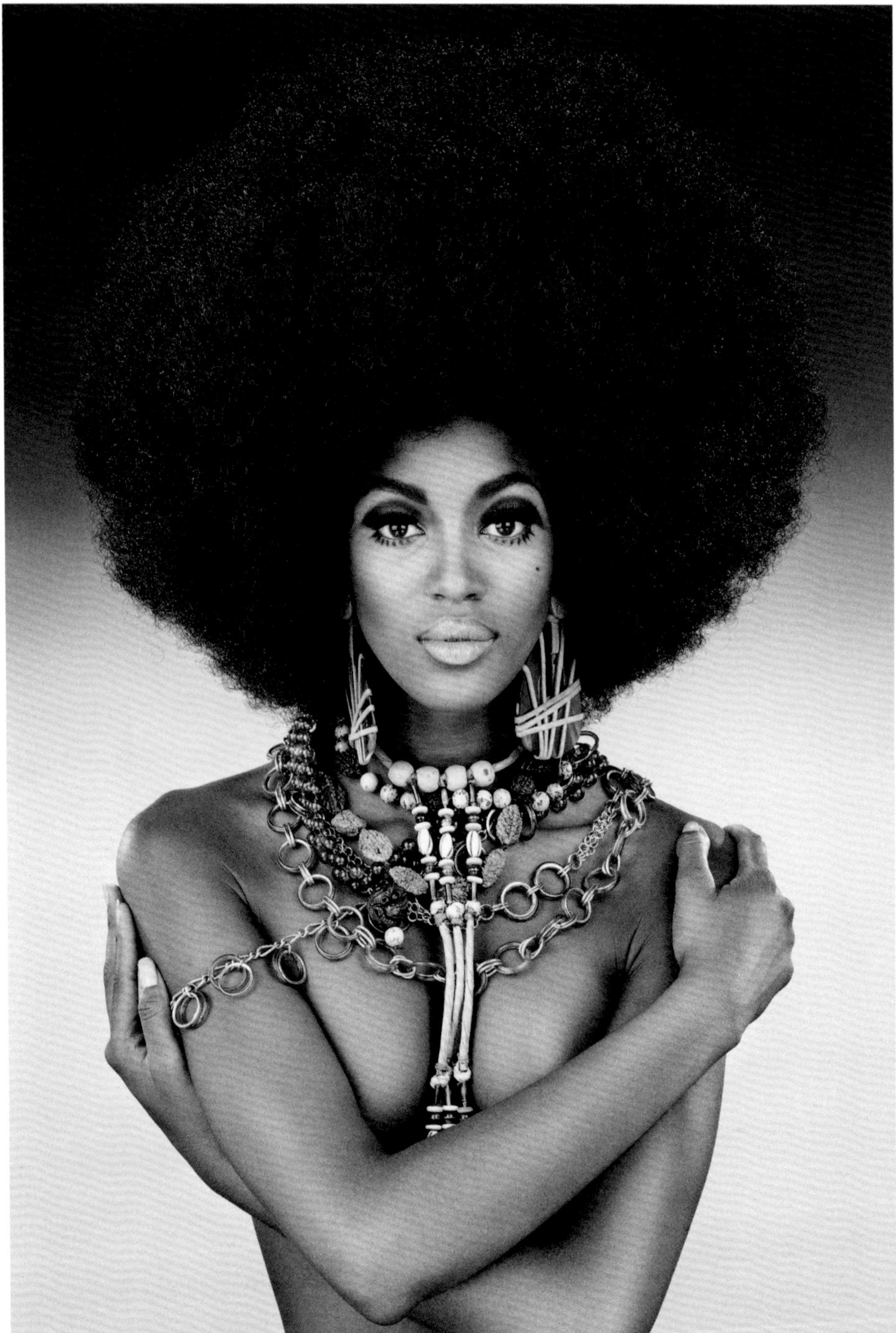

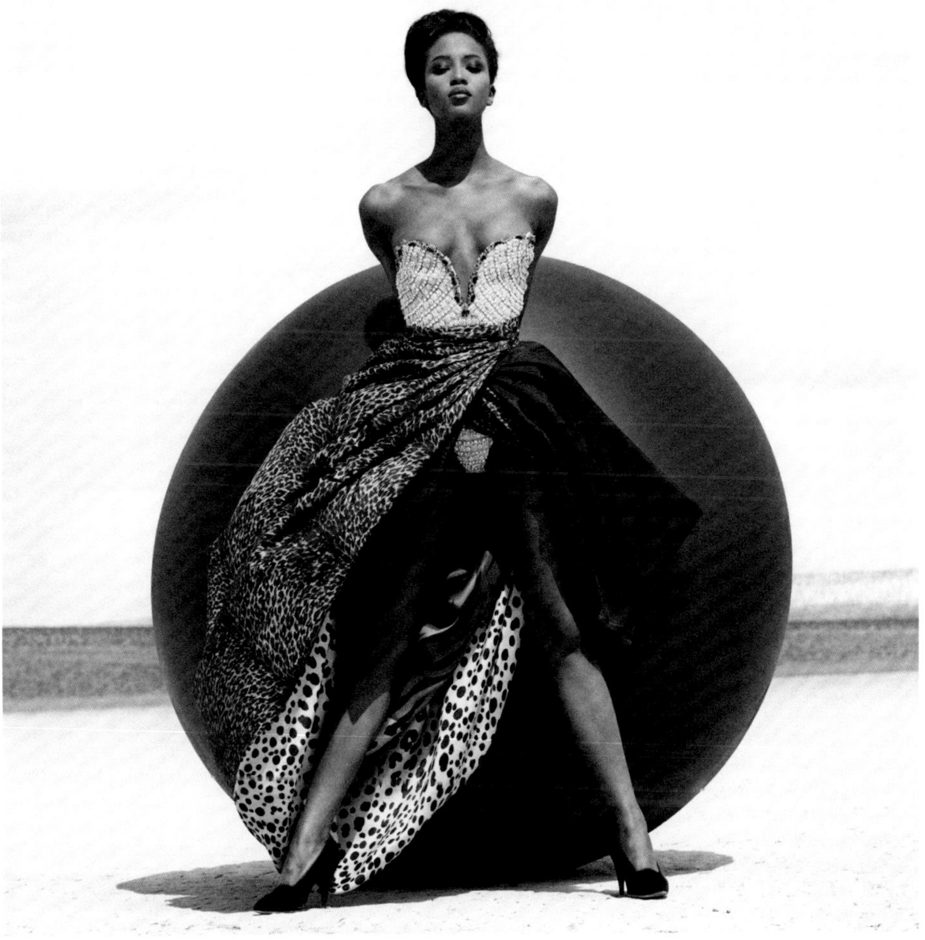

Edward (Maxey) Mapplethorpe, 1990 • Herb Ritts, 1990

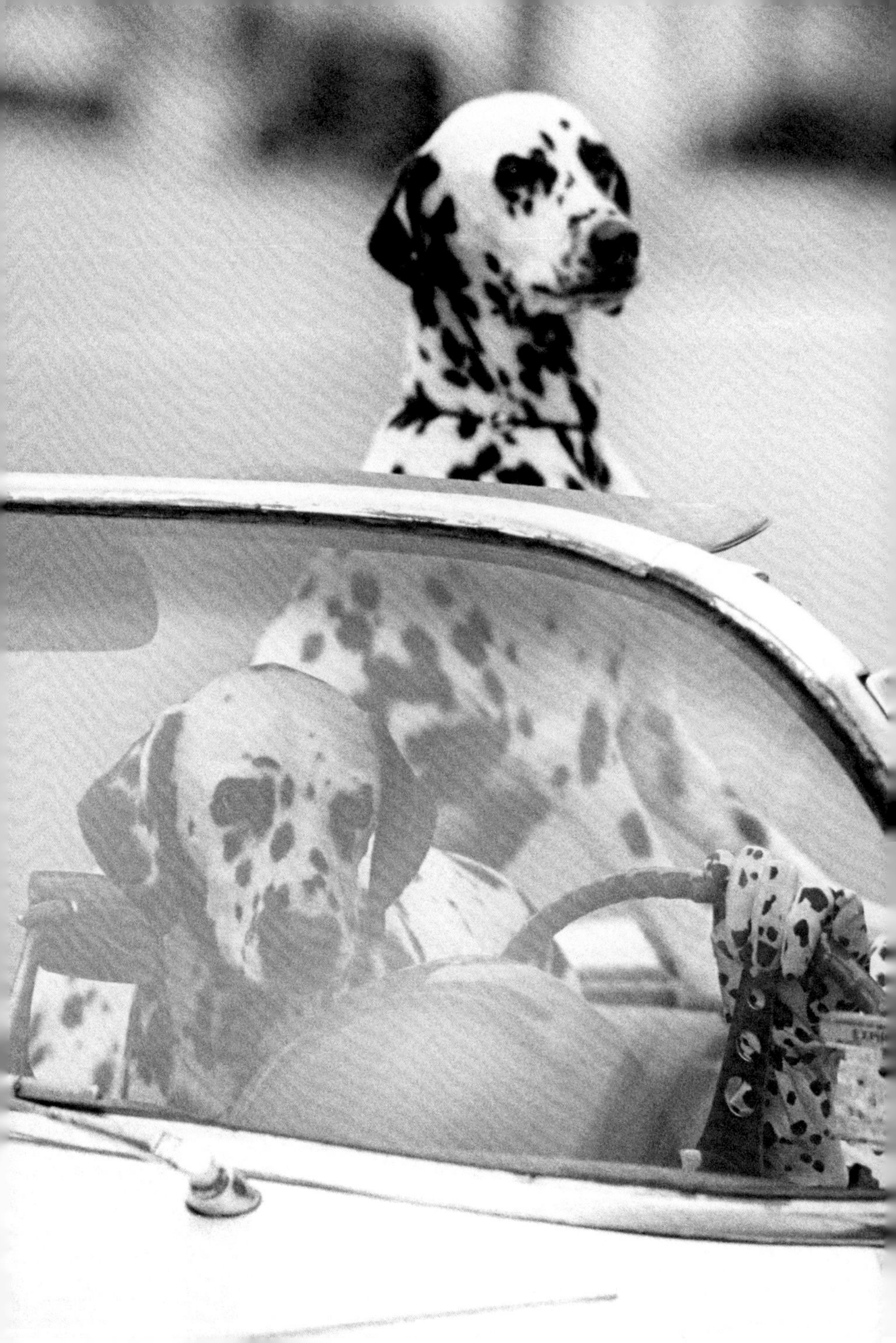

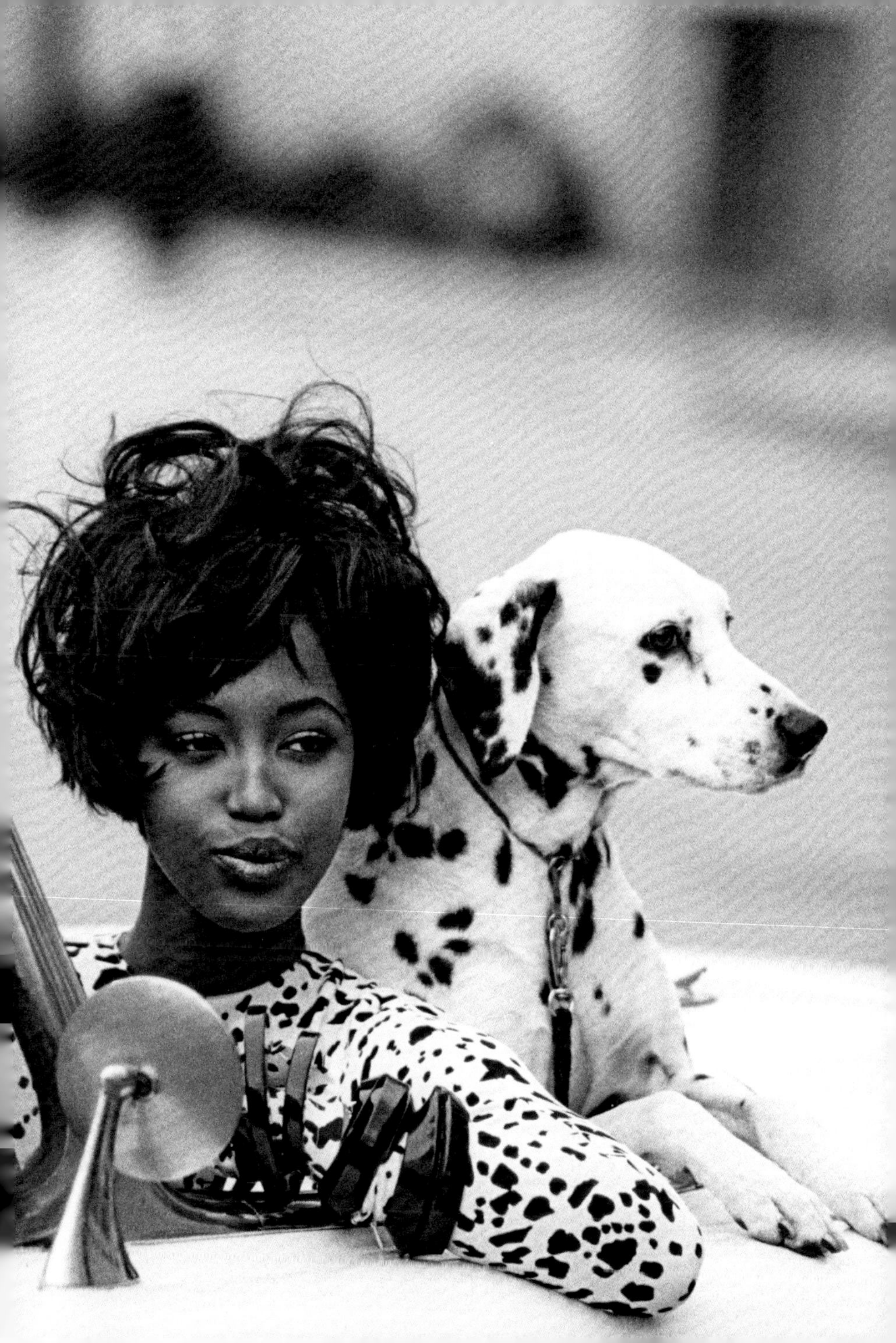

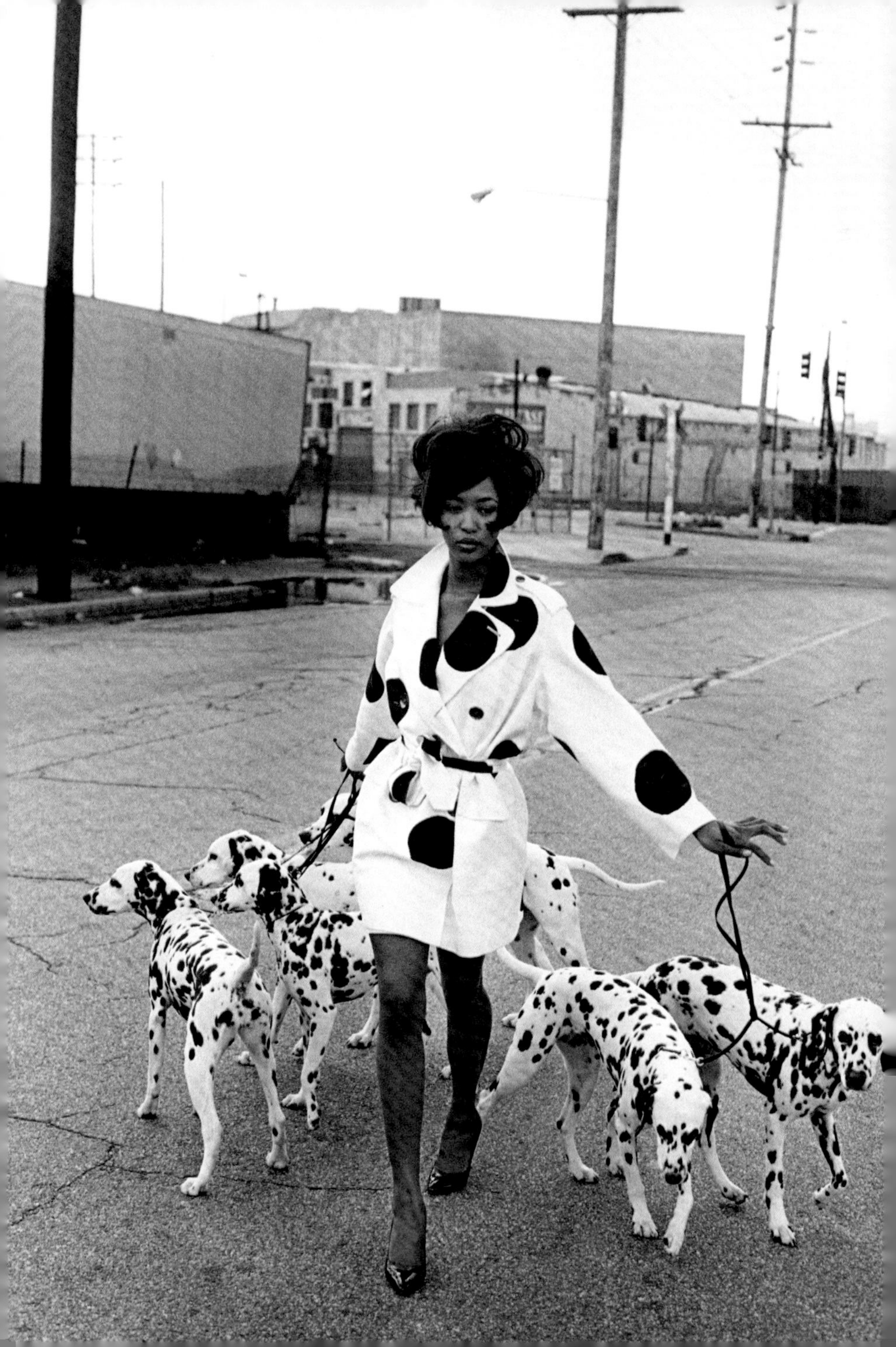

(Previous Spread & Opposite) **Peter Lindbergh, 1990**

WHEN I LOOK AT IMAN AND BEVERLY JOHNSON AND NAOMI SIMS AND PEGGY DILLARD, AND ALL THE OTHERS, I APPRECIATE THE FACT THAT THEY OPENED THE DOOR FOR ME. IF THEY HAD NOT COME BEFORE, I WOULD NEVER BE AS FAR ALONG AS I AM NOW. AND I HOPE THAT I'M OPENING THE DOOR FOR PEOPLE WHO'RE BEHIND ME. IT'S GOTTEN BETTER. IT'S GETTING BETTER.

NAOMI CAMPBELL

Ellen von Unwerth, 1990

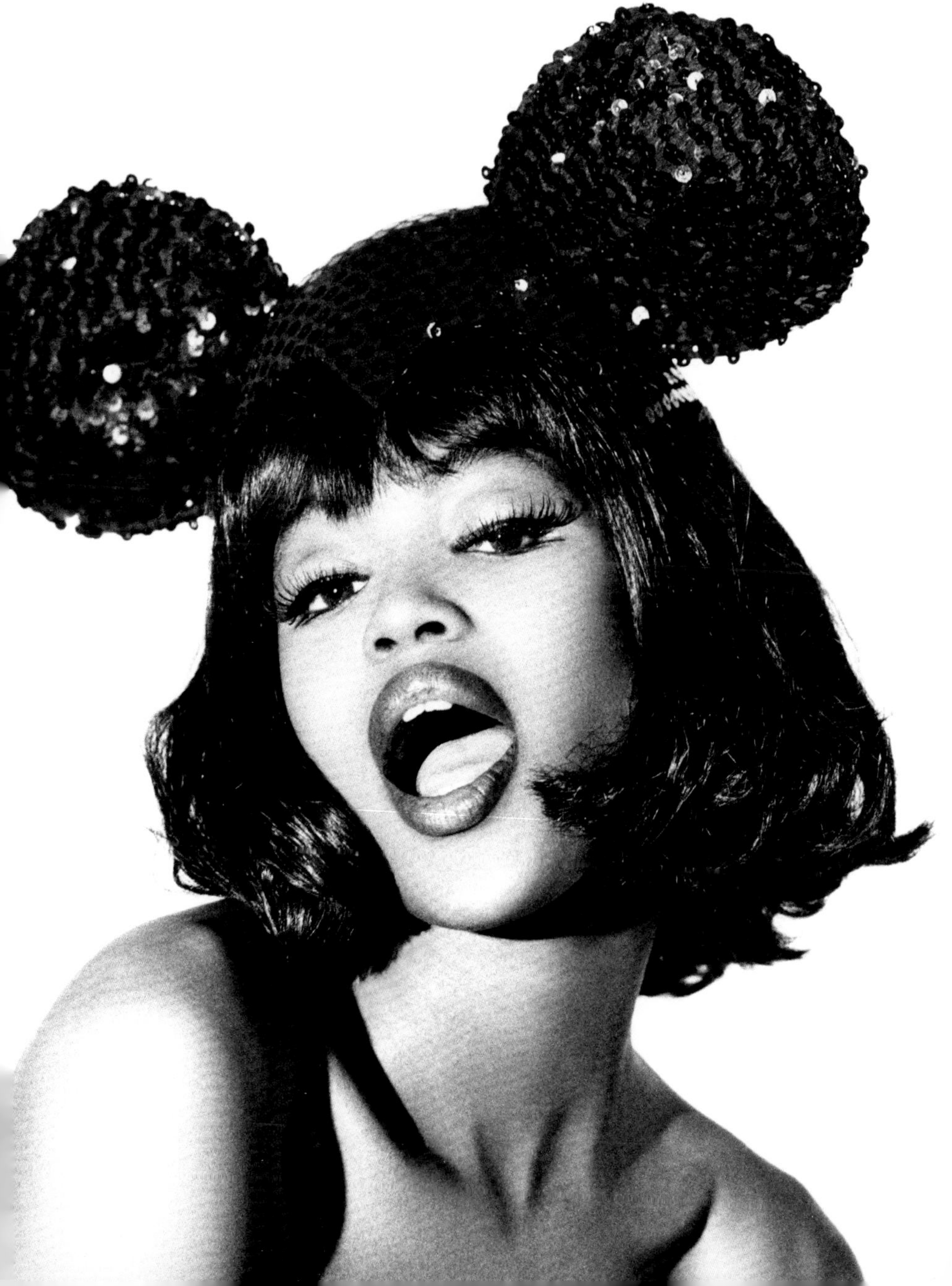

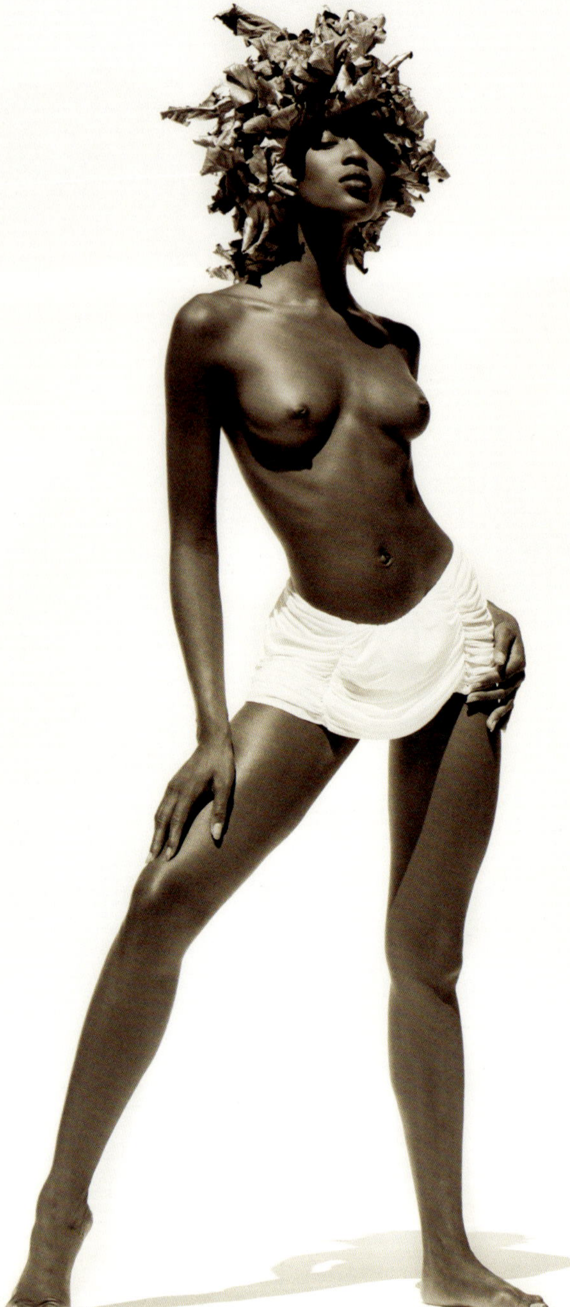

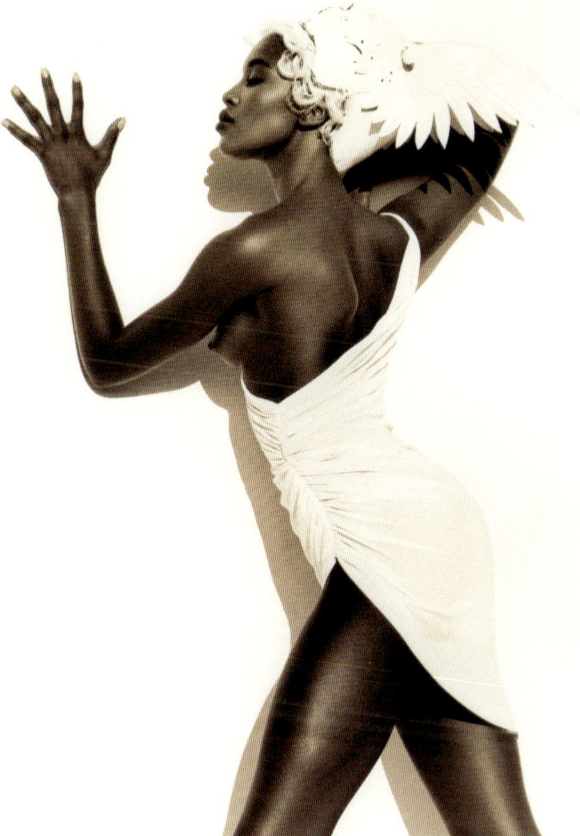

Herb Ritts, 1990

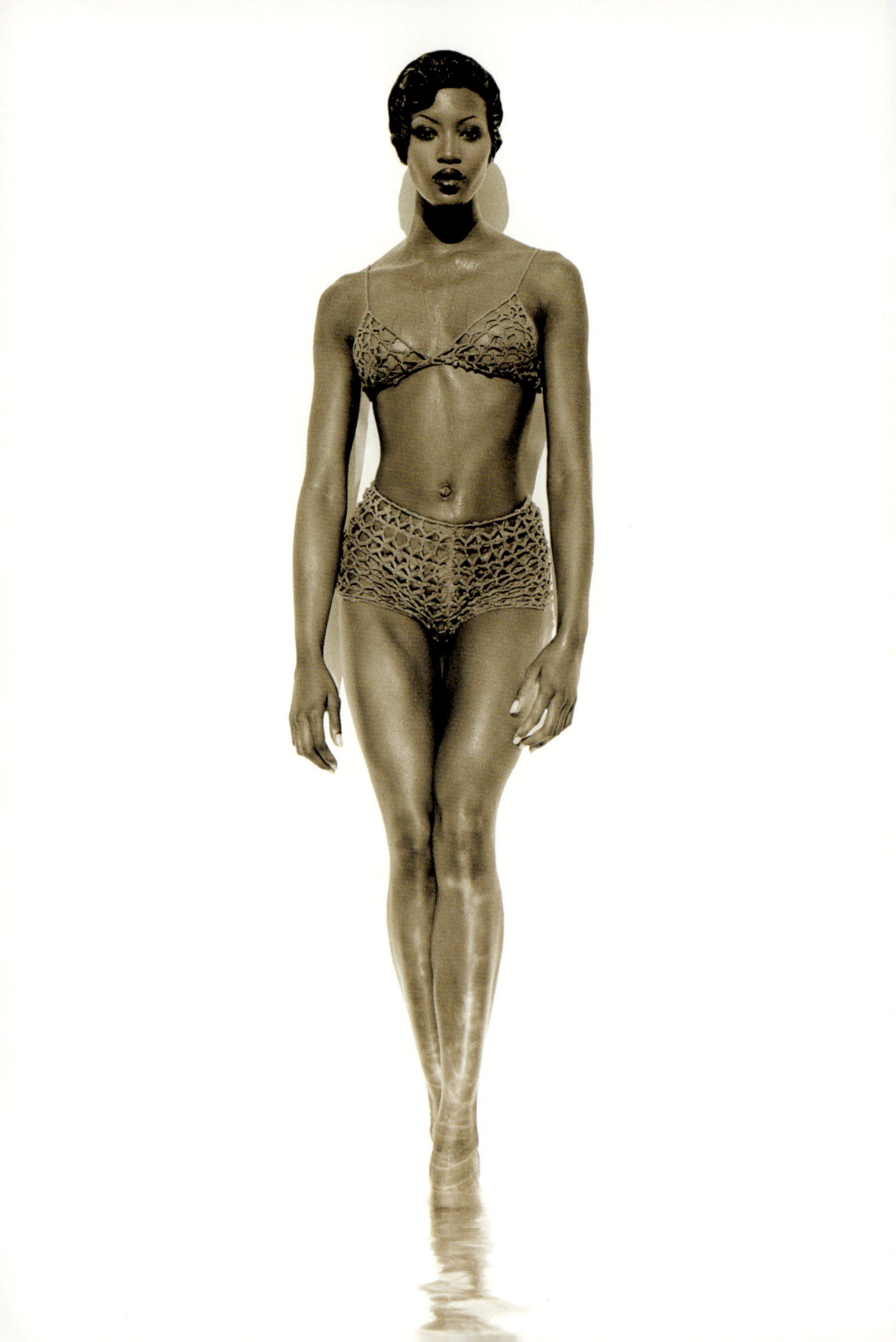

NAOMI IS A GLOBAL ICON THAT BRIDGES ALL CULTURES AND ART FORMS. SHE IS A UNIQUE HUMAN BEING THAT I AM PROUD TO CALL MY FRIEND.

BRIAN GRAZER

Herb Ritts, 1993

SHE'S A BLACK BARDOT,
AN AFRICAN MARILYN,
THE JOSPEHINE BAKER OF
THE NINETIES.
HALF KITTEN, HALF TIGRESS,
SEXY AND INNOCENT,
A FLOWER CHILD IN A
CAREER WOMAN'S BODY.

VANITY FAIR

Max Vadukul, 1992

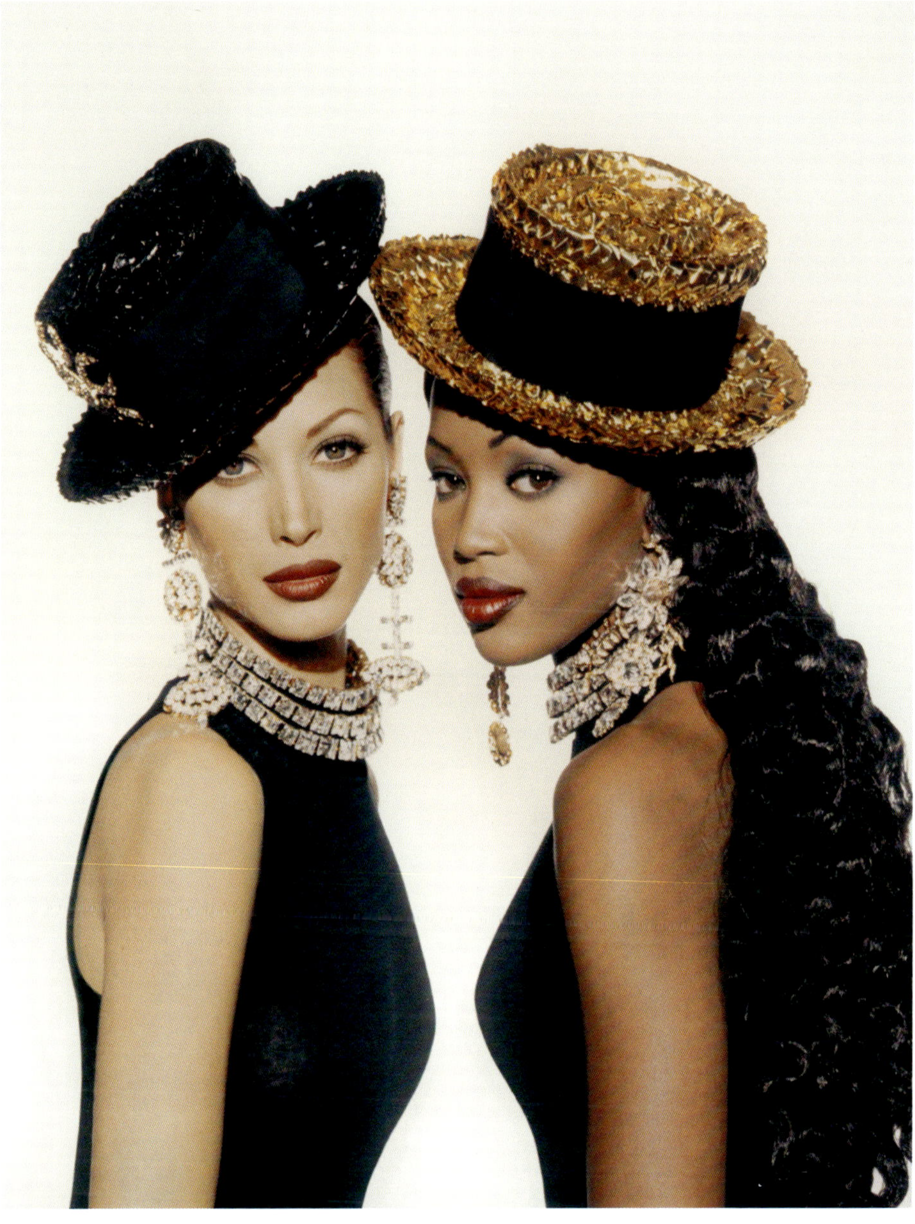

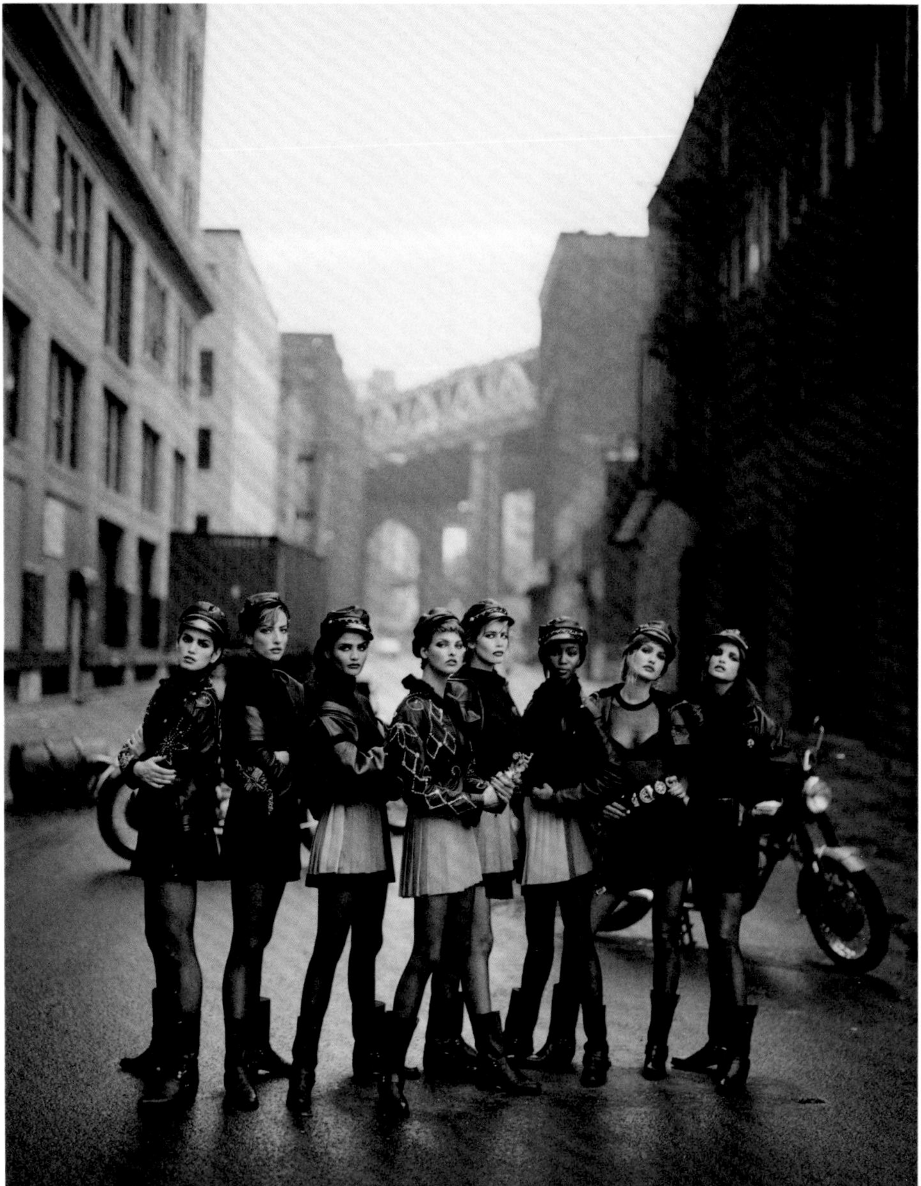

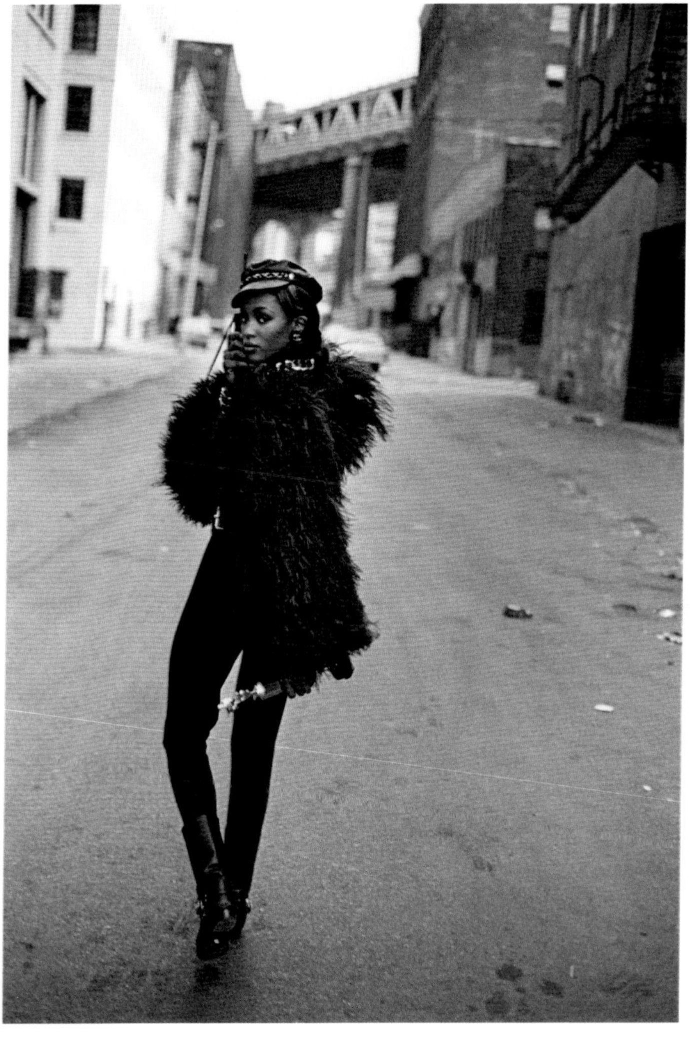

Peter Lindbergh, 1991

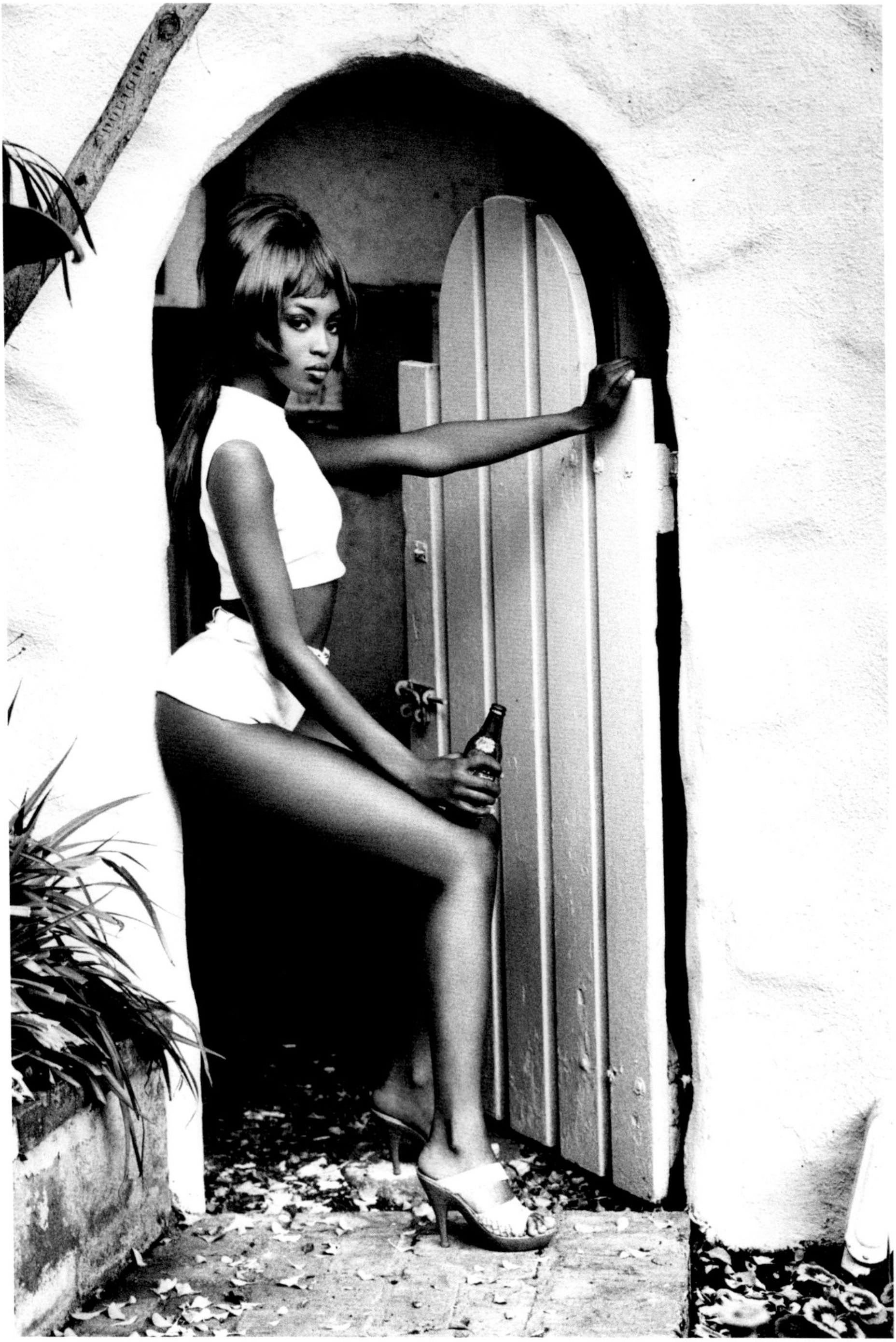

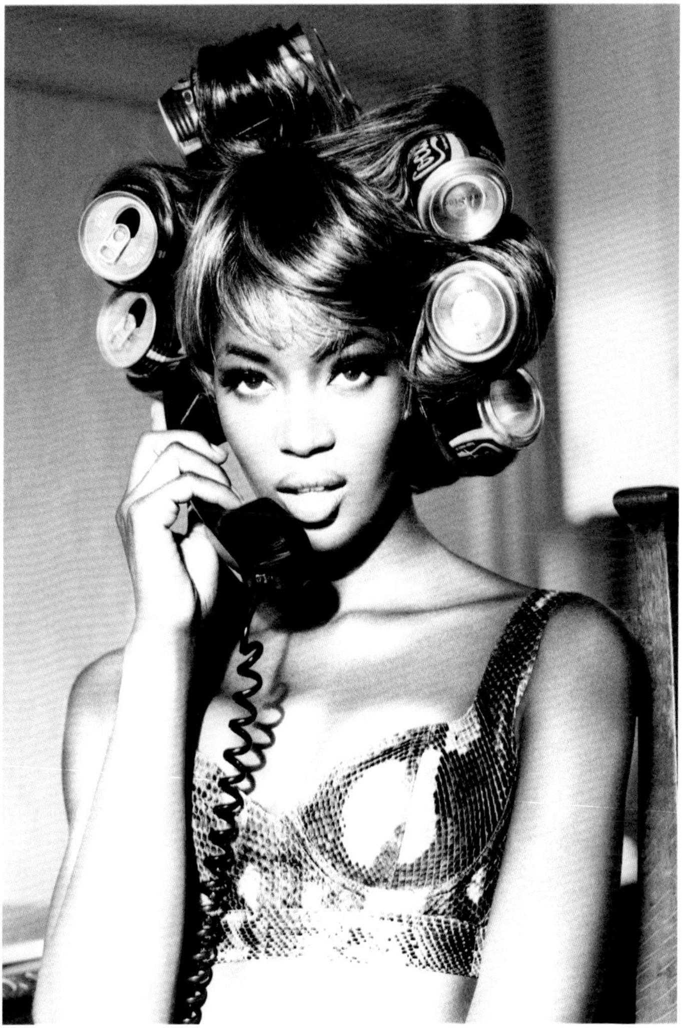

Ellen von Unwerth, 1991

NAOMI IS CHILD TO
WOMAN WRAPPED UP IN ONE.
HER SMILE – INTOXICATING.
HER SENSITIVITY – ALLURING.
HER RANGE IS INFINITE,
HER ENERGY UNIQUE.
SHE'S MY FAVORITE.

HERB RITTS

Herb Ritts, 1991 • *(Following Spread)* **Thierry Le Gouès, 1992**

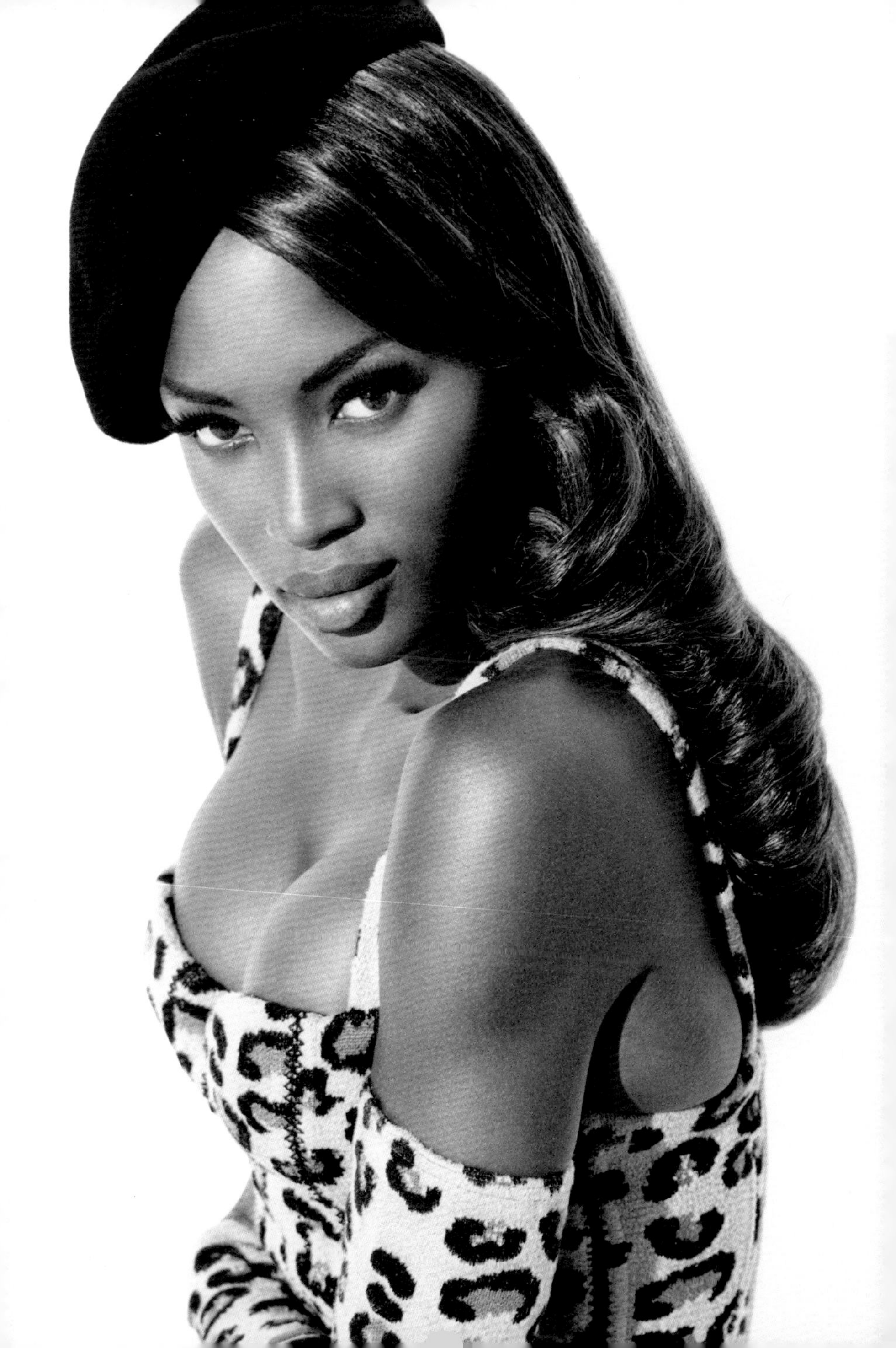

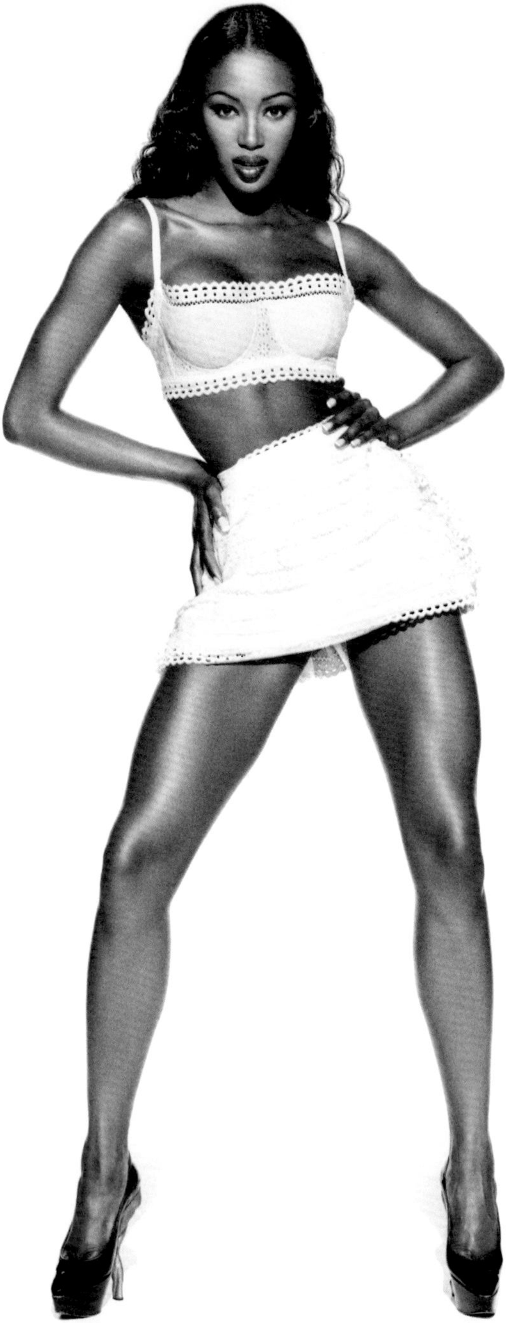

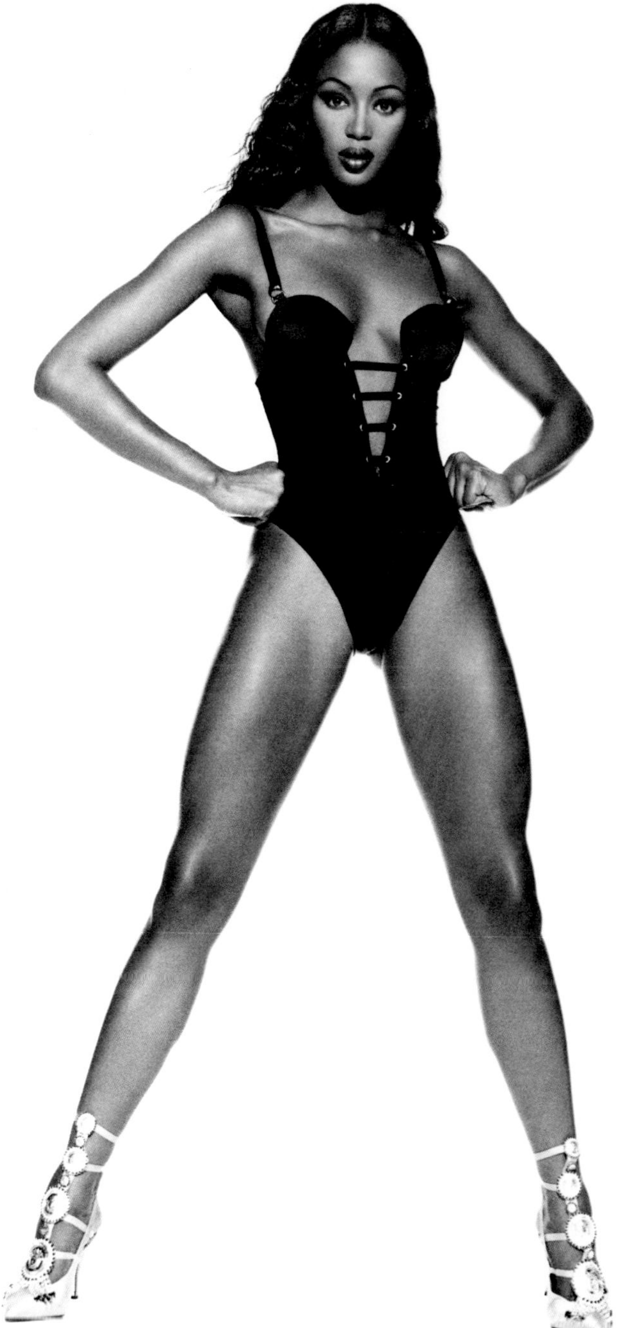

HER BEAUTY, HER STYLE,
HER SENSE OF HUMOR AND
MISCHIEVOUS WAYS.
THERE IS ONLY ONE NAOMI.

STEVEN MEISEL

Peter Lindbergh, 1992

NAOMI IS LIKE
A SILENT MOVIE STAR
IN AN AGE OF NOISE.

BONO

Peter Lindbergh, 1992

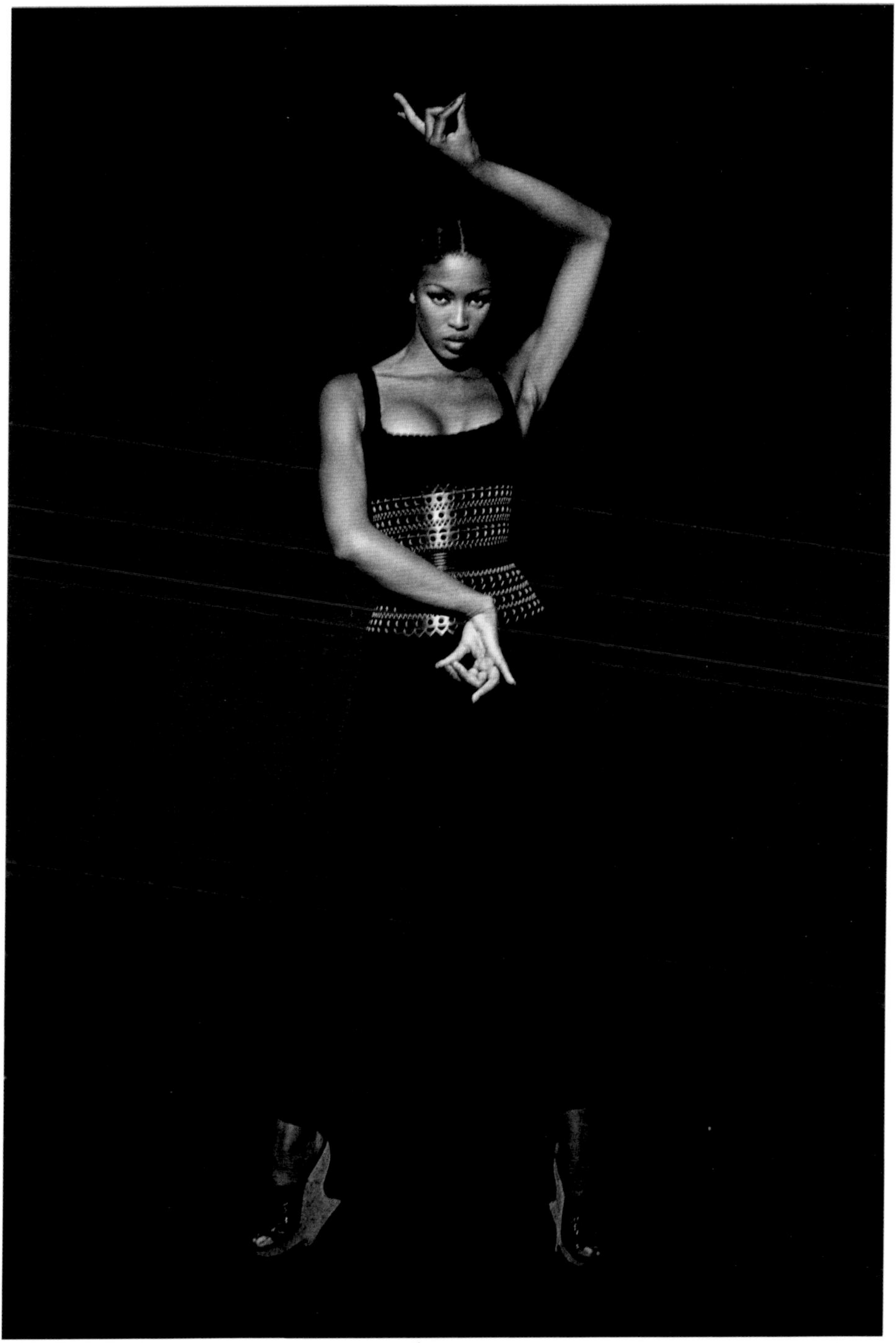

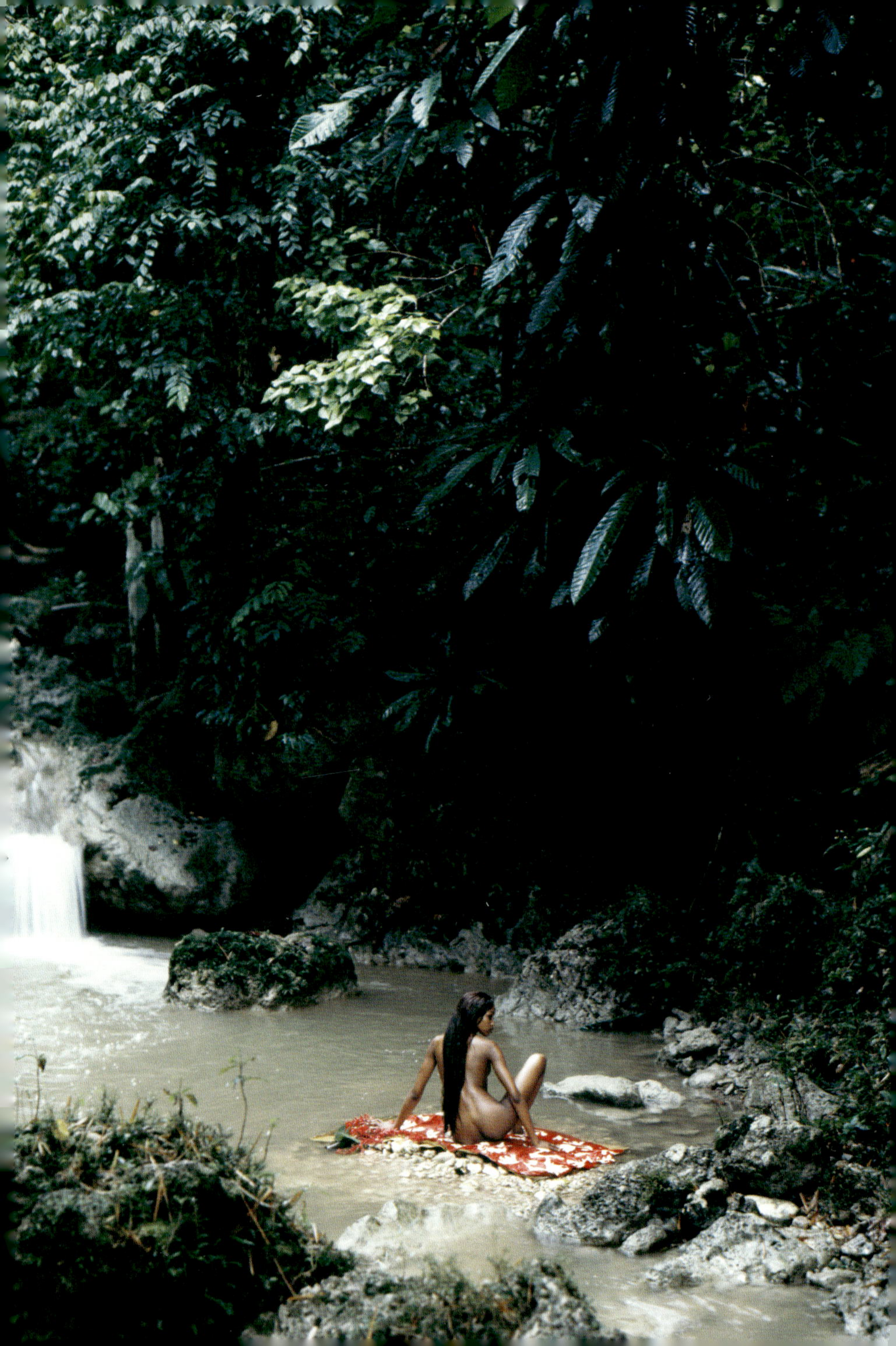

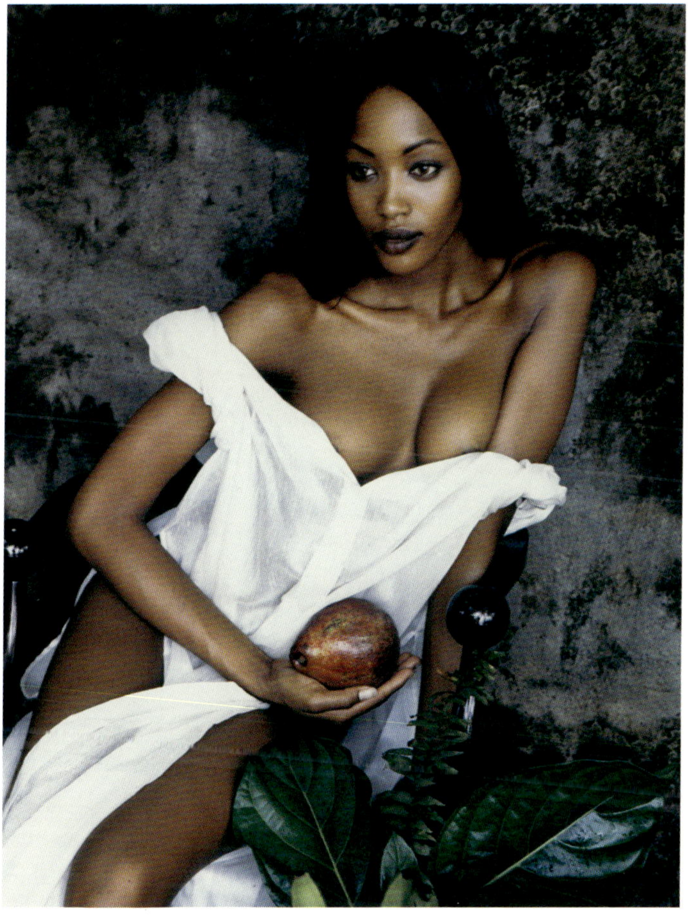

(This & Following Spread) **Peter Lindbergh, 1992**

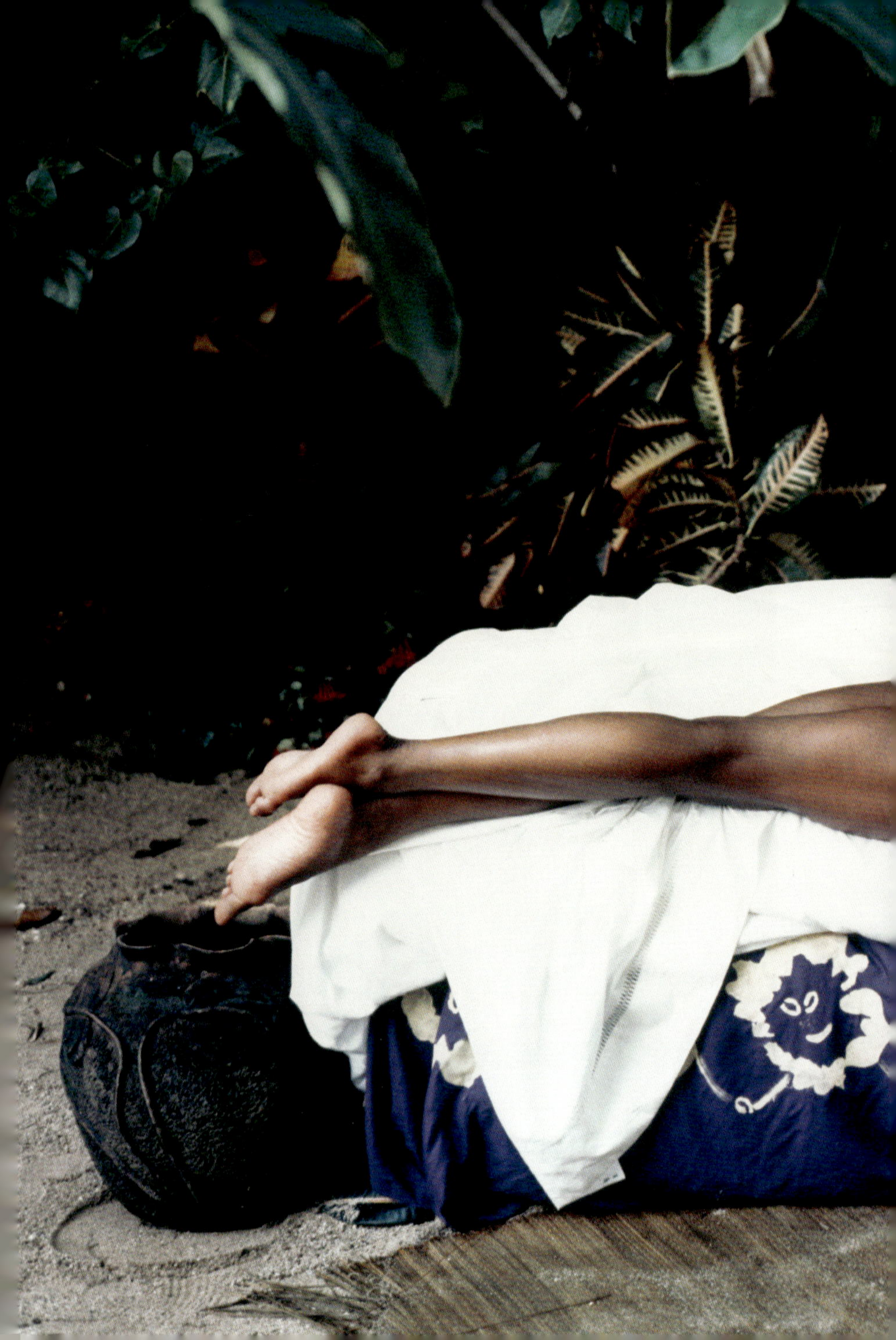

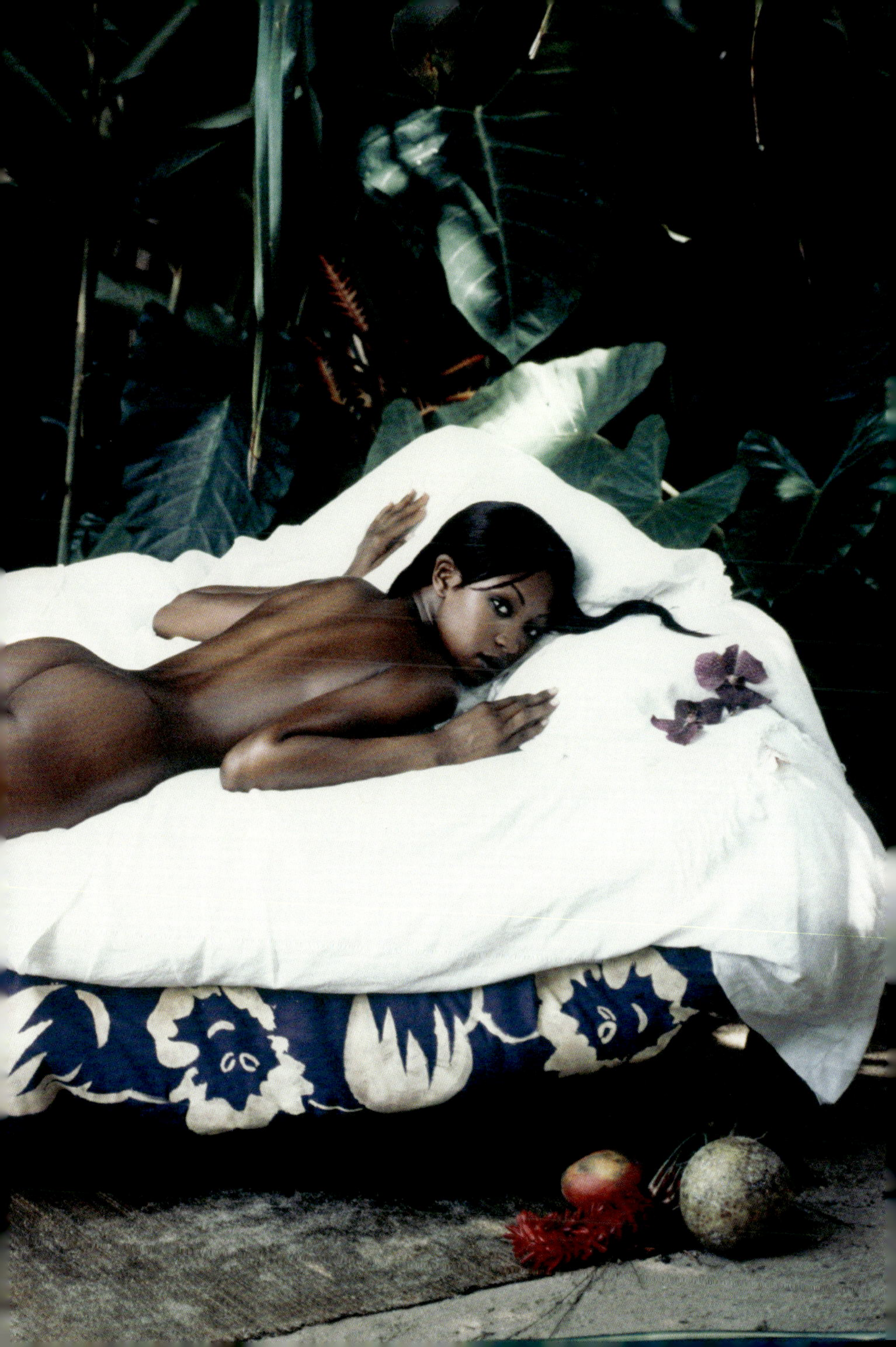

Steven Meisel, 1992

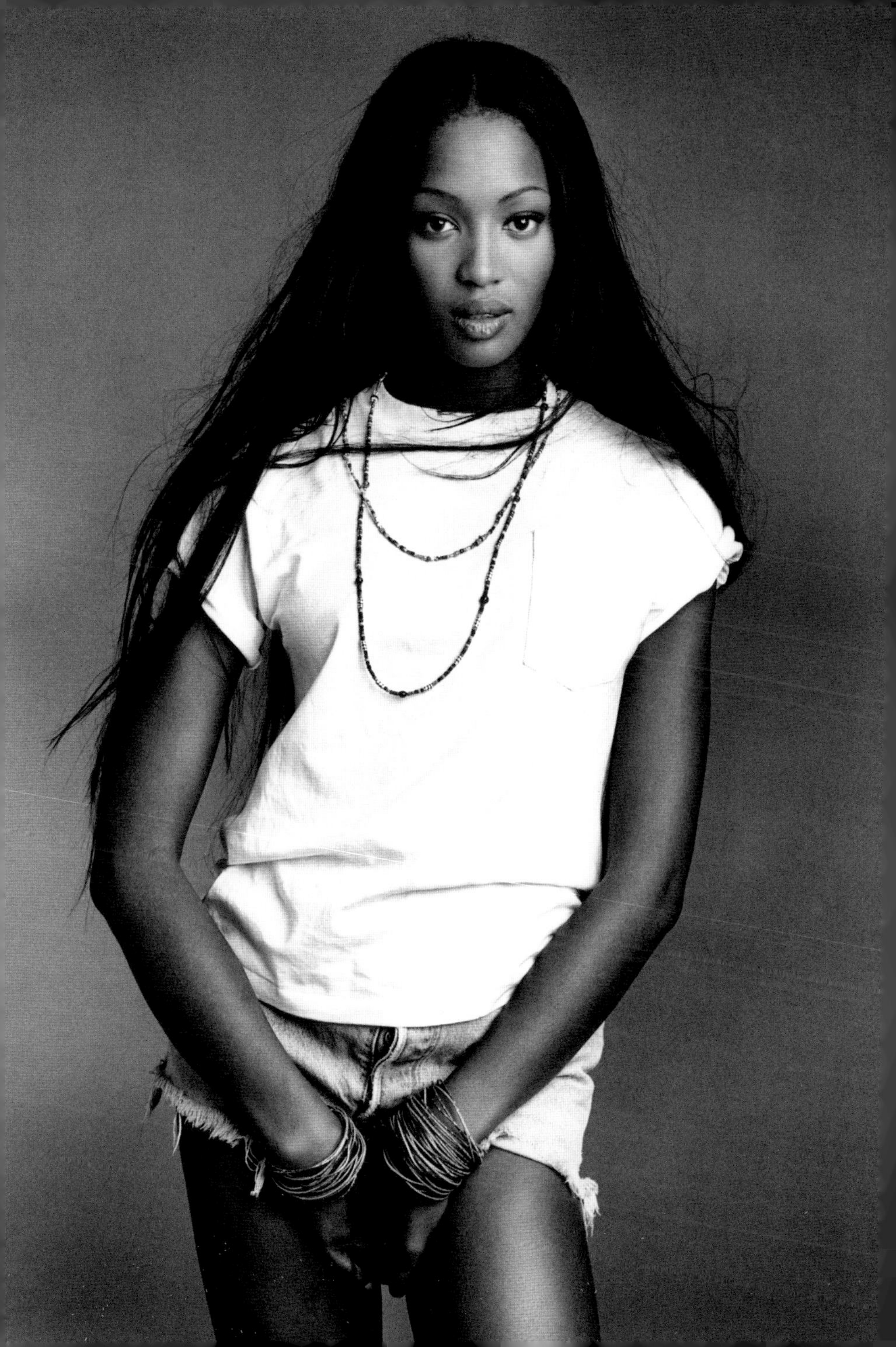

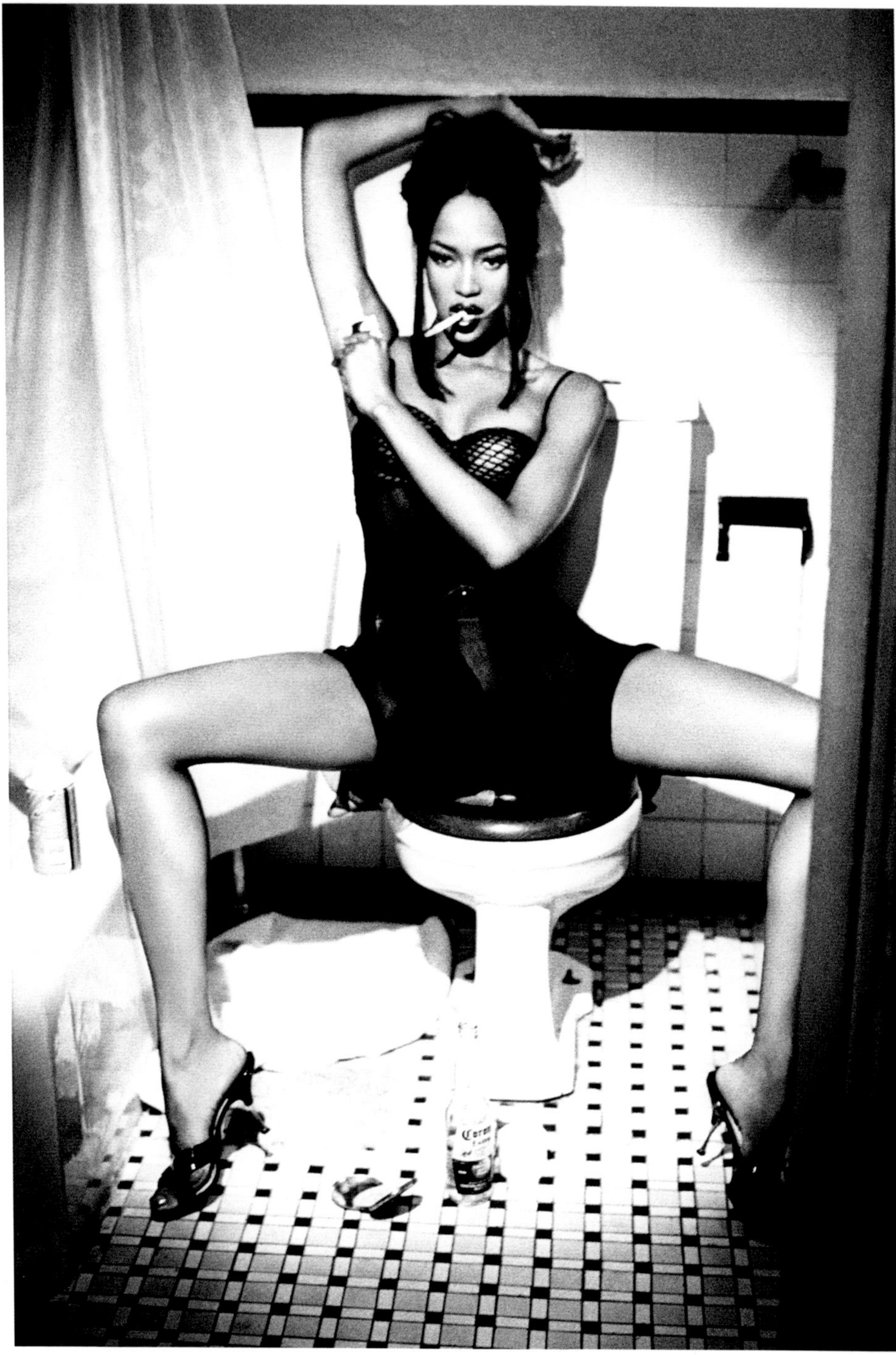

PHOTOGRAPHY IS A MIRROR IN WHICH WE SEE OURSELVES REFLECTED. NAOMI GAVE A LOT OF YOUNG BLACK WOMEN A SUPPORTIVE AND BEAUTIFUL REFLECTION.

IMAN

Ellen von Unwerth, 1994

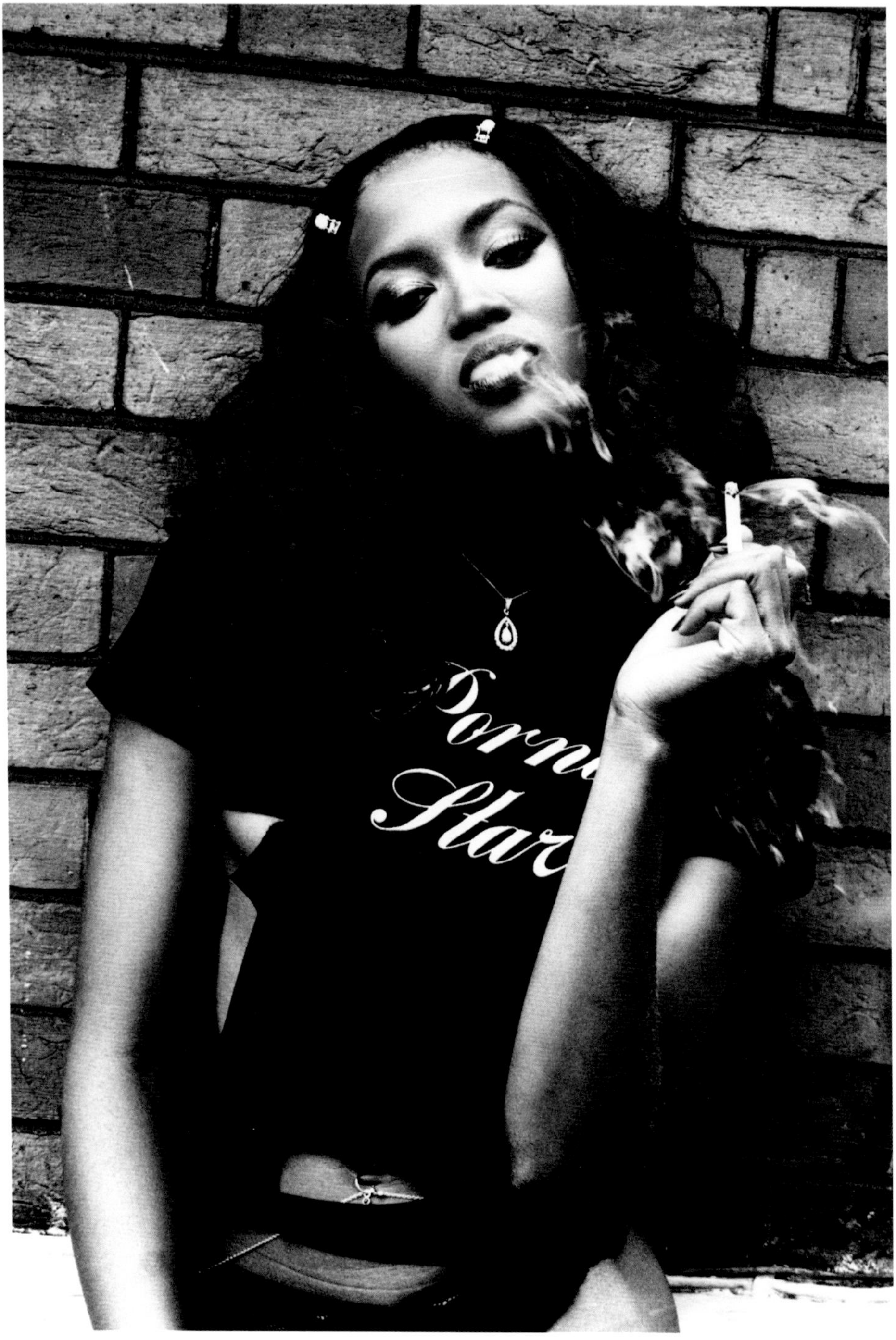

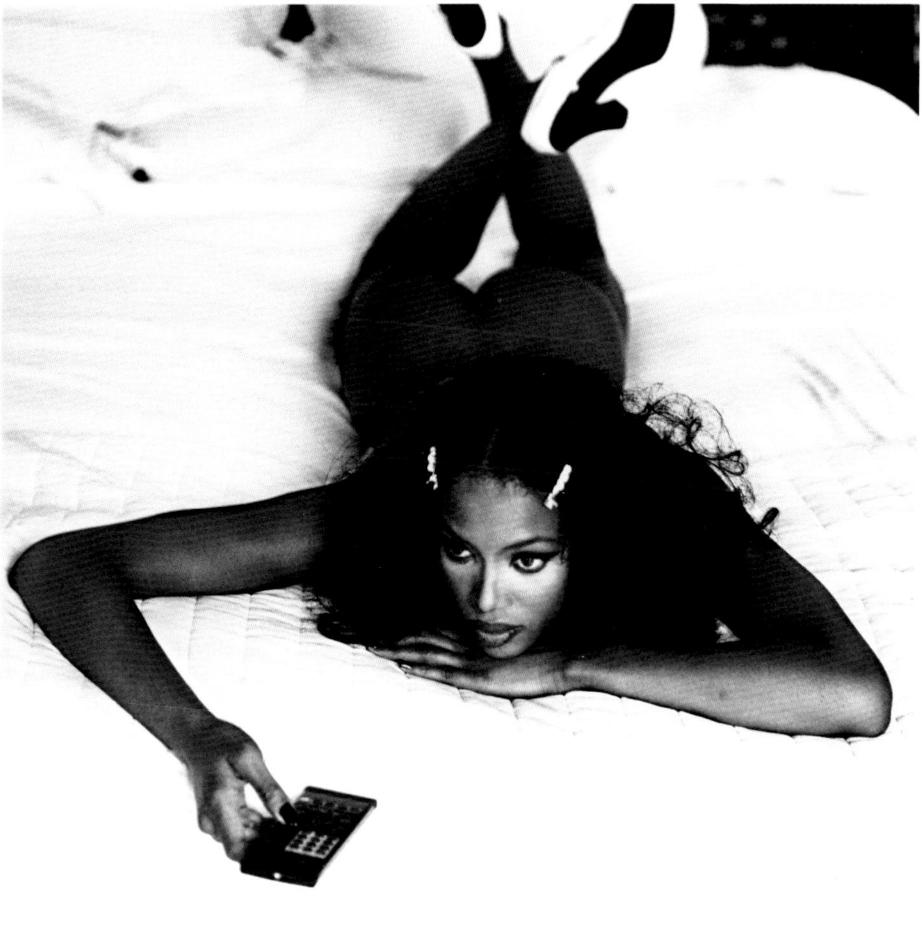

Anton Corbijn, 1994

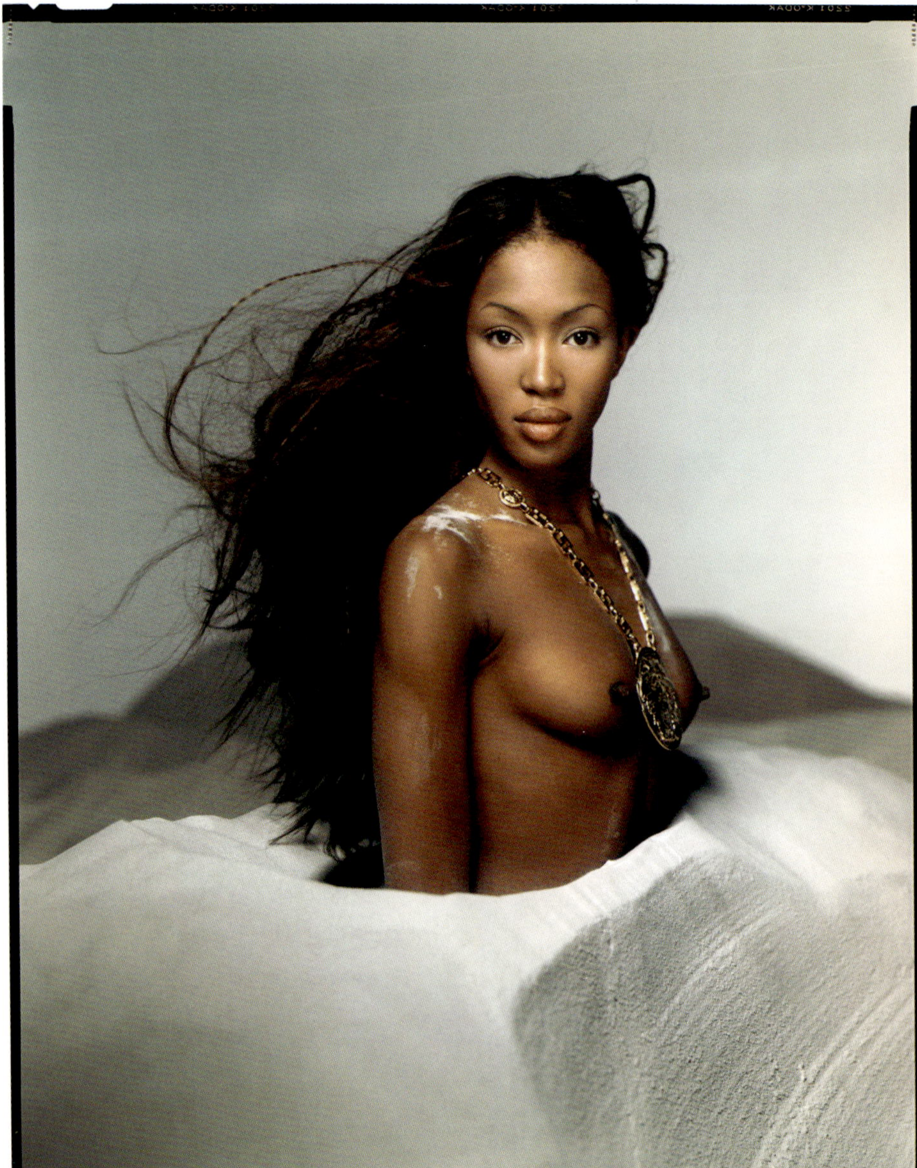

Richard Avedon, 1992

I FIRST PHOTOGRAPHED
NAOMI WHEN SHE WAS 16
AND VERY NEW TO MODELLING.
SHE WAS GORGEOUS, AND
ALTHOUGH SHY SHE HAD
SOMETHING AMAZING ABOUT
HER. SHE WAS A SURPRISE
OF LIFE!

MARIO TESTINO

Anton Corbijn, 1994

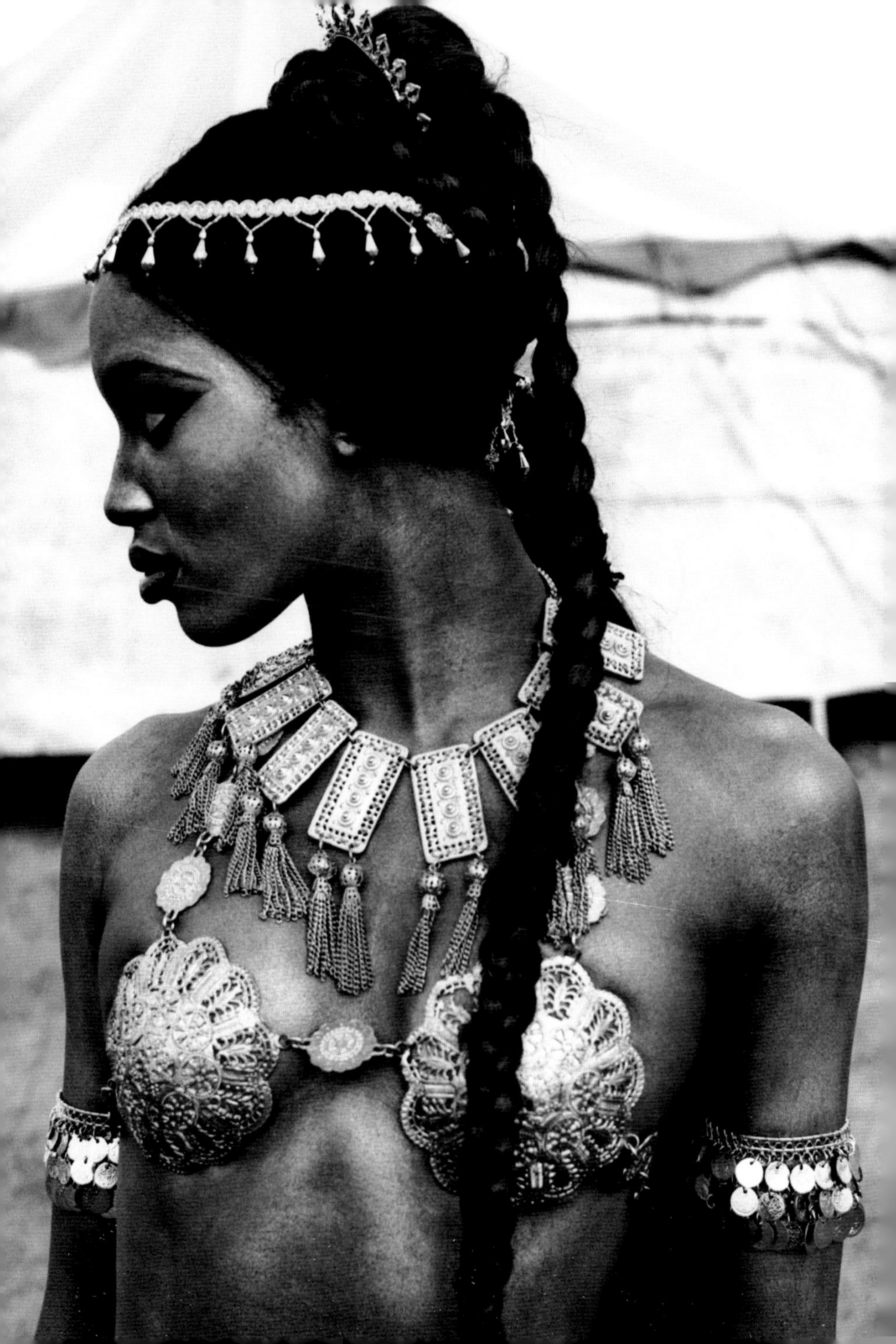

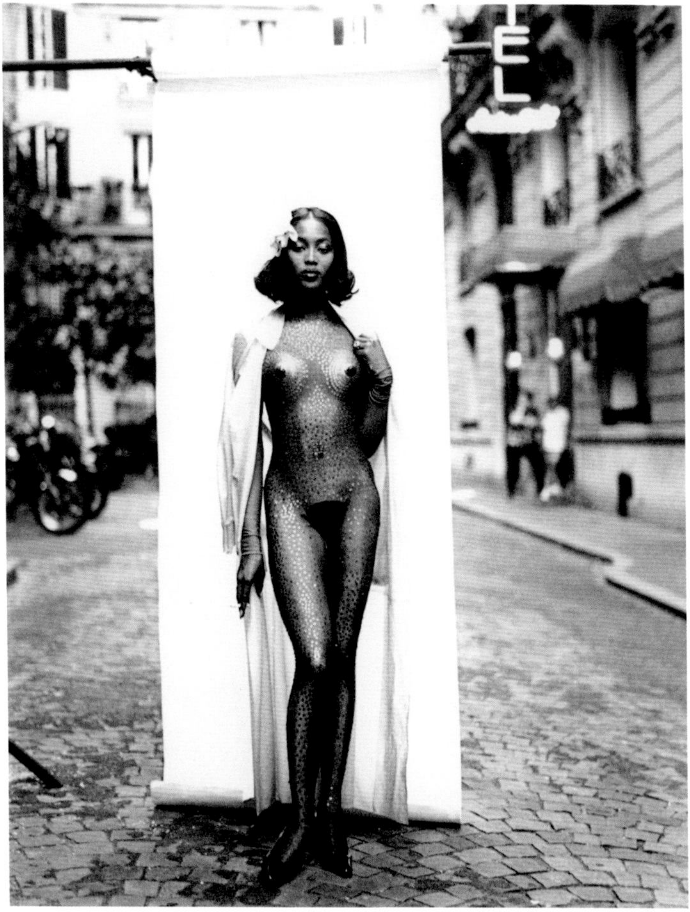

Paolo Roversi, 1994 • Paolo Roversi, 1997

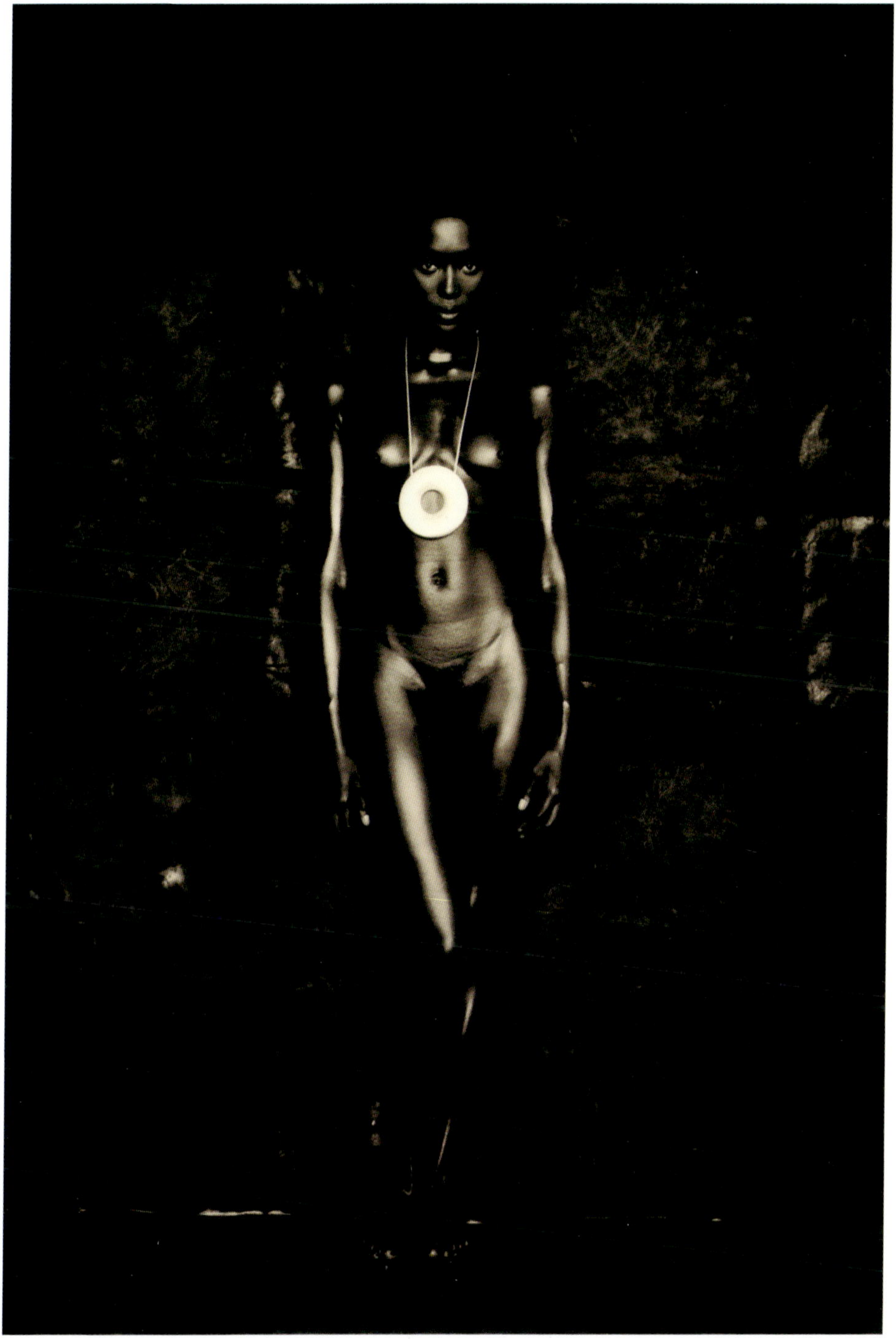

WHEN...YOU SAY NO,
YOU'RE A BITCH. YOU CAN'T
WIN. THEY'RE GOING TO
CALL YOU A BITCH EITHER
WAY. IF I'M A BITCH,
I'M A HARD WORKING BITCH.

NAOMI CAMPBELL

Pierre et Gilles, 1997 • *(Following Spread)* **Peter Lindbergh, 1997**

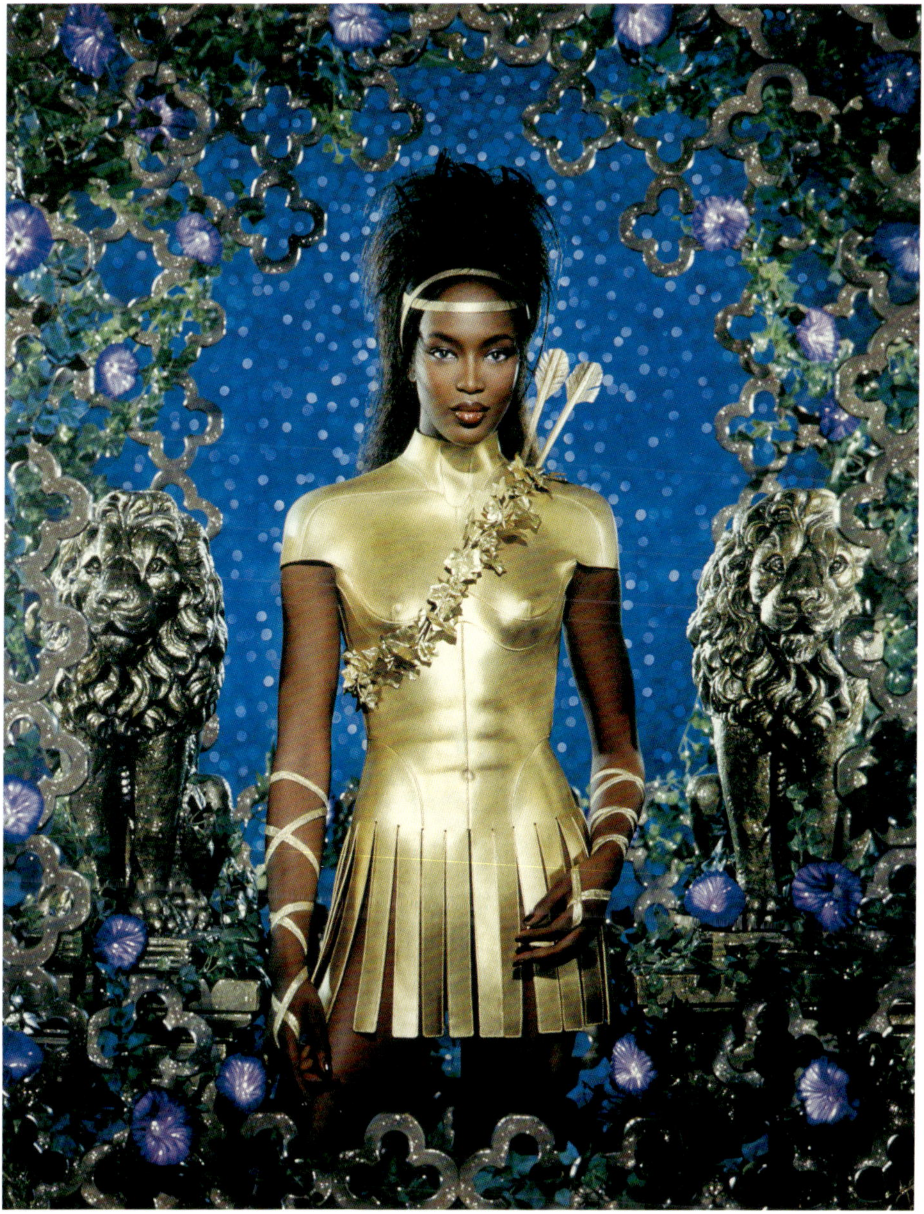

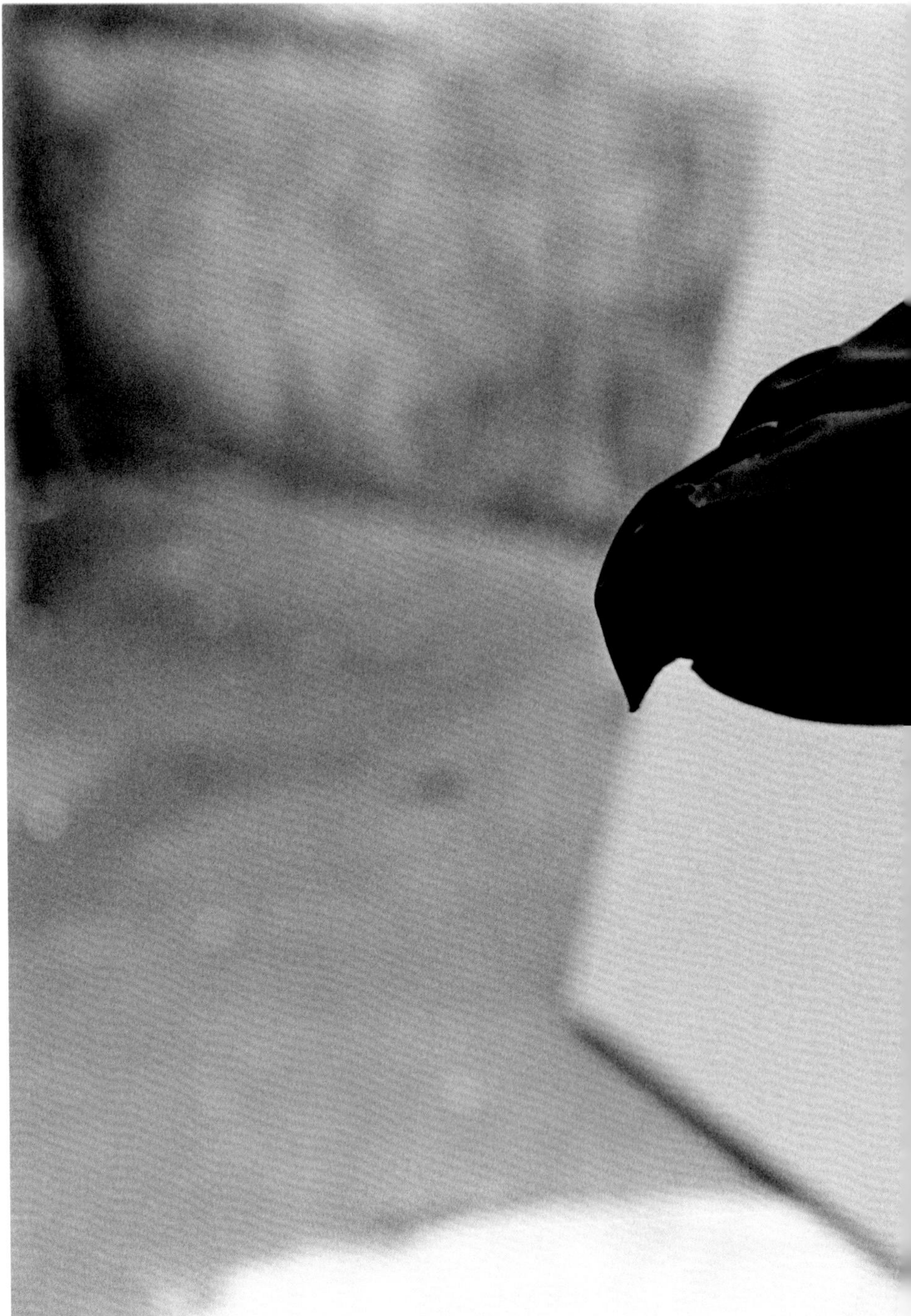

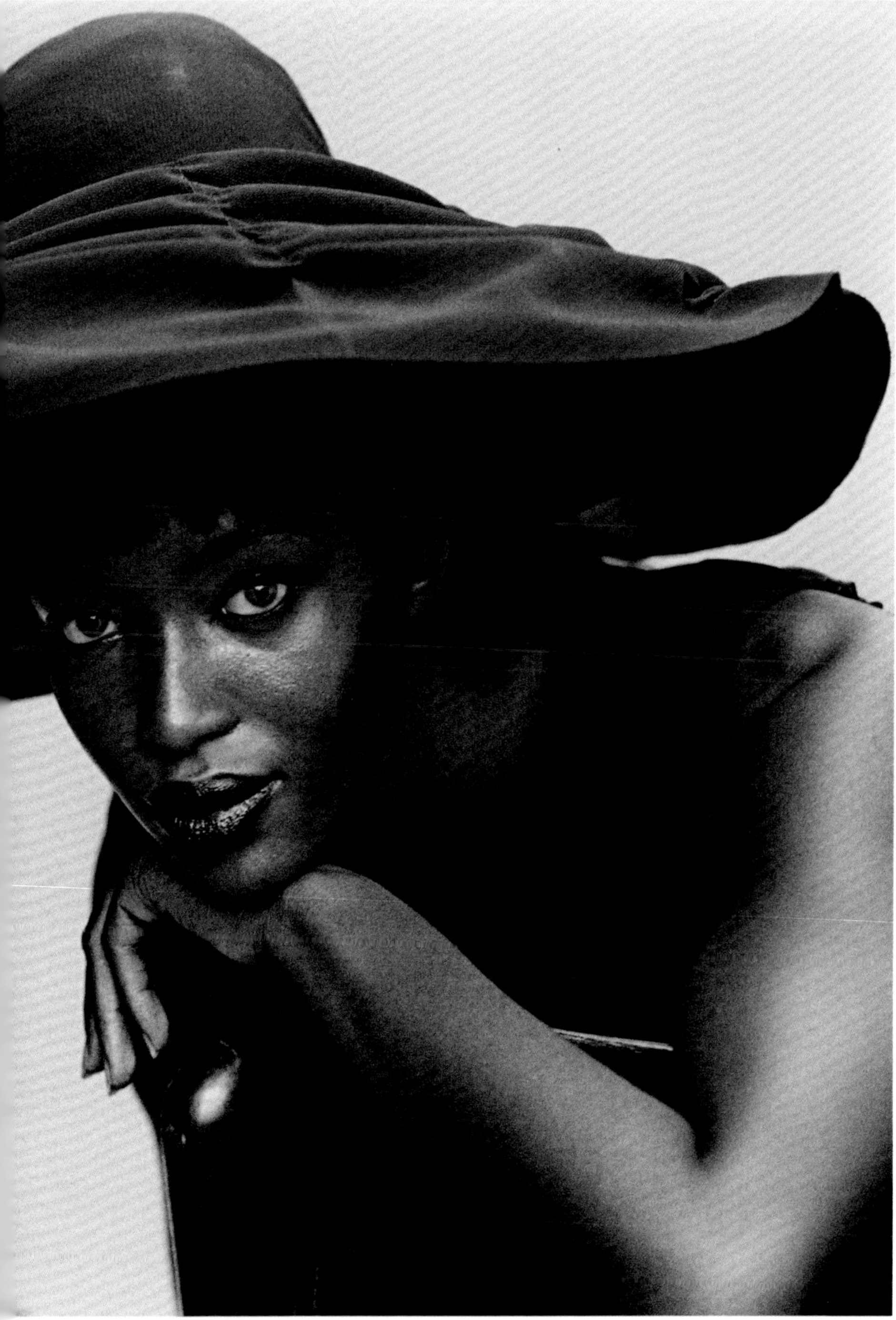

IN CANNES WITH HER,
I THOUGHT I WAS WITH
MARILYN MONROE.
WE HAD MORE ATTENTION
THAN ANY ACTRESS IN
ANY FILM. HOW CAN YOU
BE UPSET ABOUT THAT?
IT WAS BETTER THAN BEING
WITH ELIZABETH TAYLOR.

MARC JACOBS

Mario Testino, 1996

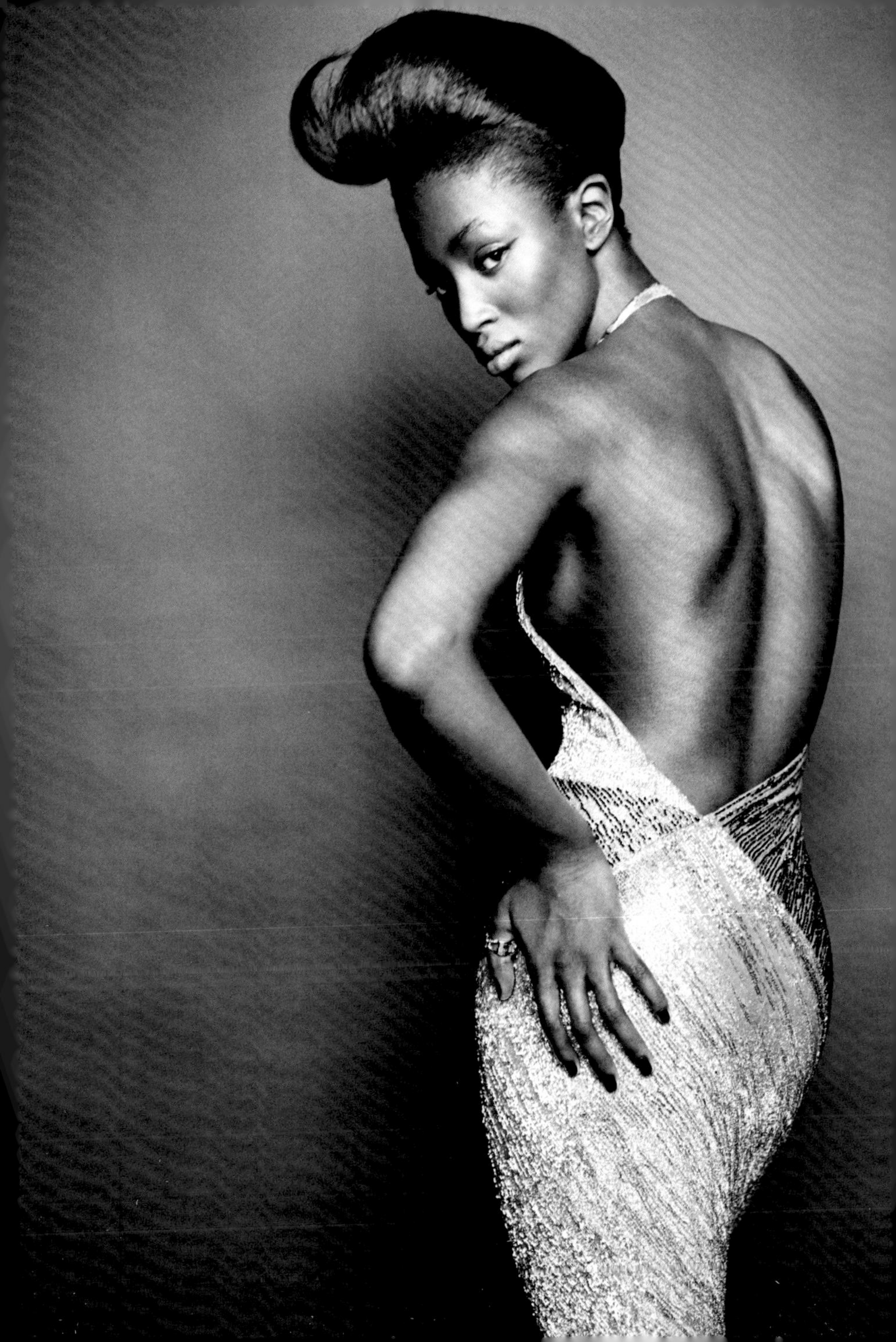

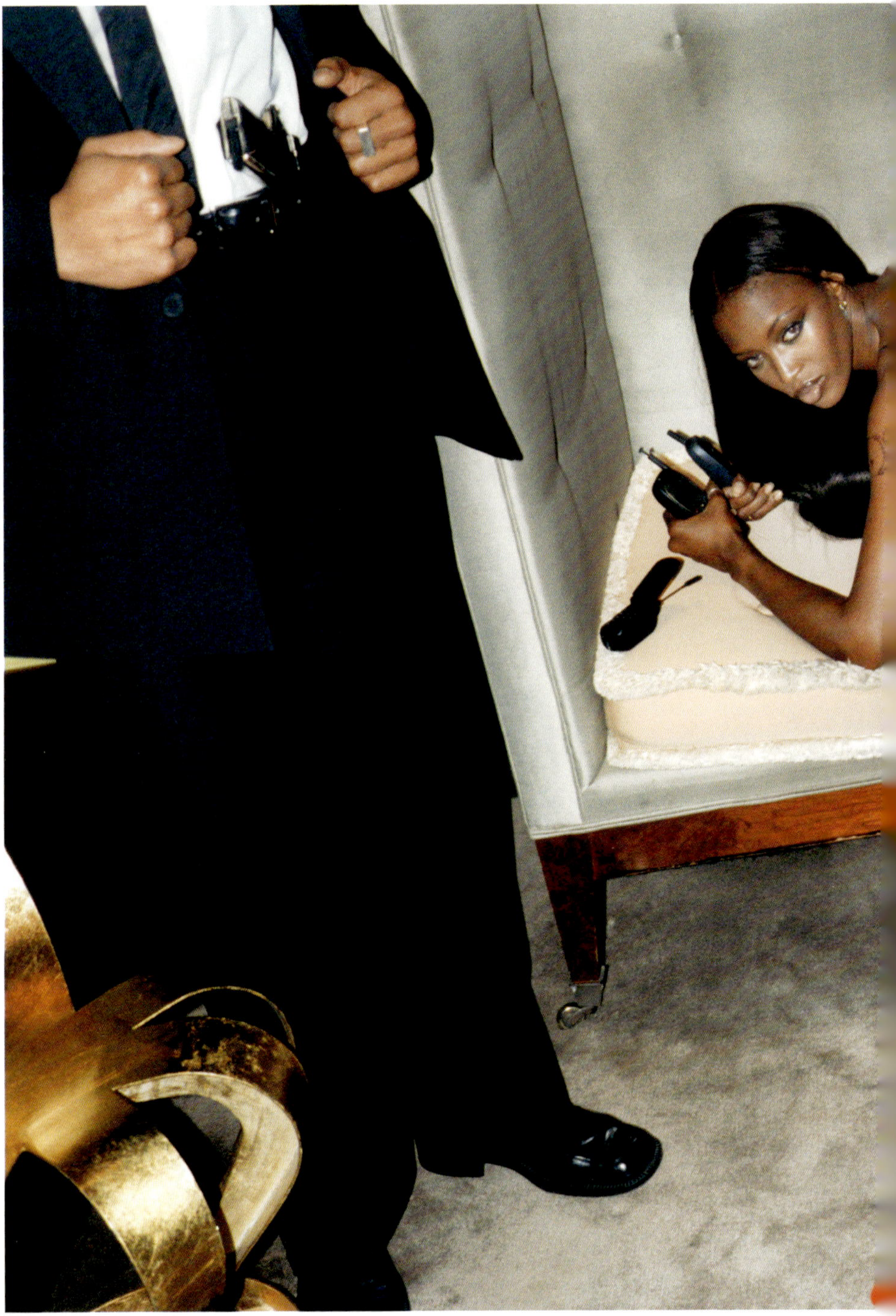

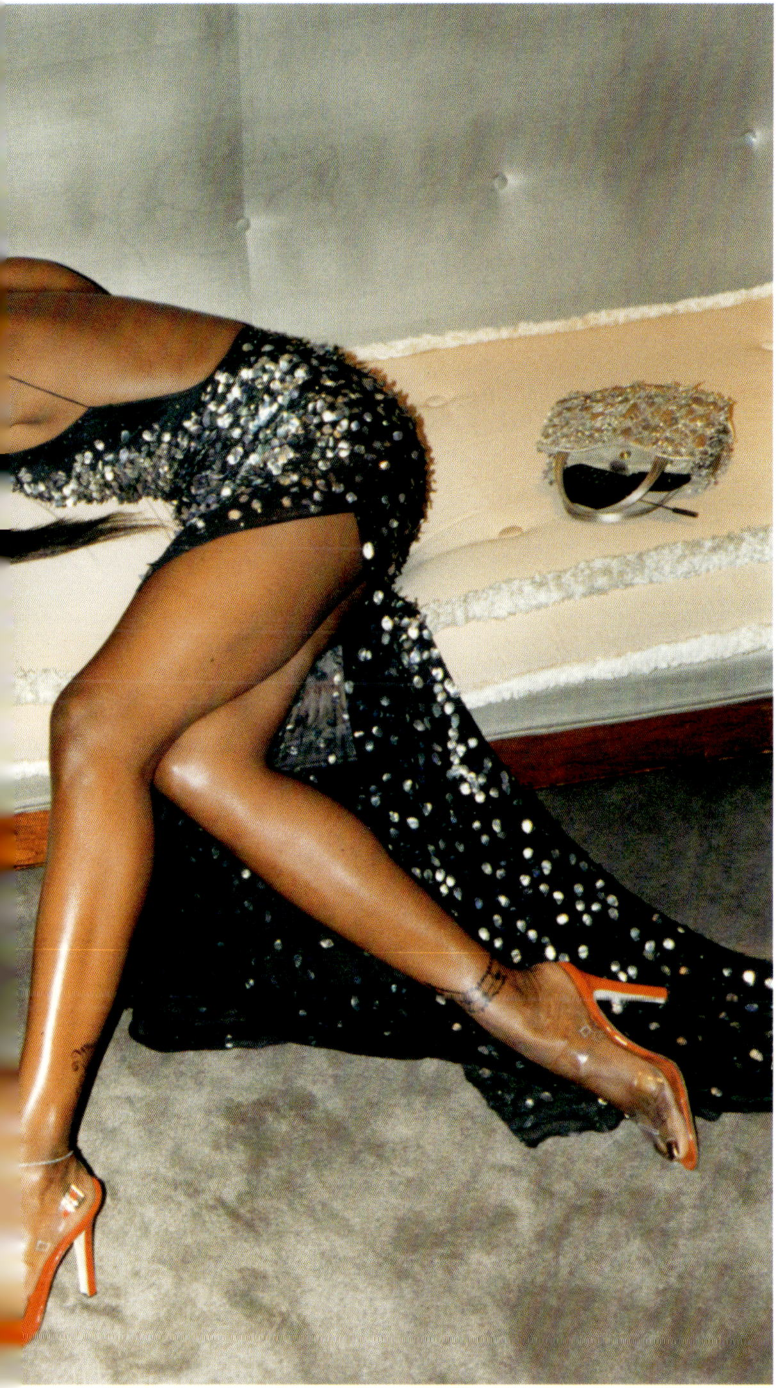

I HAVE FILMED HER, PHOTOGRAPHED HER AND MADE SCULPTURES OF HER, AND IN EACH OF THESE MEDIUMS HER INCREDIBLE BEAUTY AND STRENGTH HAS ENABLED ME TO CREATE IMPORTANT IMAGES OF A MODERNITY, POWER AND RELEVANCE TO THE TIME WE LIVE IN.

NICK KNIGHT

(Previous Spread) **Helmut Newton, American *Vogue*, 1999**
Helmut Newton, Cap d'Antibes, 1998

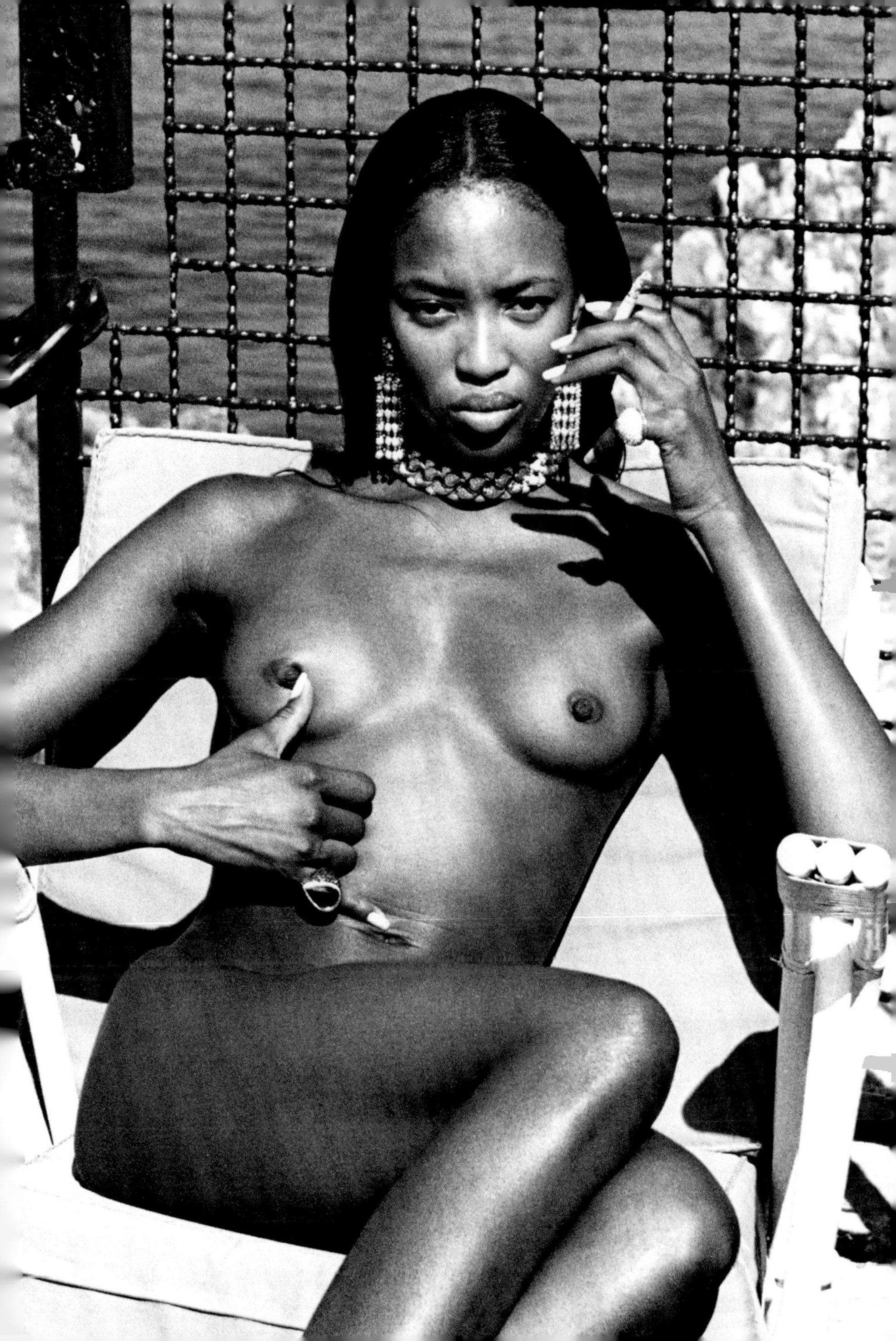

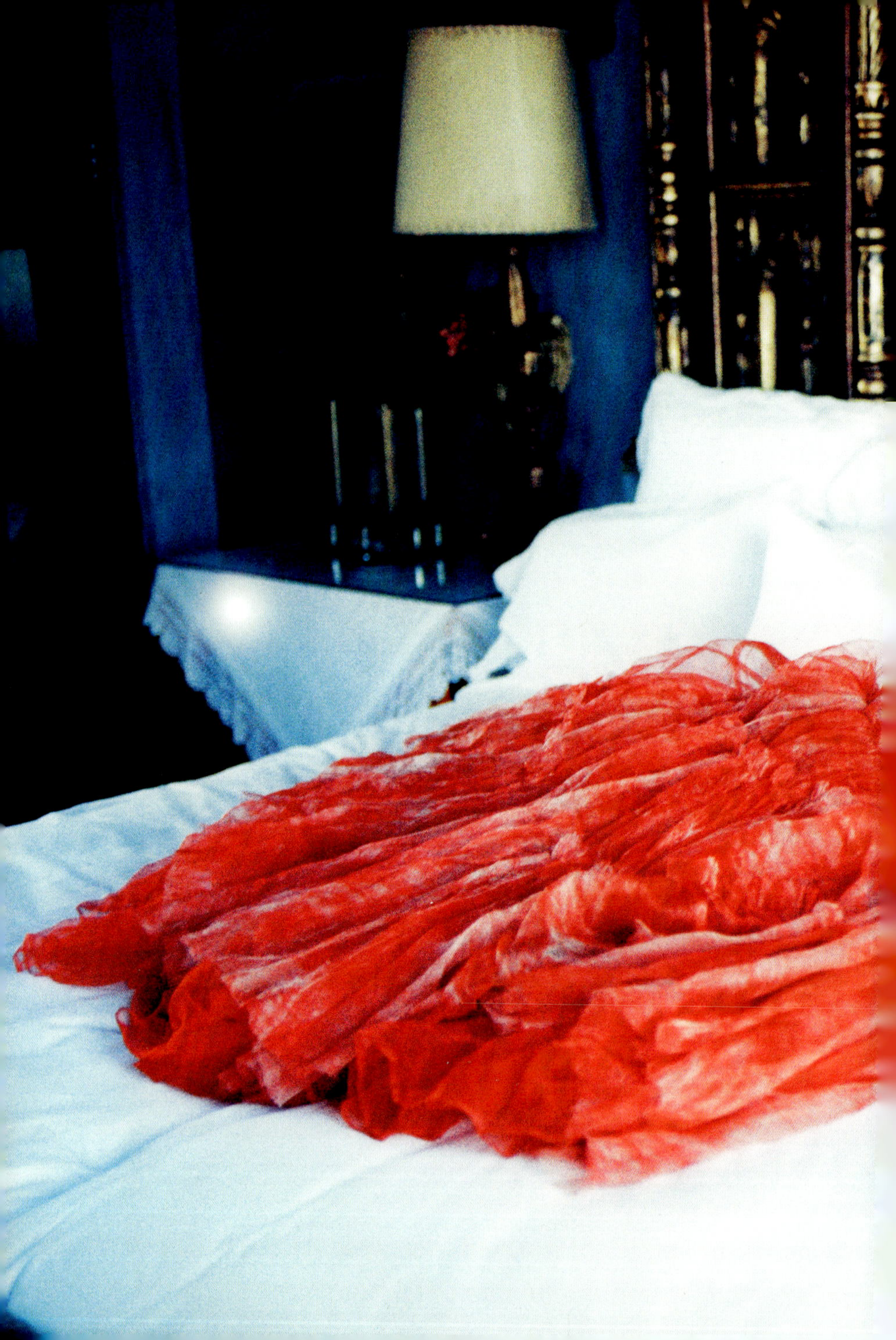

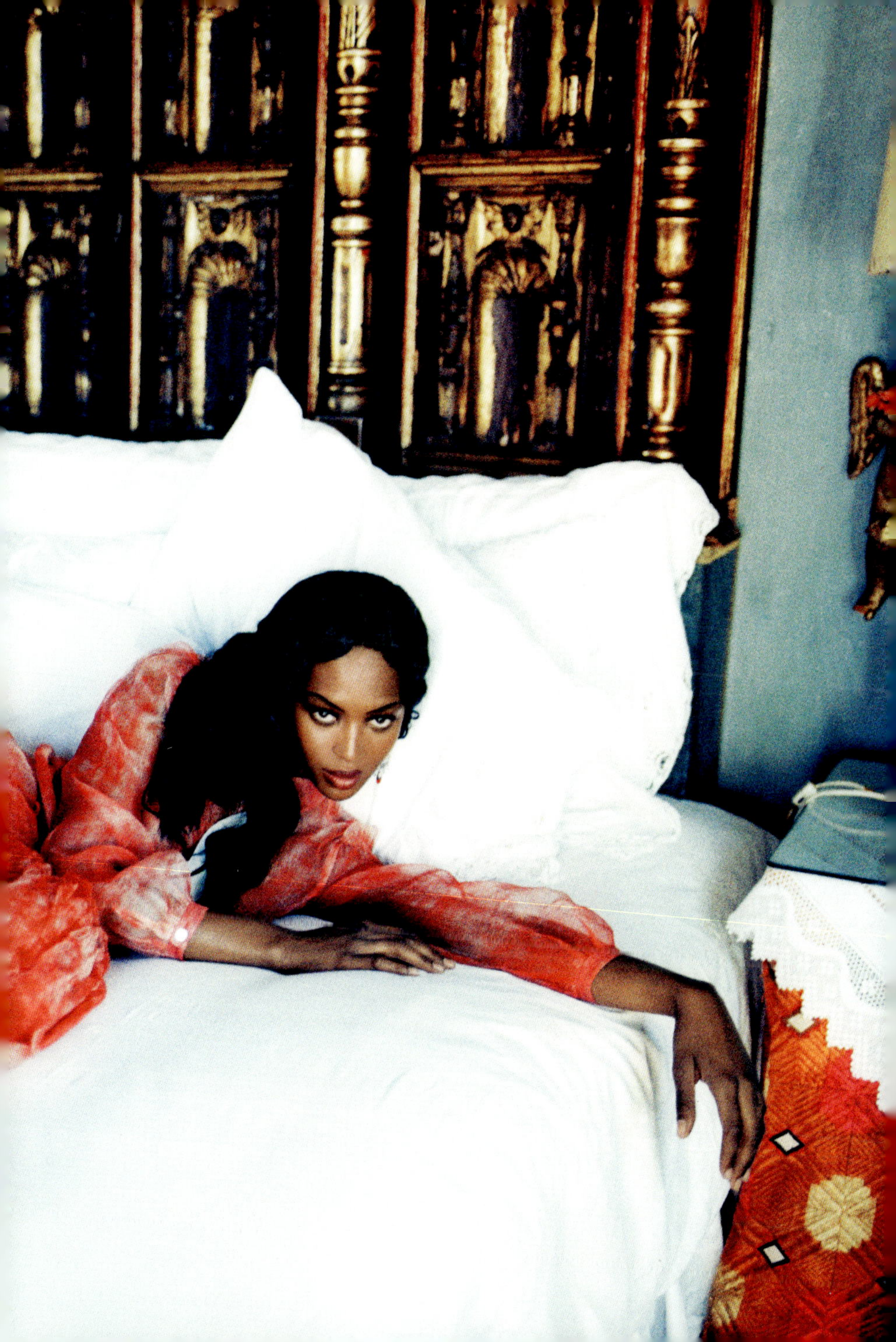

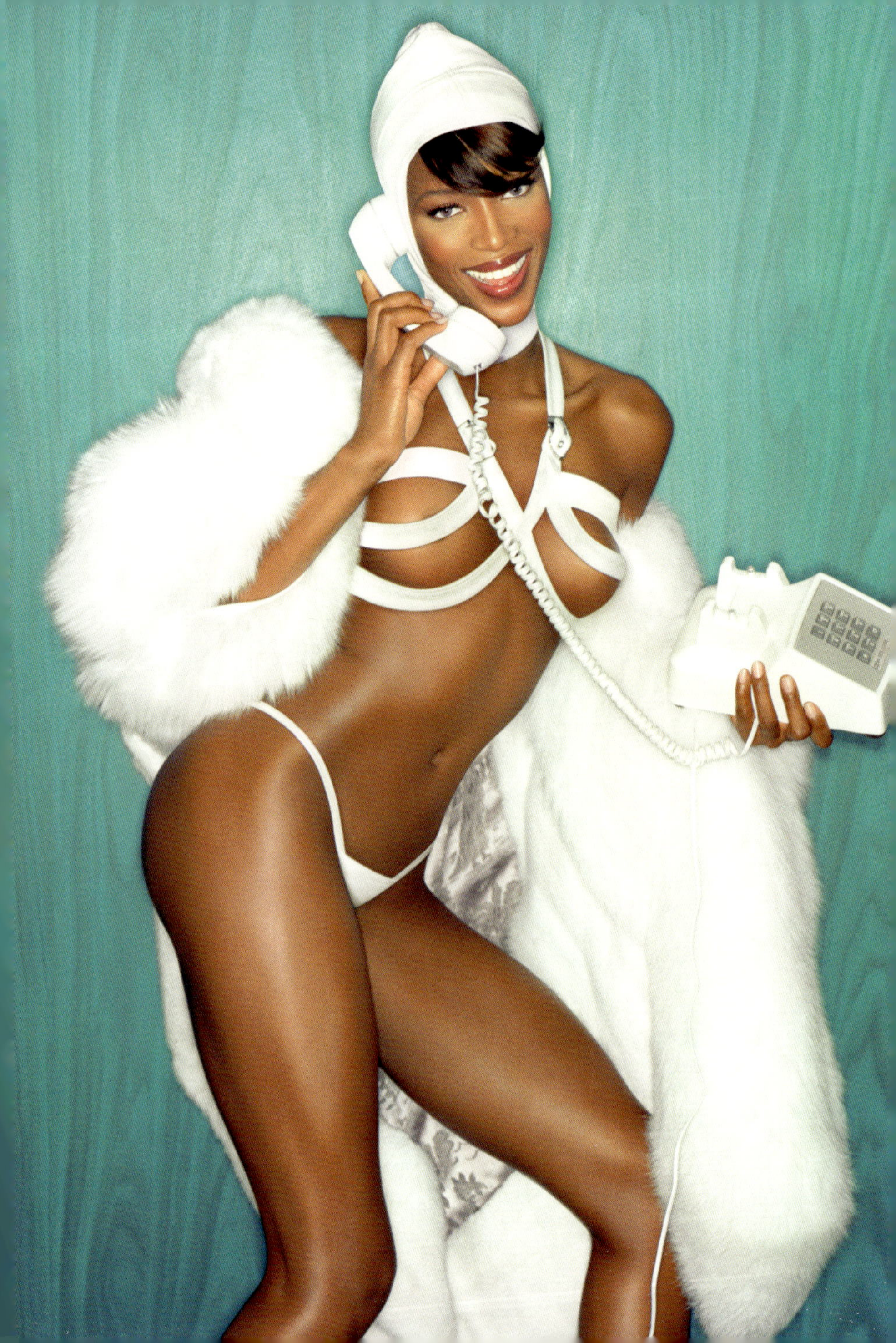

(Previous Spread) **Ellen von Unwerth, 1998**
(Opposite & Following Spread) **David LaChapelle, 1999**

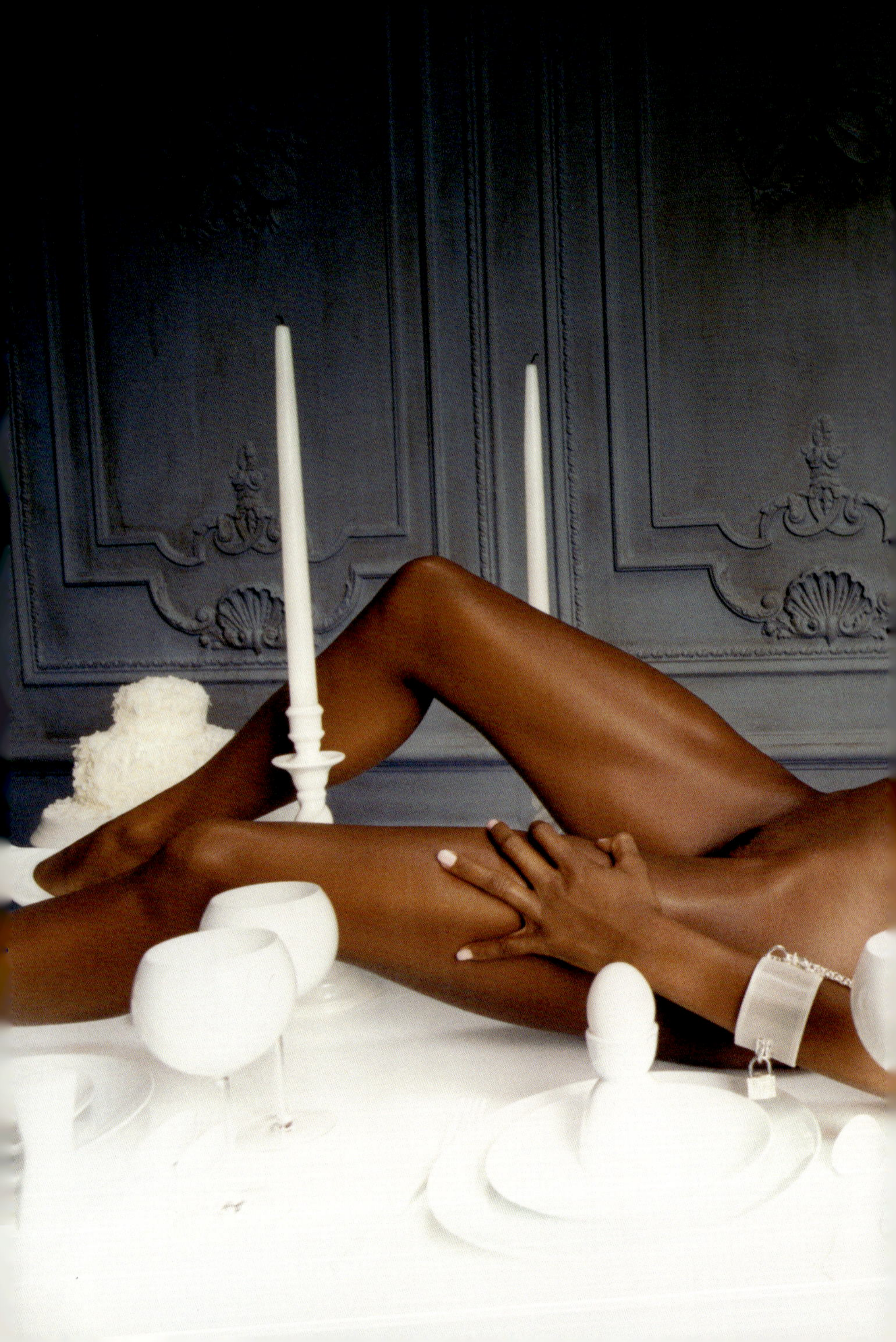

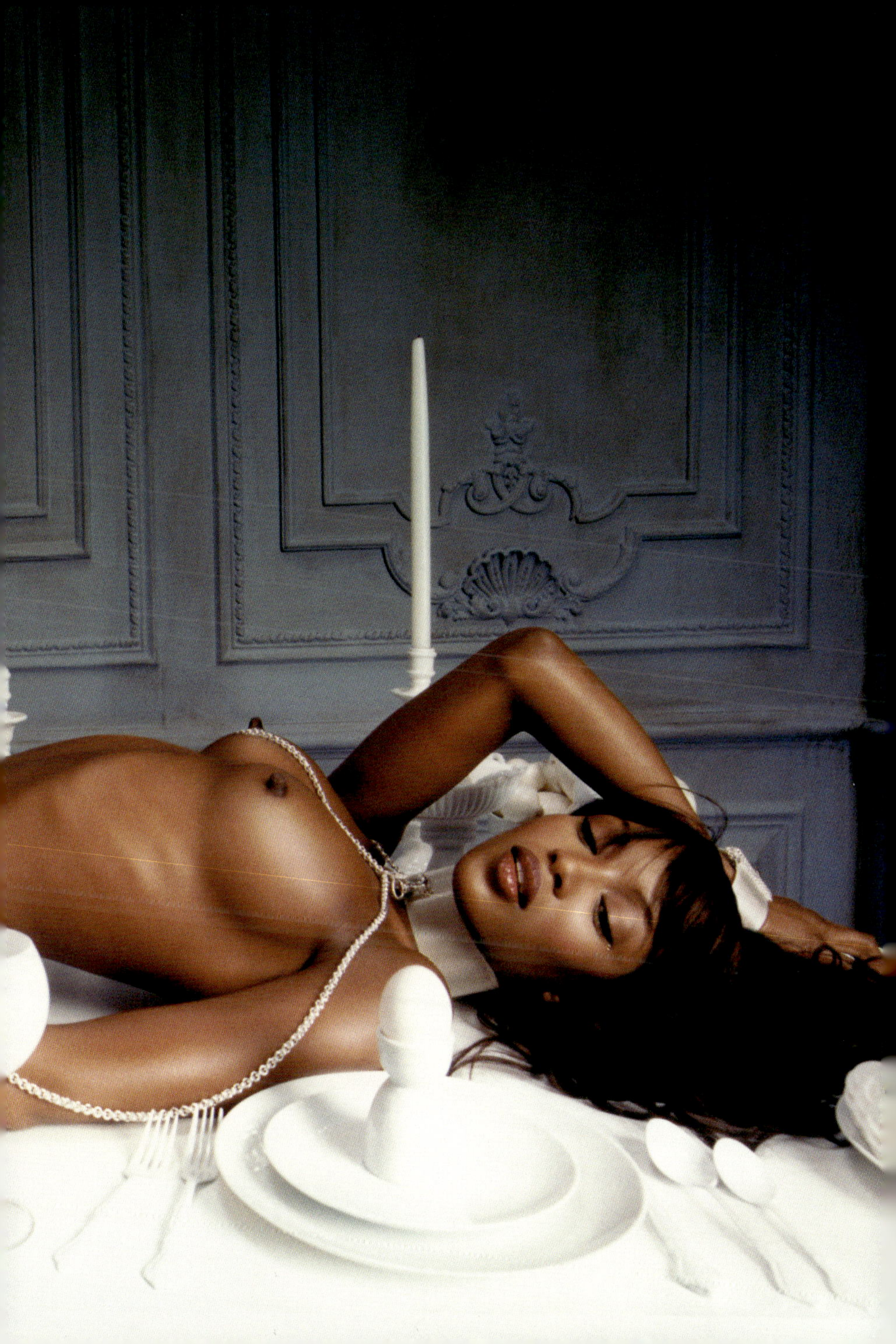

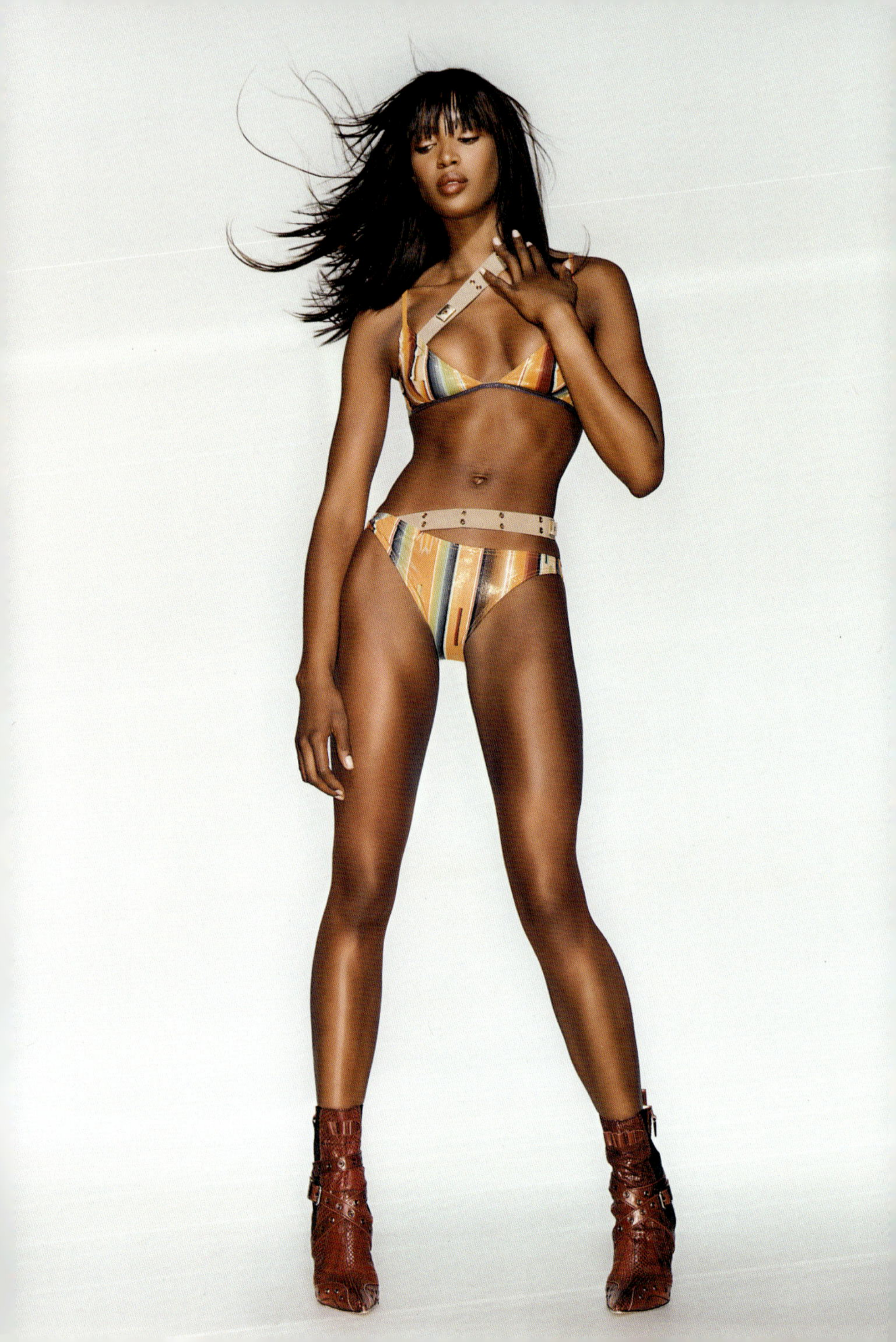

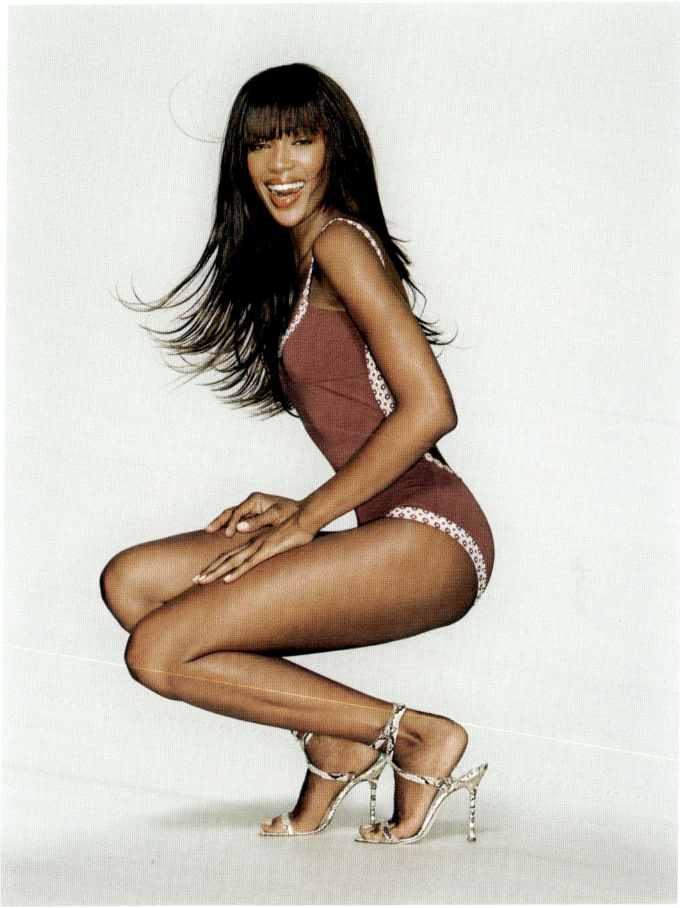

Gilles Bensimon, 2002

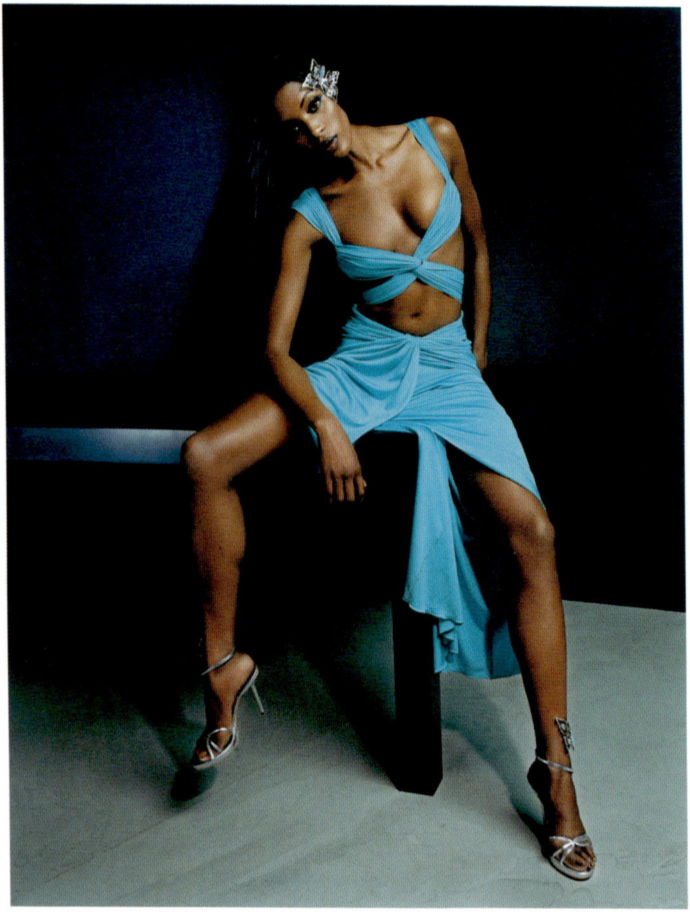

Mario Testino, 2003 • *(Following Spread)* **Mert Alas & Marcus Piggott, 2003**

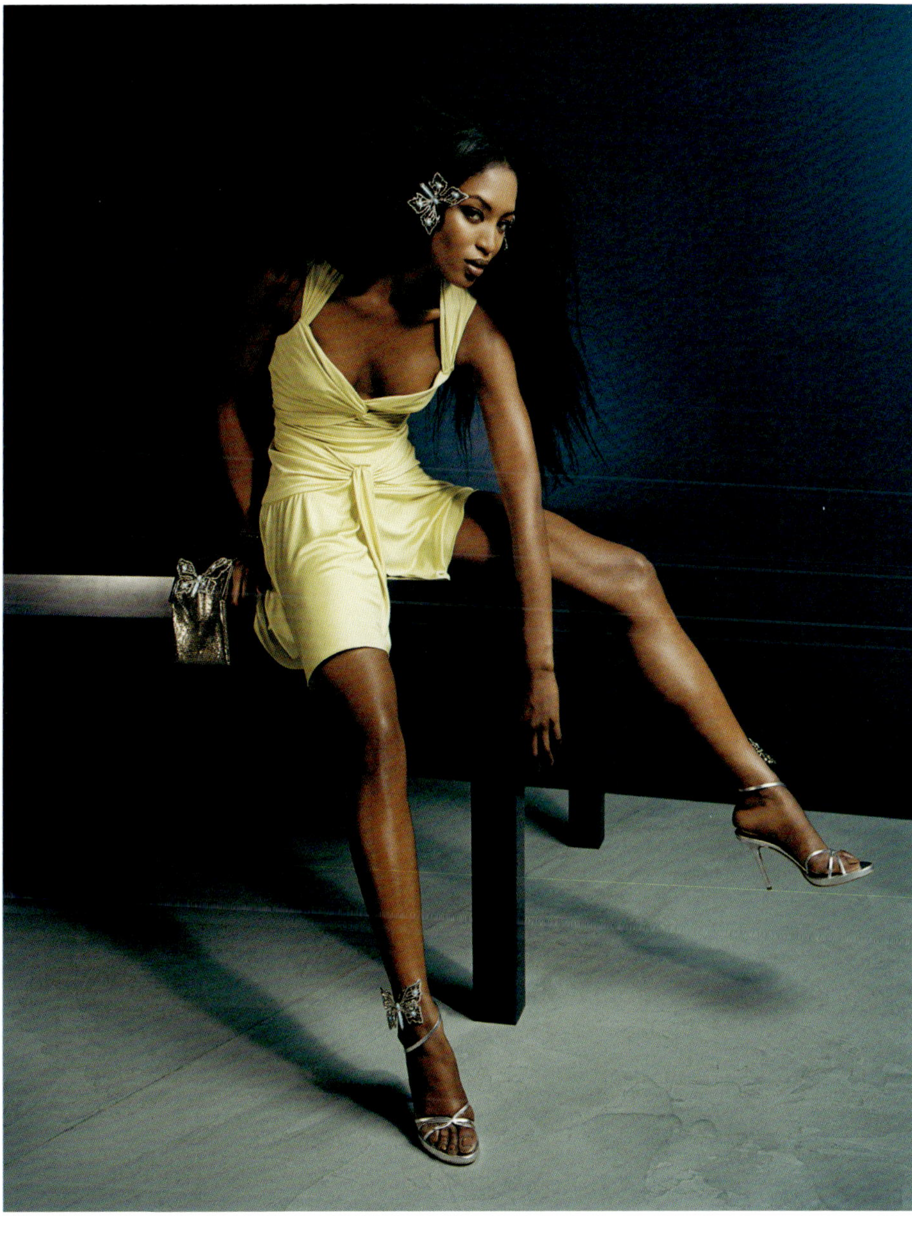

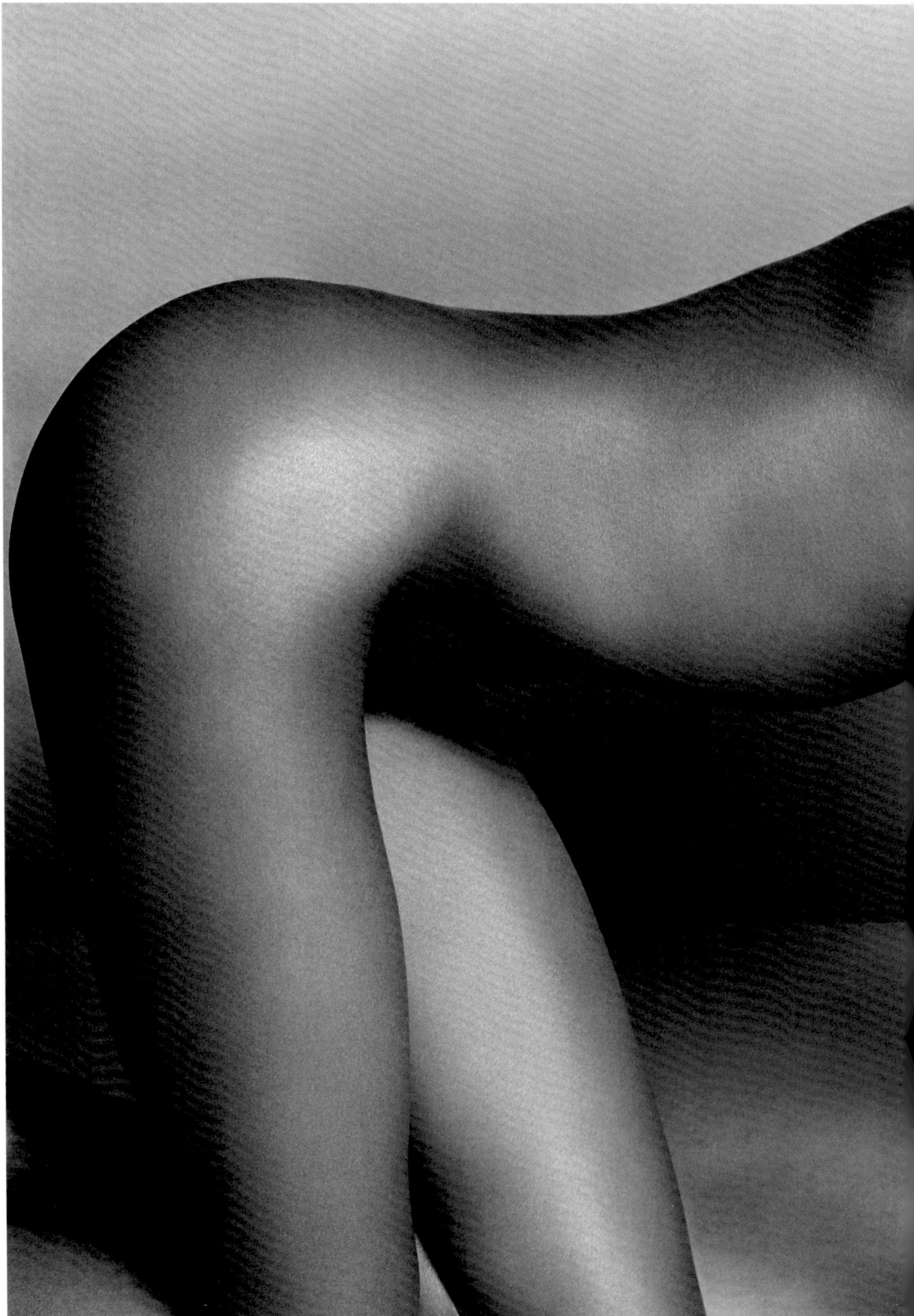

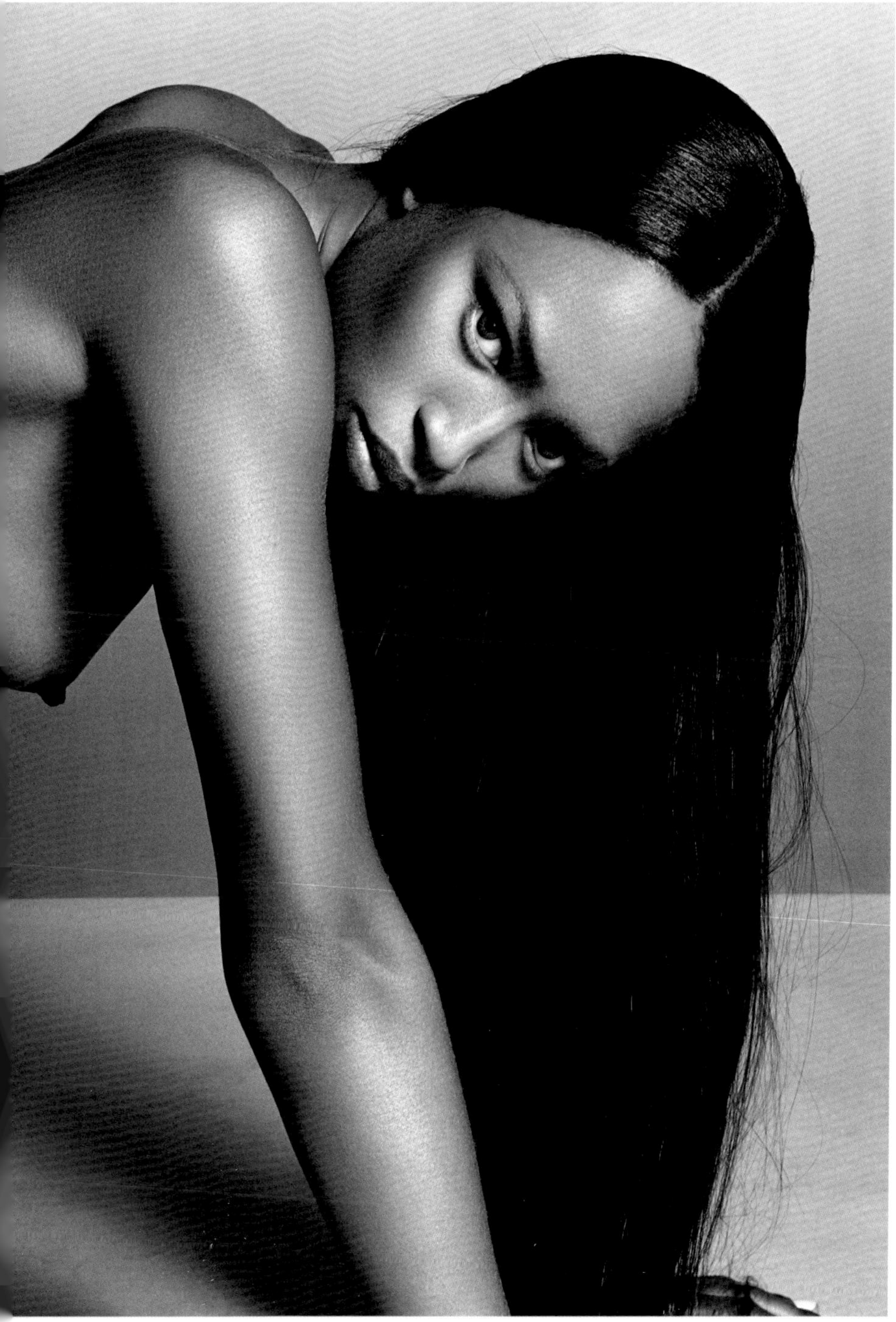

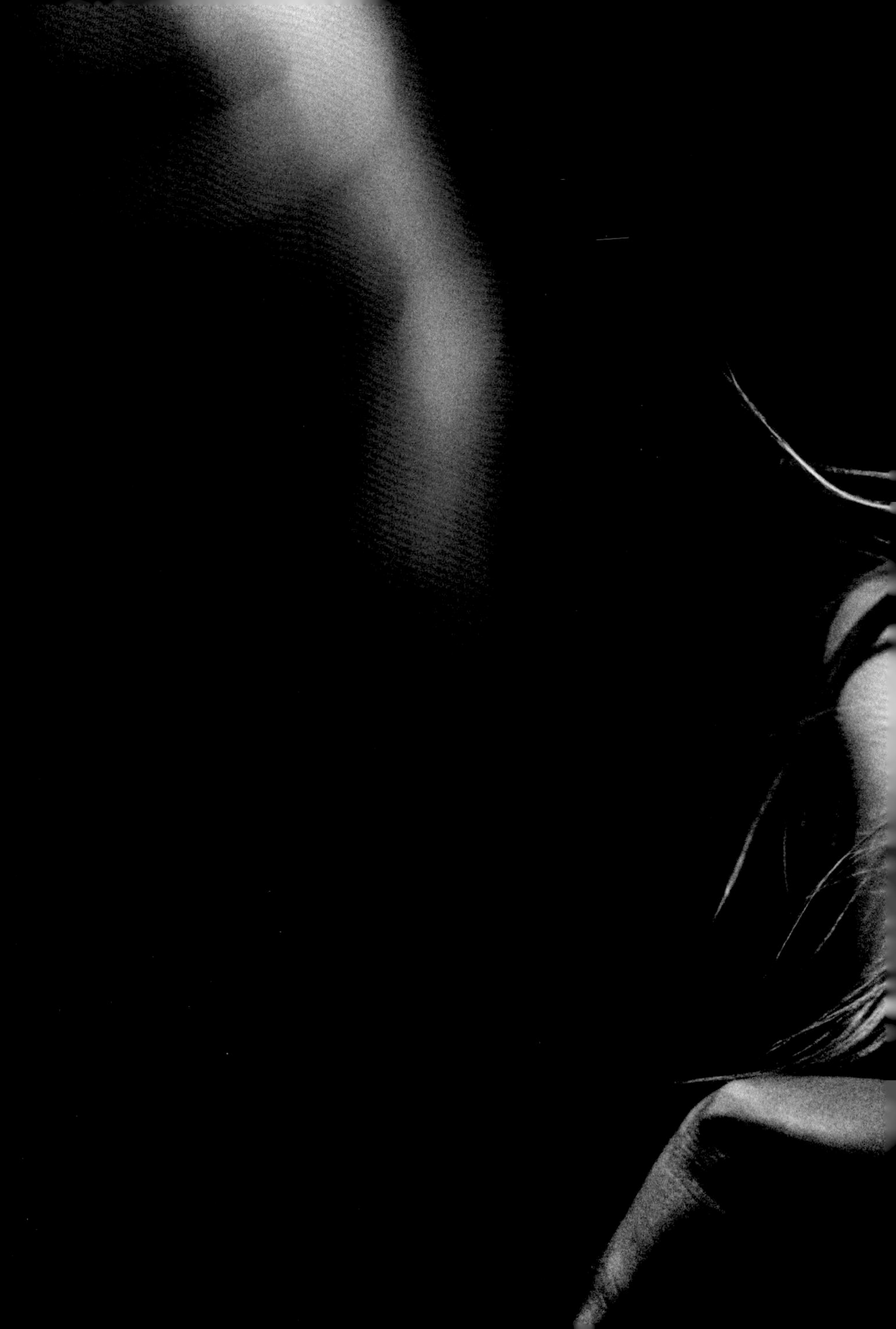

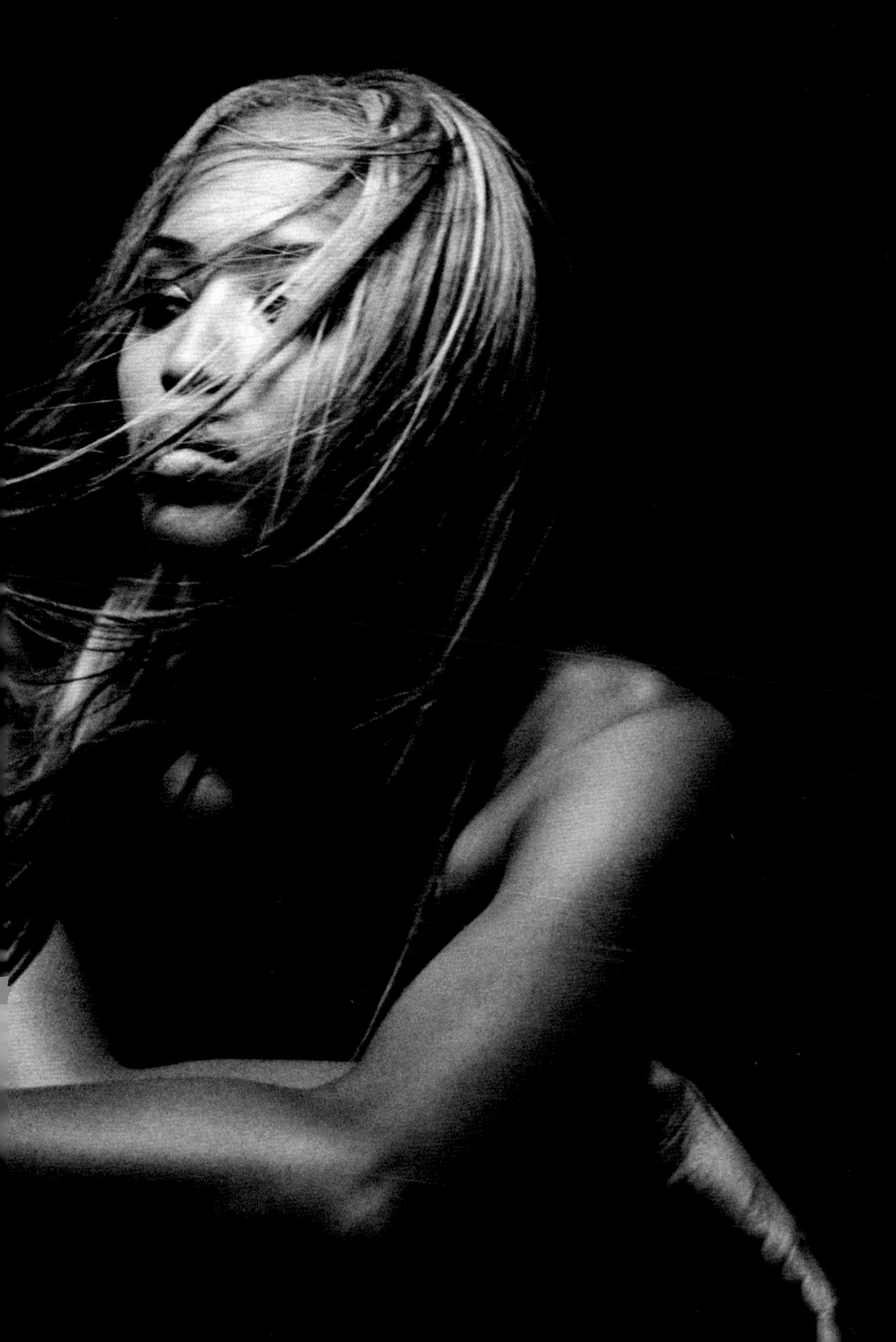

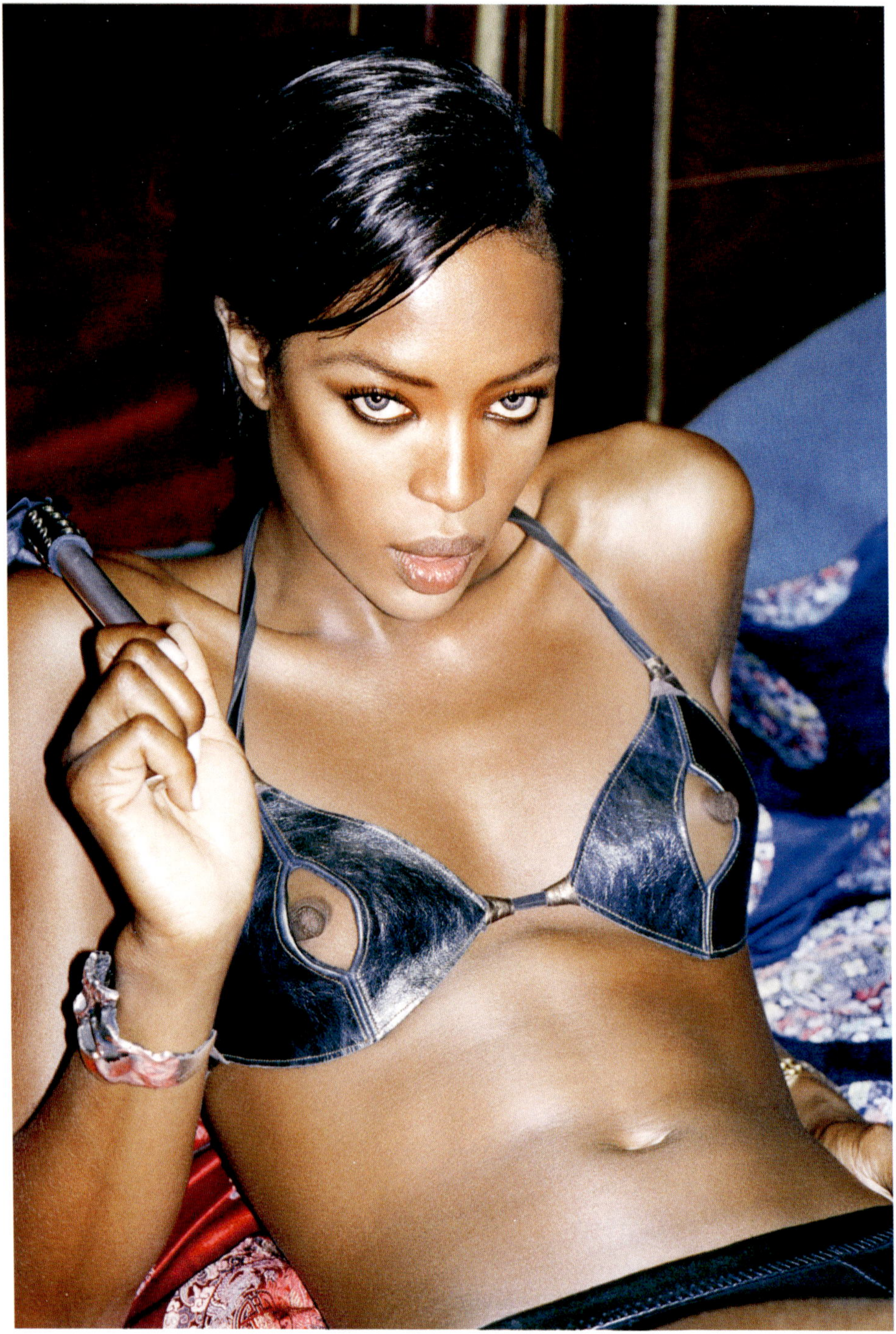

(Previous Spread) **Peter Lindbergh, 2005 • Ellen von Unwerth, 2003**

NAOMI IS AN ENDURING BEAUTY WITH A UNIQUE CHARACTER – SHE HAS GREAT STRENGTH, WHICH RESONATES THROUGH HER PERSONALITY AND HER BEING, AND WHICH DRIVES HER TO PERFECTION.

ZAHA HADID

(Opposite & Following Spreads) **Mert Alas & Marcus Piggott, 2007**

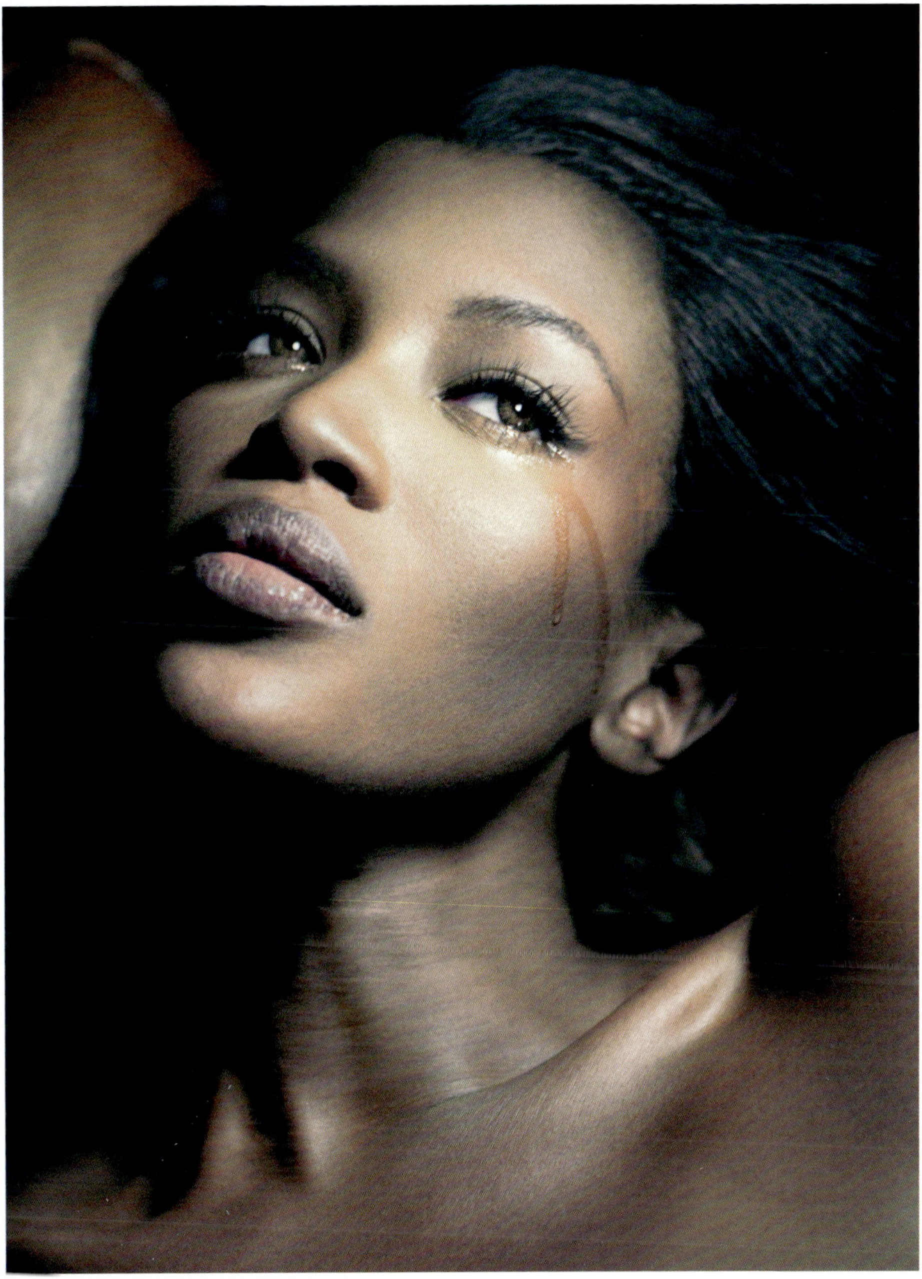

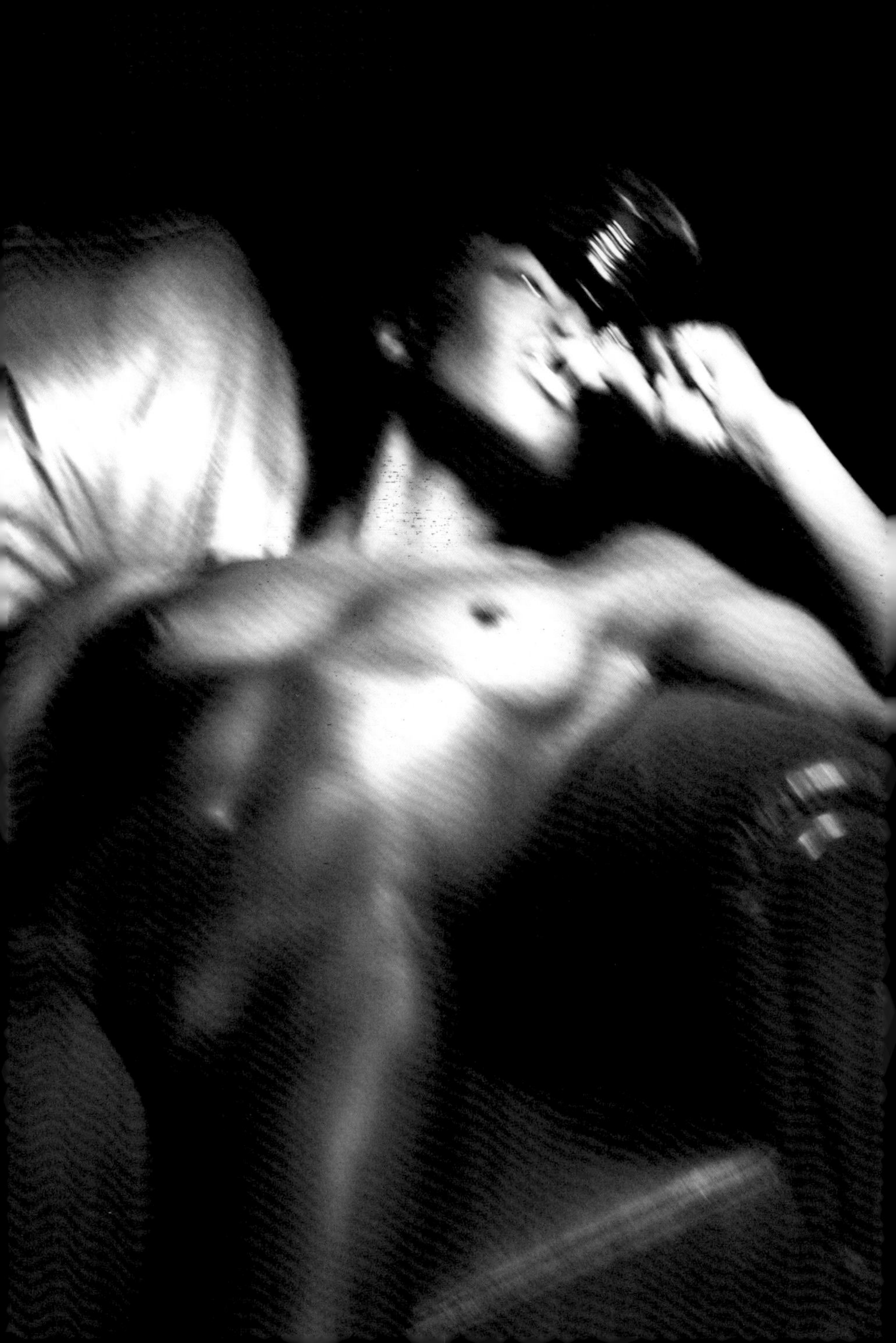

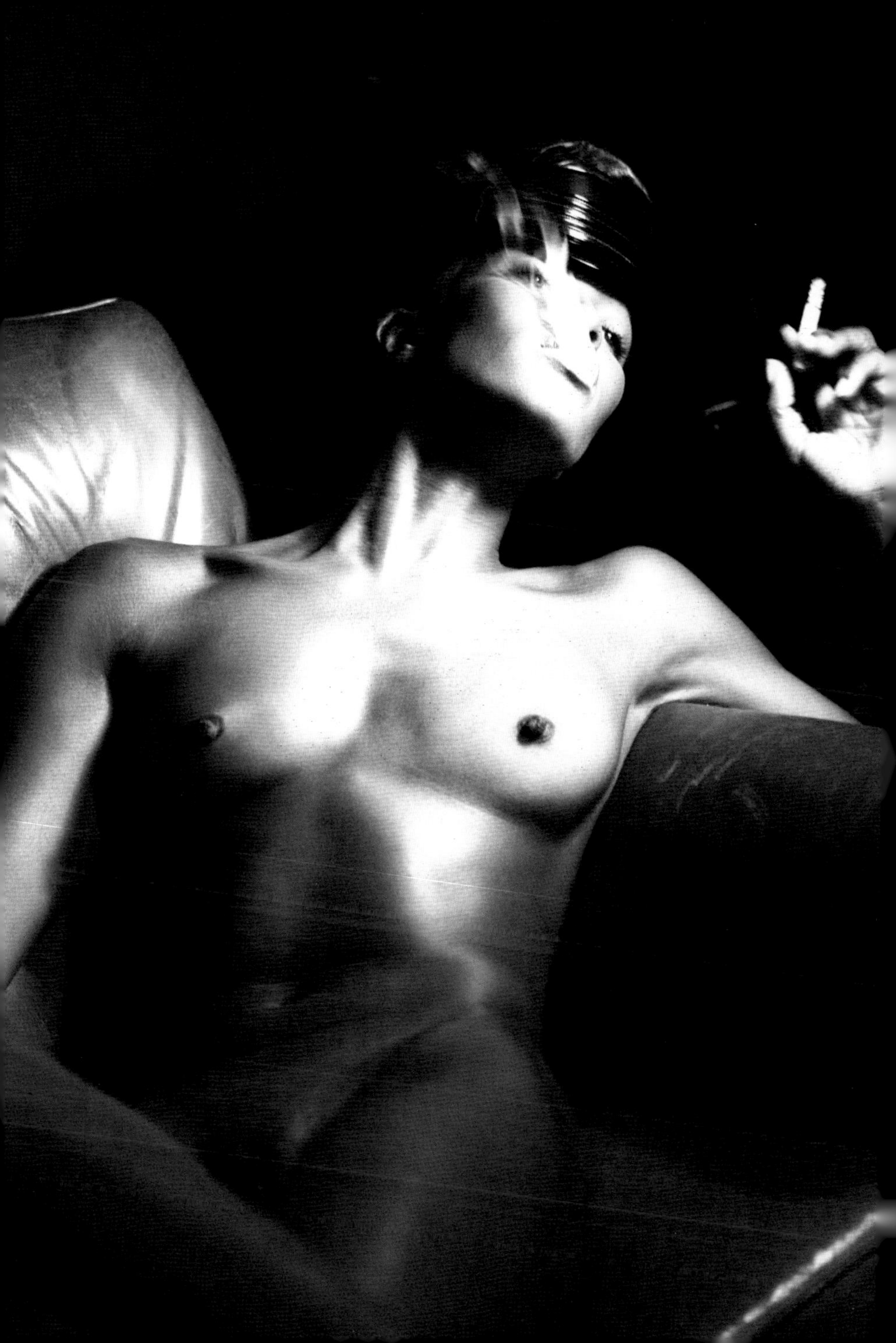

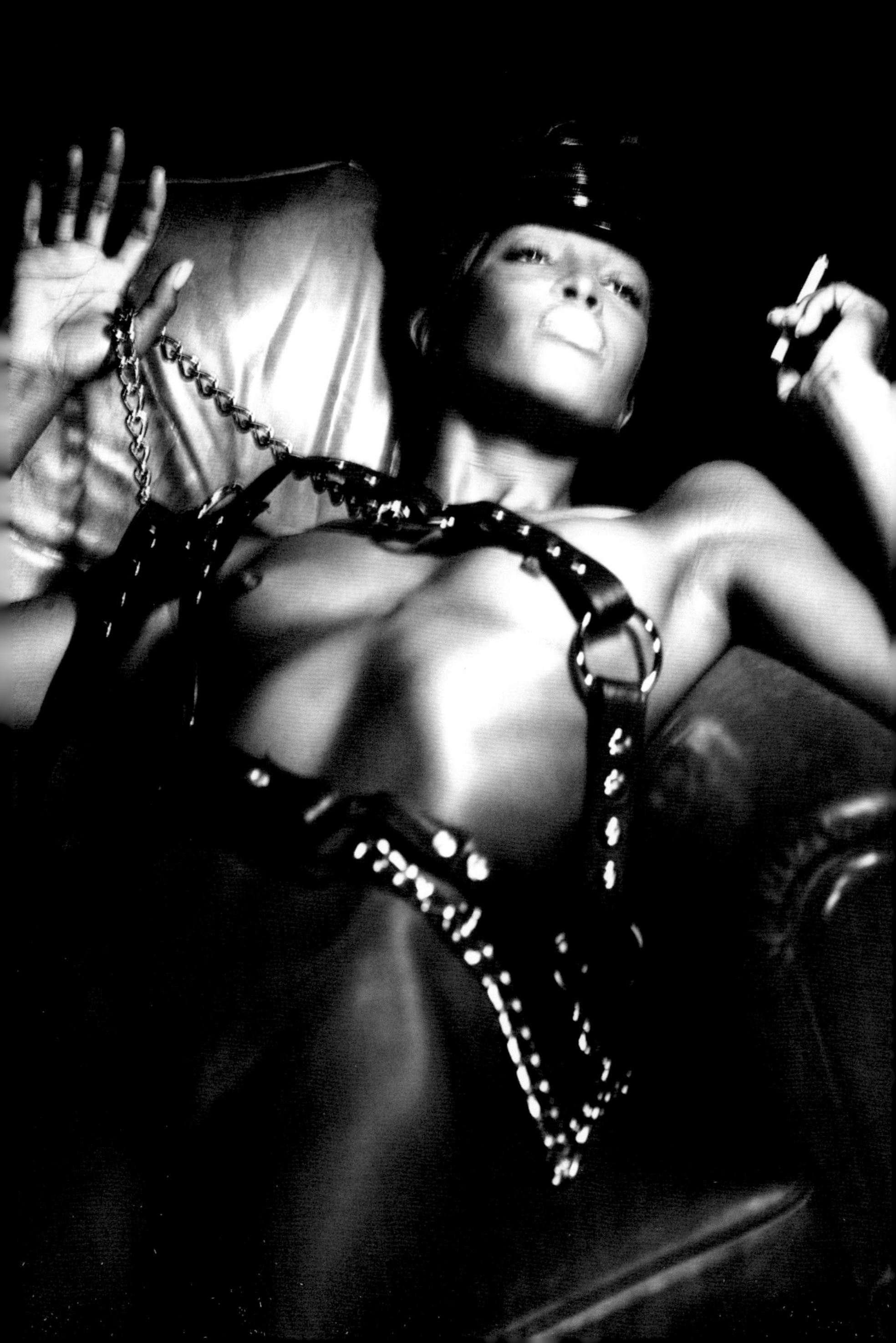

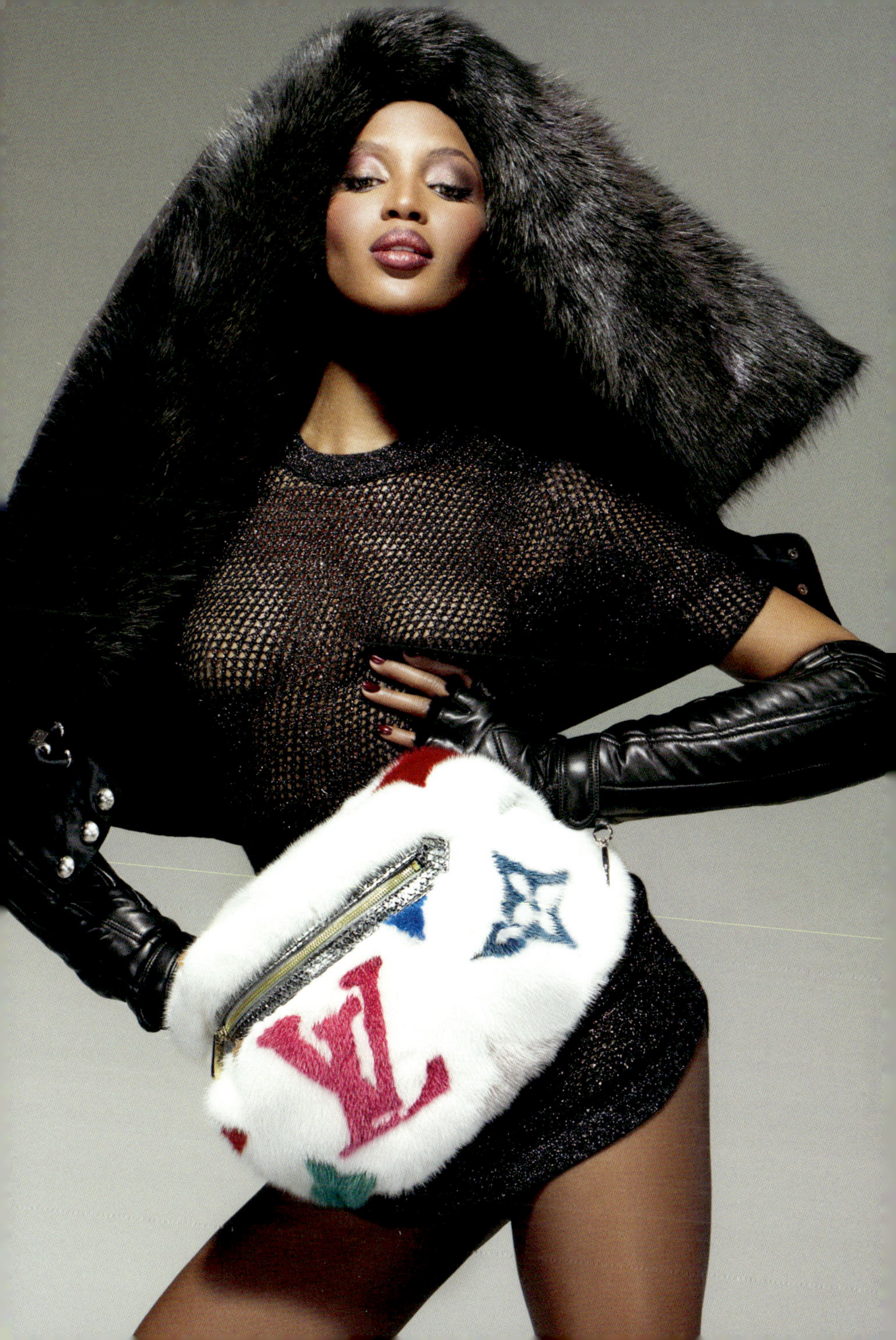

WHAT MAKES HER SO AMAZING? SHE IS ABSOLUTELY BEAUTIFUL AND RAZOR SHARP SMART, WITH A POWERFUL PERSONALITY AND A DAZZLING SMILE. NAOMI HAS IT ALL. YOU HAVE TO LOVE HER.

JONATHAN NEWHOUSE

Mario Sorrenti, 2007

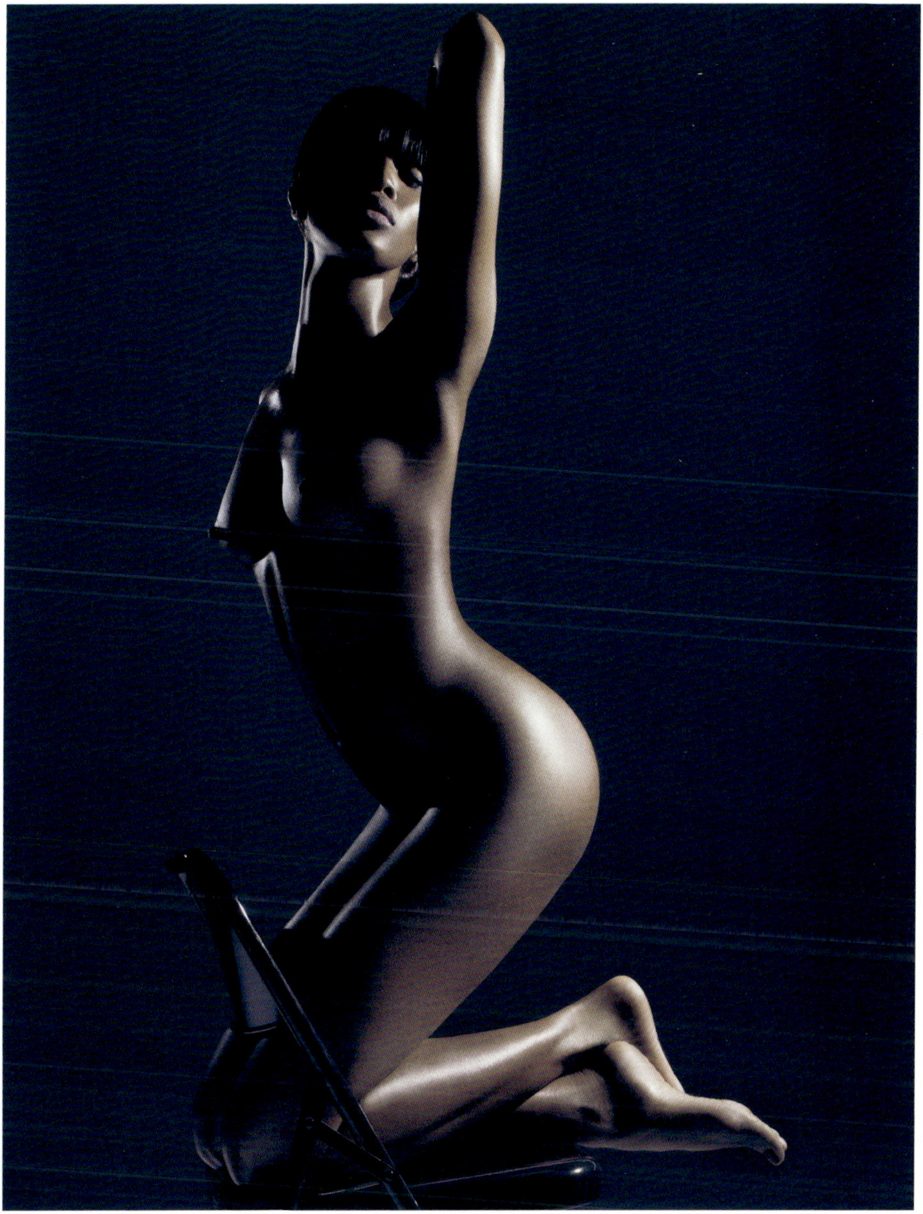

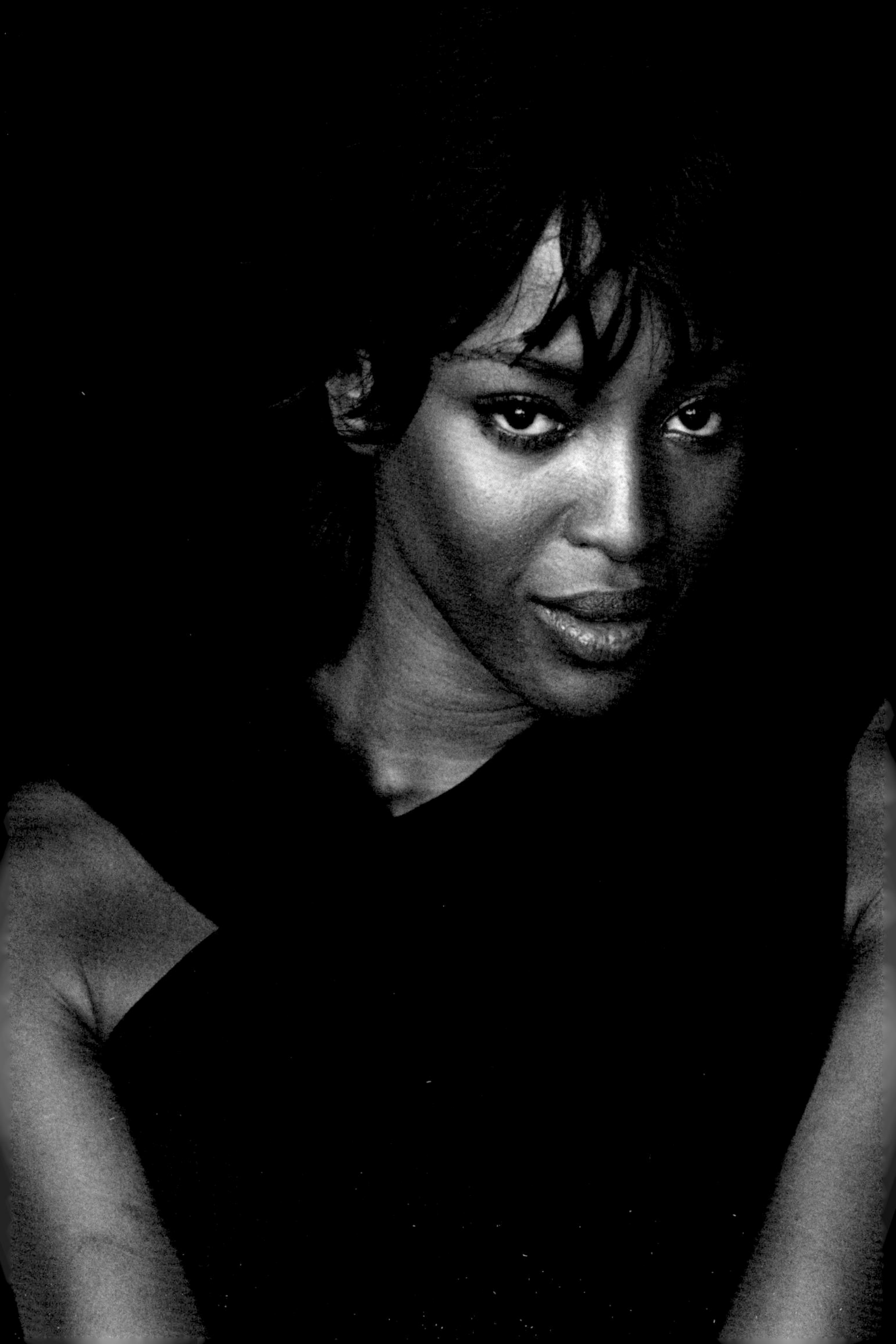

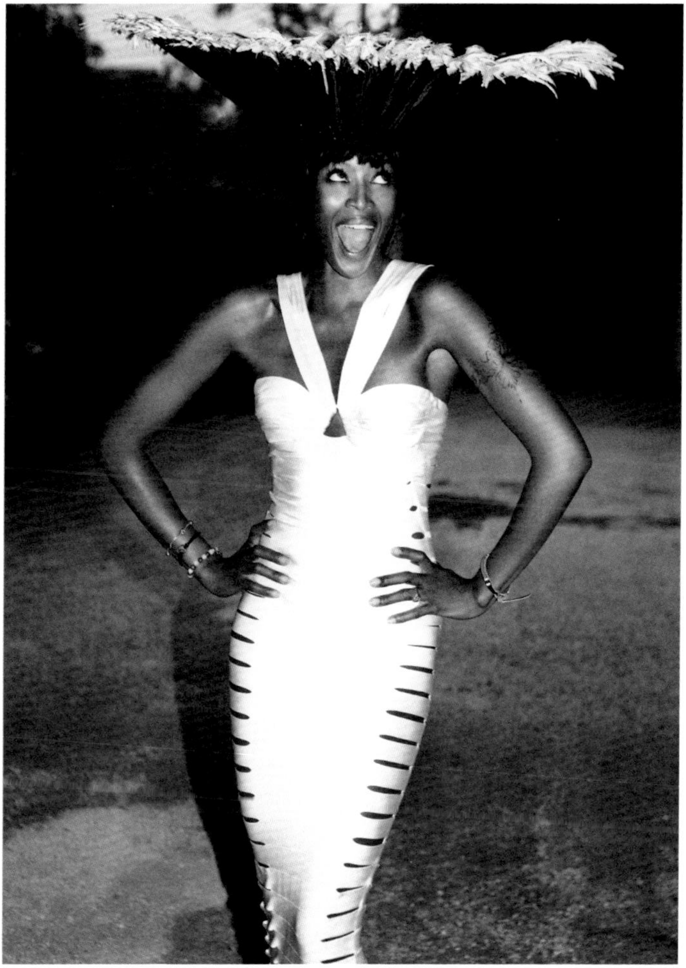

Peter Lindbergh, 2007 • Simon Harris, 2008

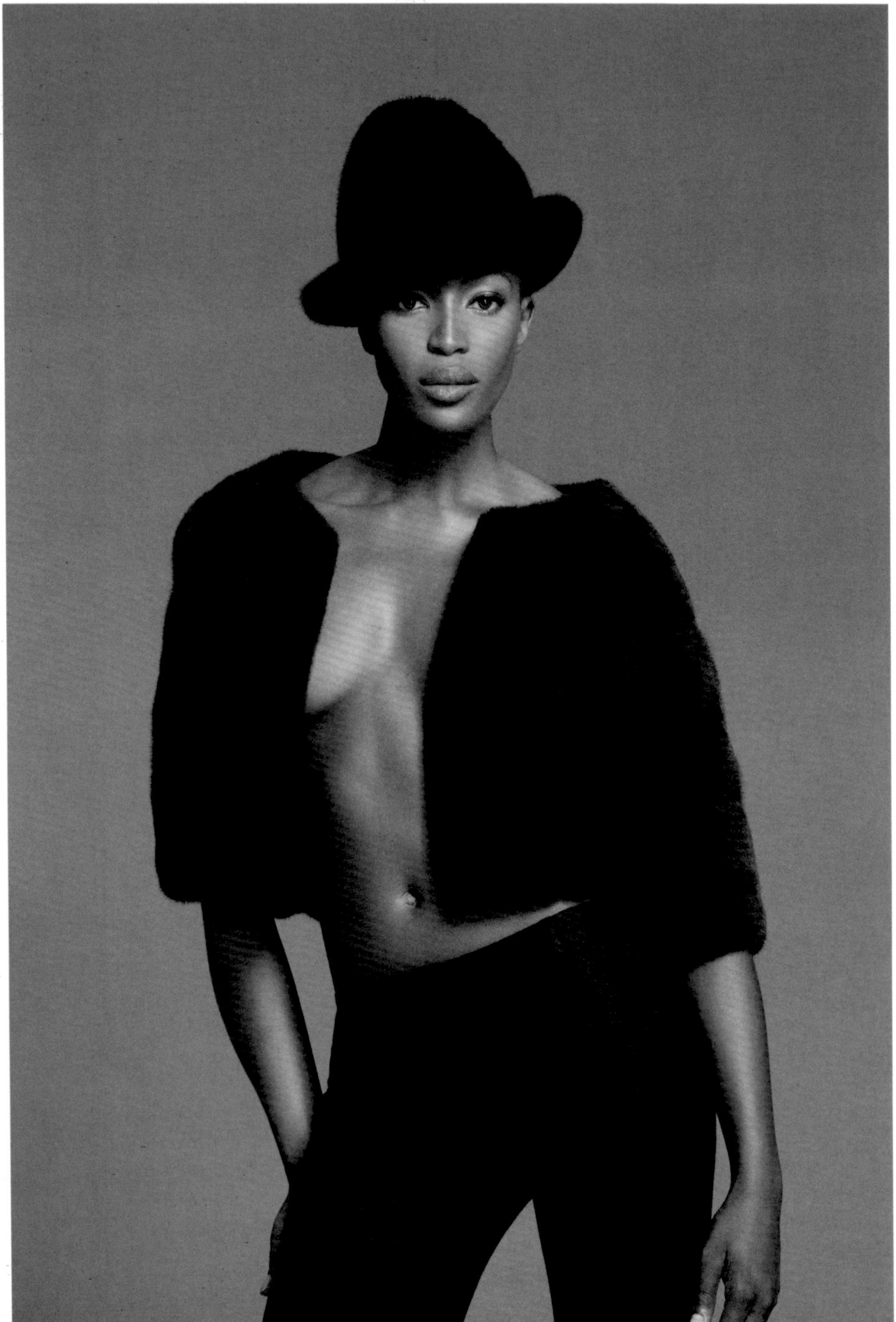

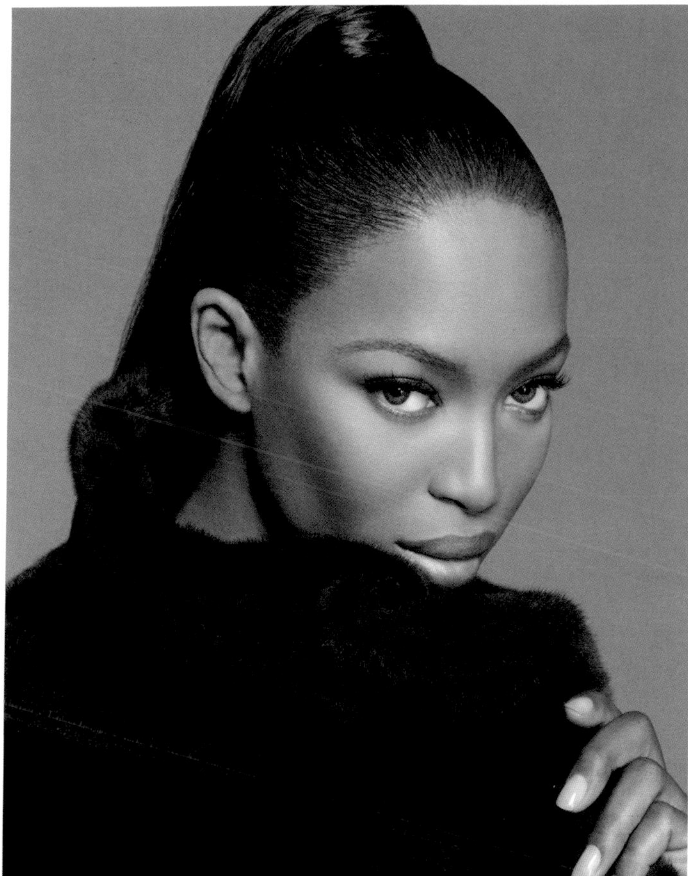

Laspata DeCaro, 2007

NAOMI HAS AN ALMOST UNTOUCHABLE POWER. SHE RADIATES LIFE AND BEAUTY AND STRENGTH.

STEFANO PILATI

Mario Sorrenti, 2008 • *(Following Spread)* **Steven Meisel, 2008**

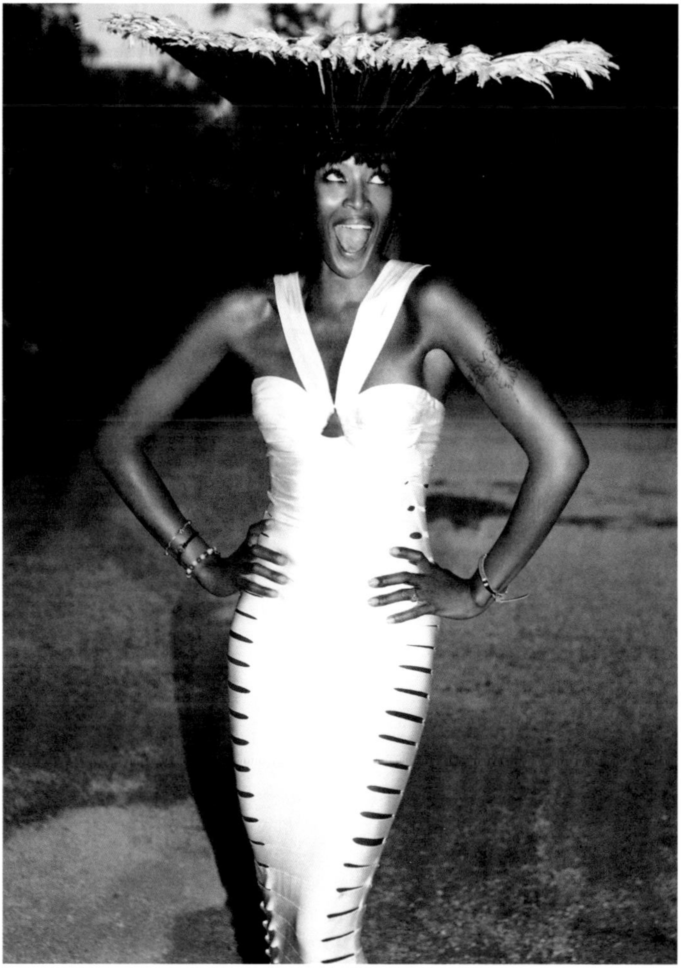

Peter Lindbergh, 2007 • Simon Harris, 2008

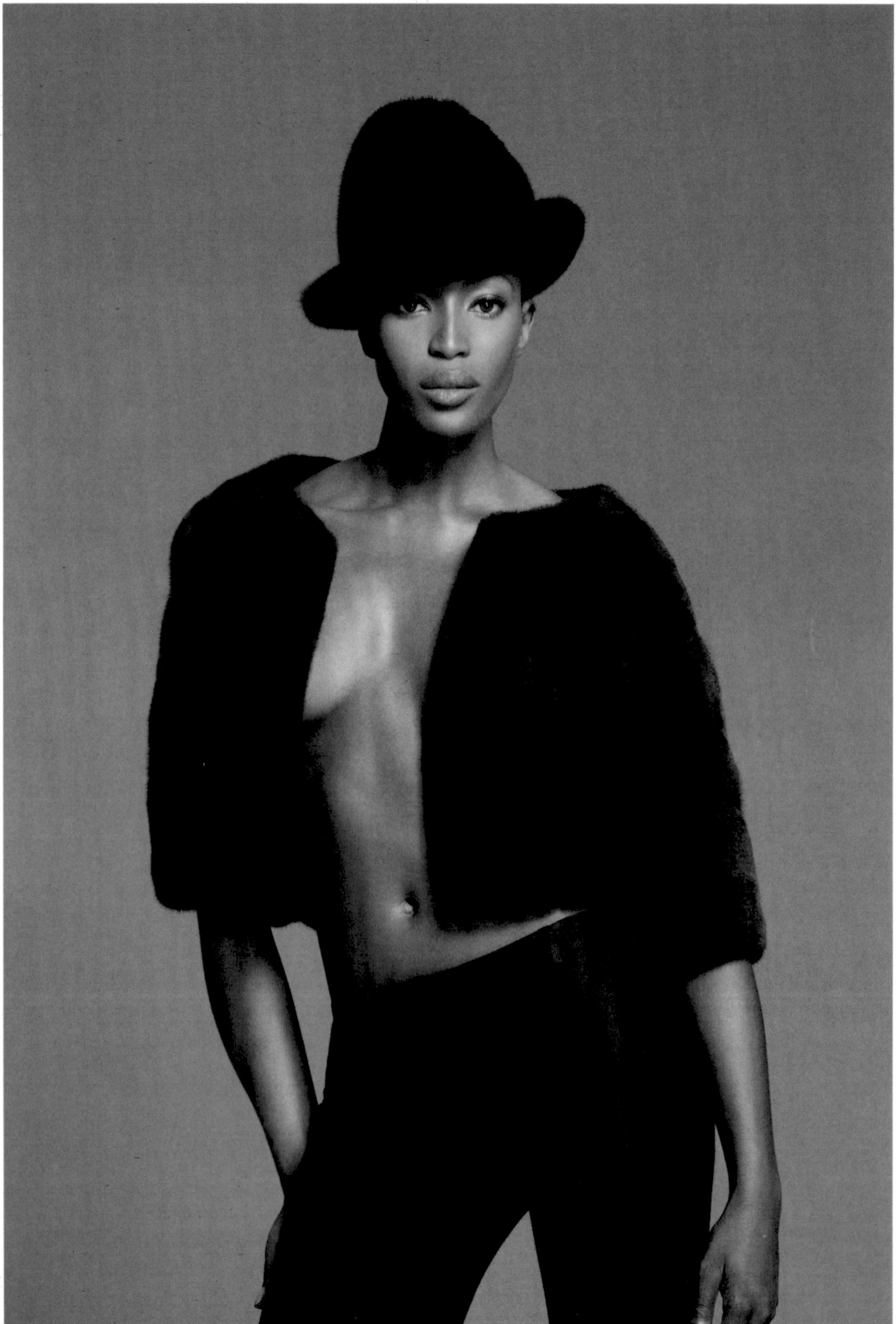

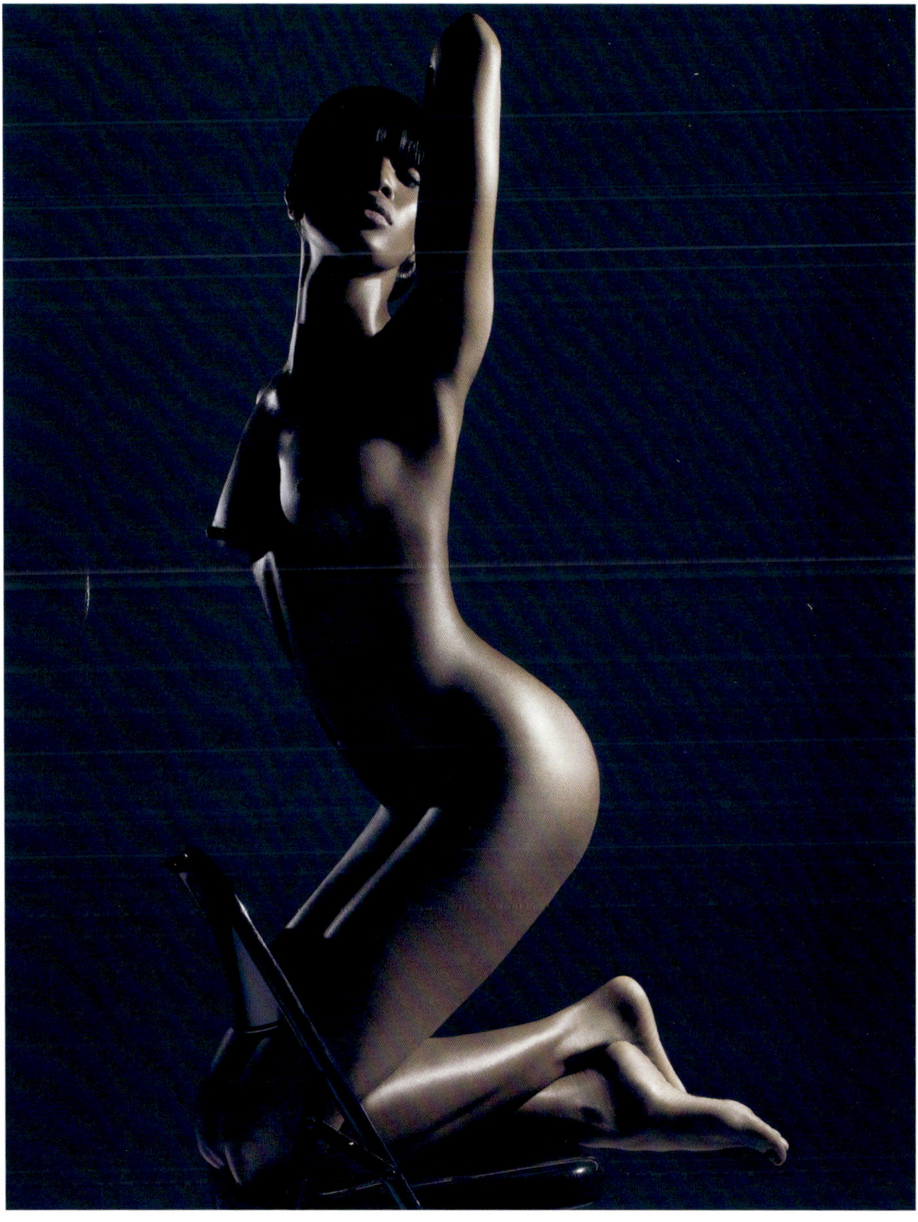

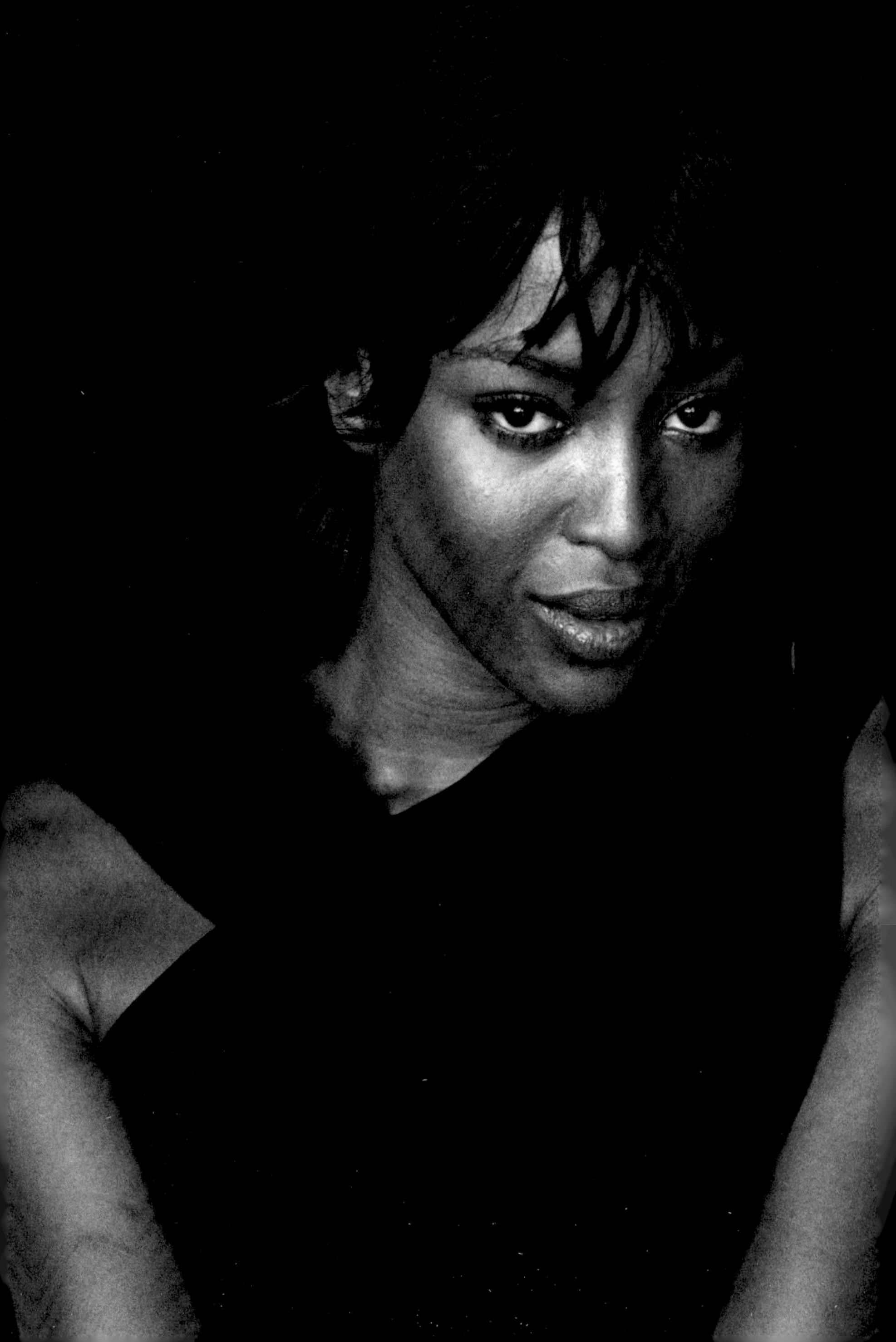

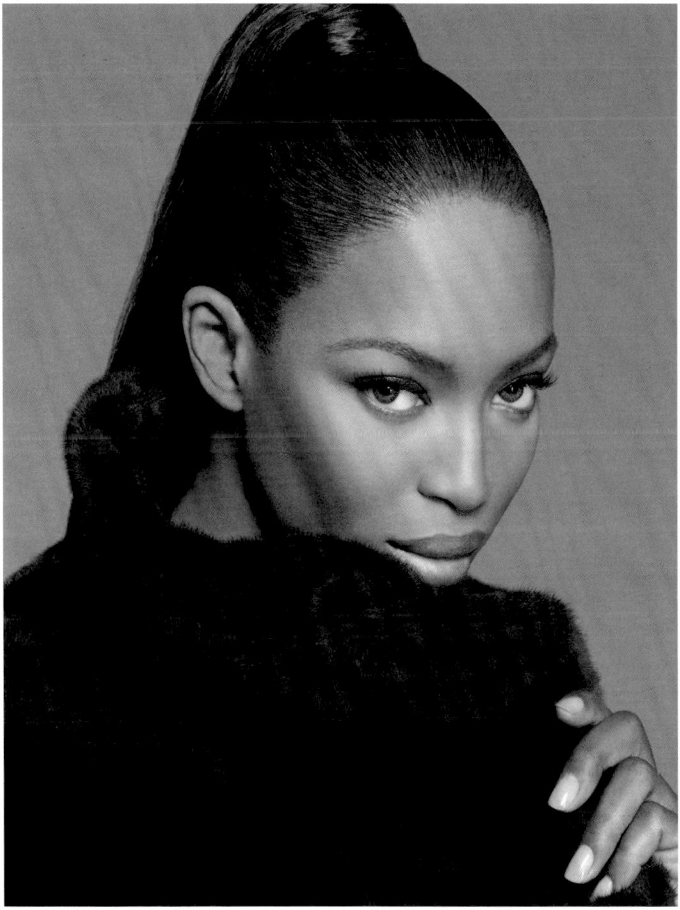

Laspata DeCaro, 2007

NAOMI HAS AN ALMOST UNTOUCHABLE POWER. SHE RADIATES LIFE AND BEAUTY AND STRENGTH.

STEFANO PILATI

Mario Sorrenti, 2008 • *(Following Spread)* **Steven Meisel, 2008**

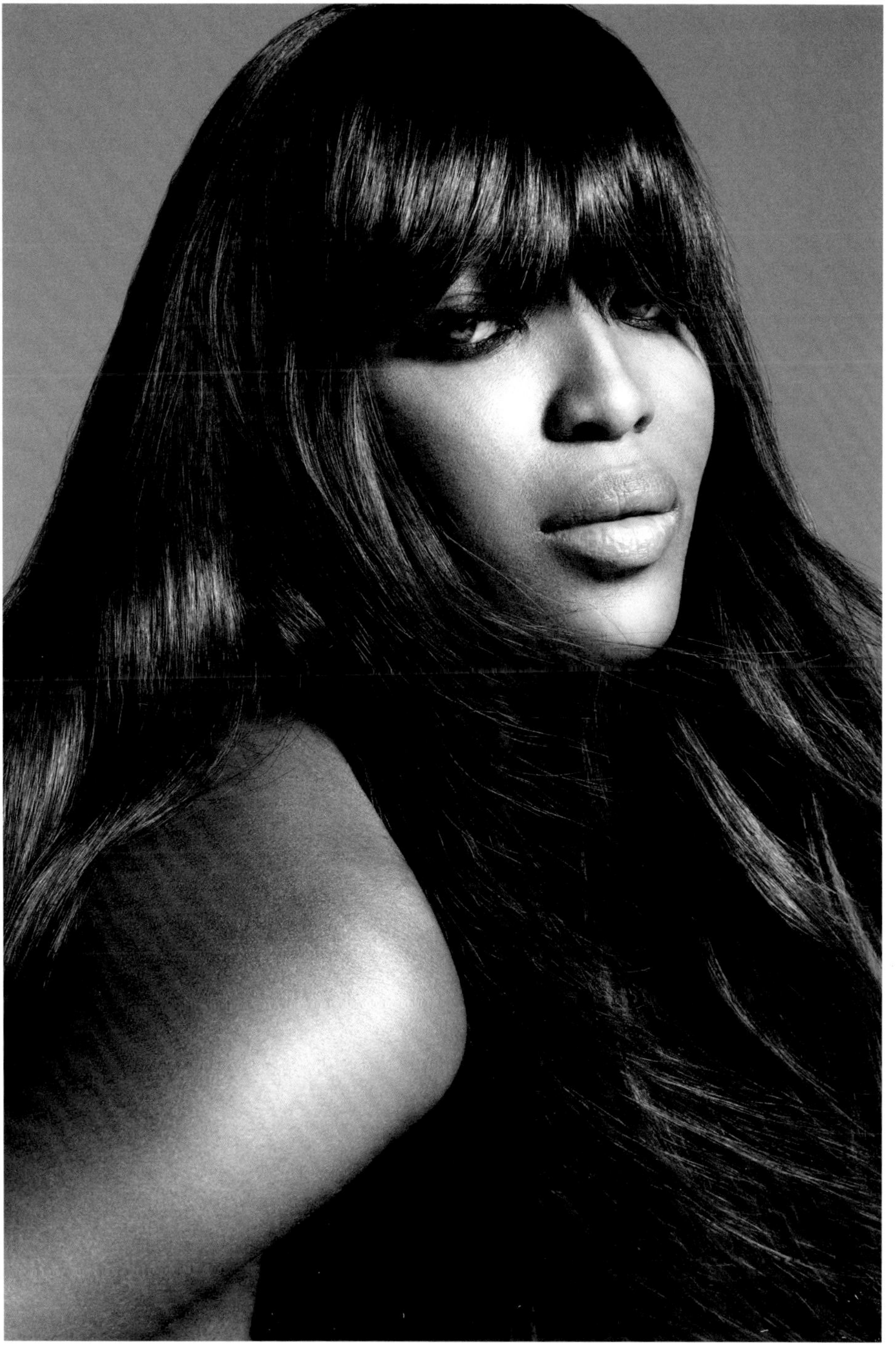

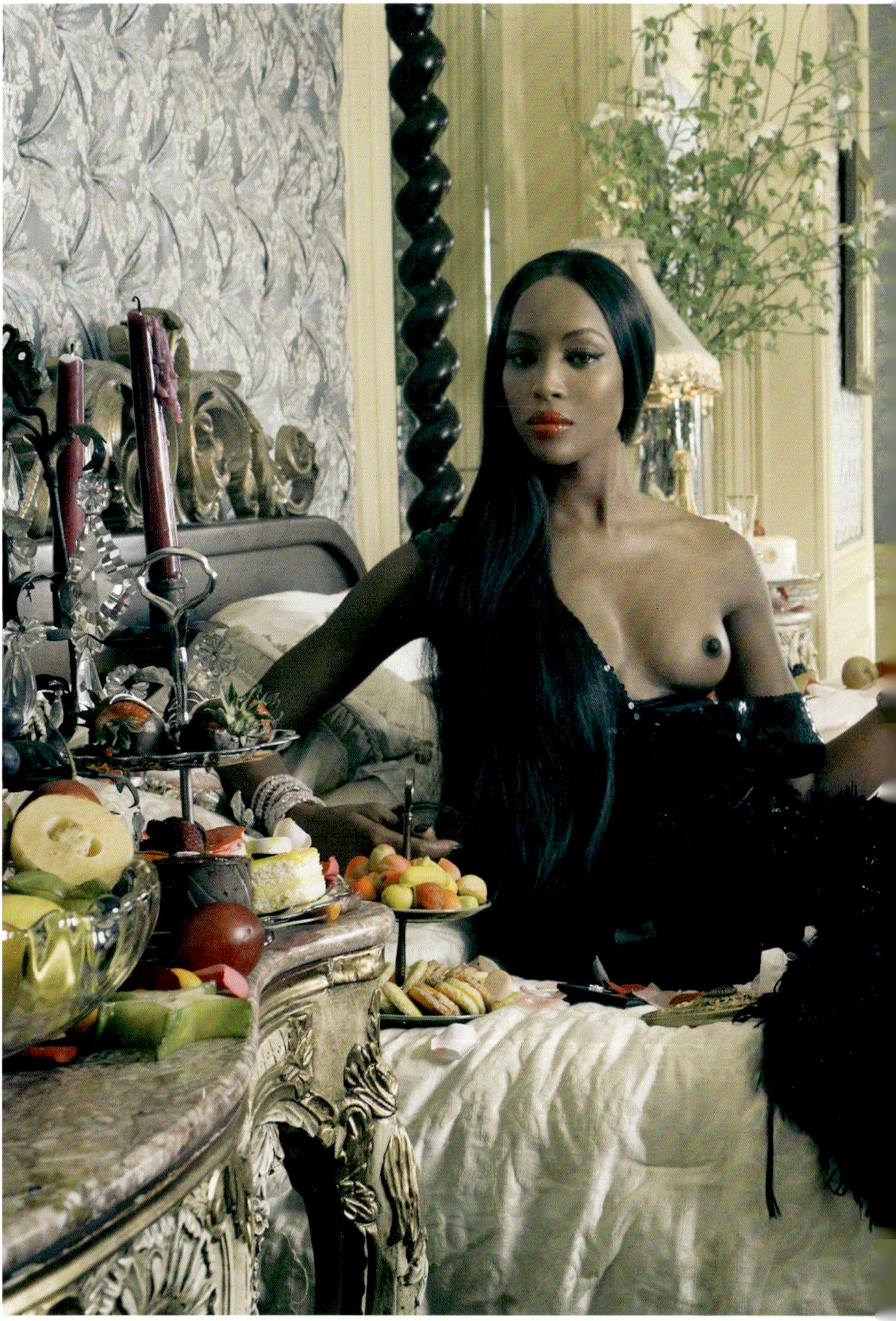

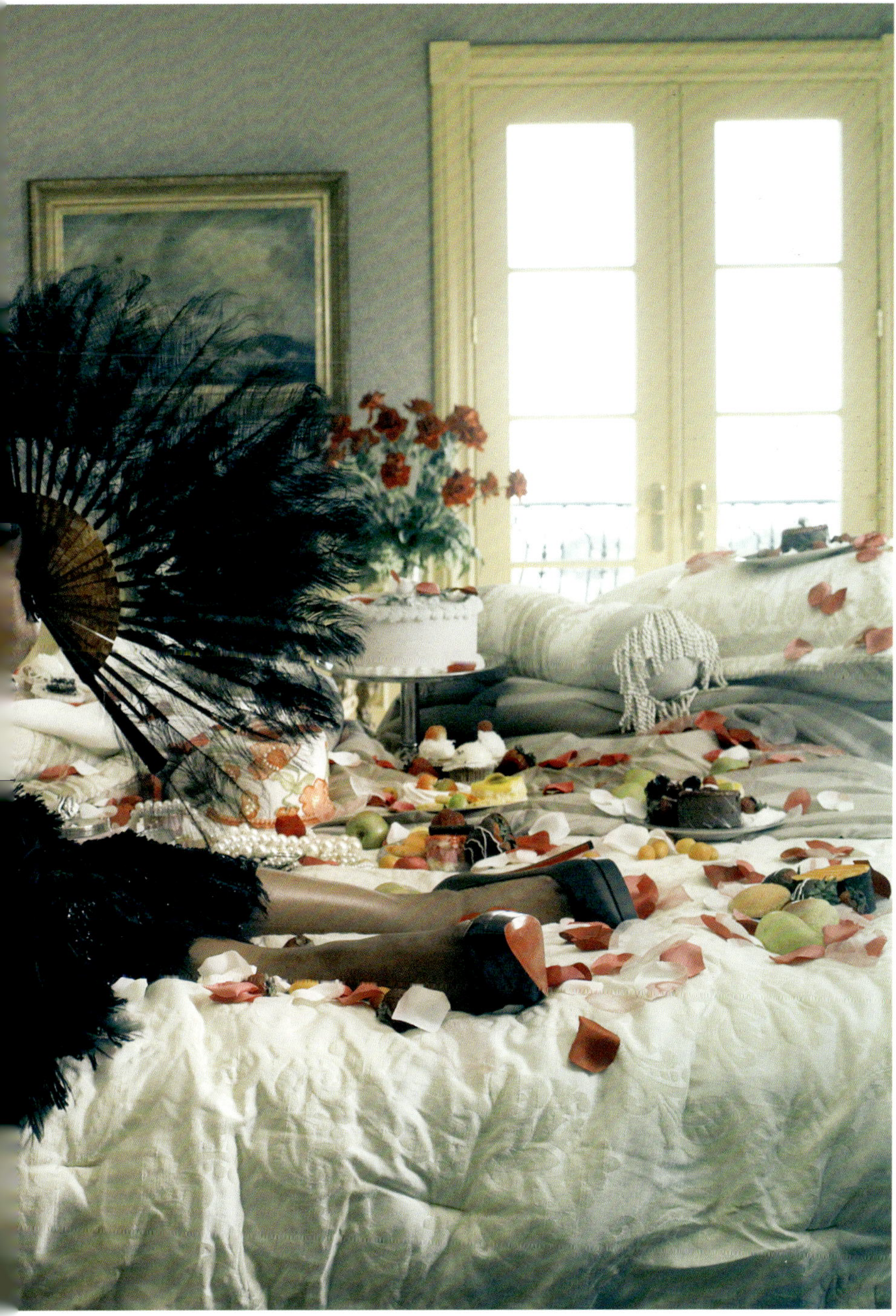

NAOMI HAS AN
OTHERWORLDLY BEAUTY . . .
BIGGER THAN JUST FASHION,
LARGER THAN LIFE;
A BLACK GODDESS
THAT WILL LIVE
FOREVER IN HISTORY.

RICCARDO TISCI

Sebastian Faena, 2008 • *(Following Spread)* **Mario Testino, 2008**

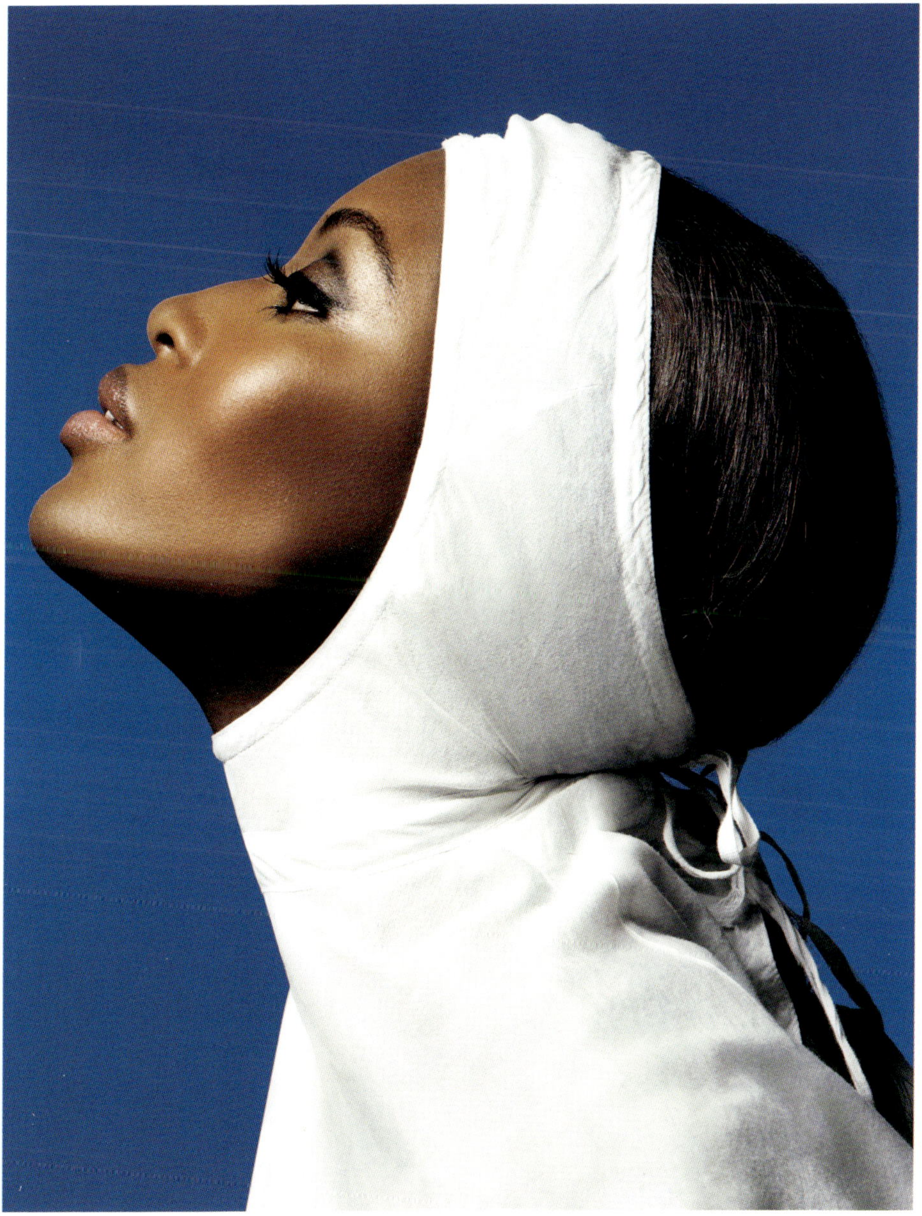

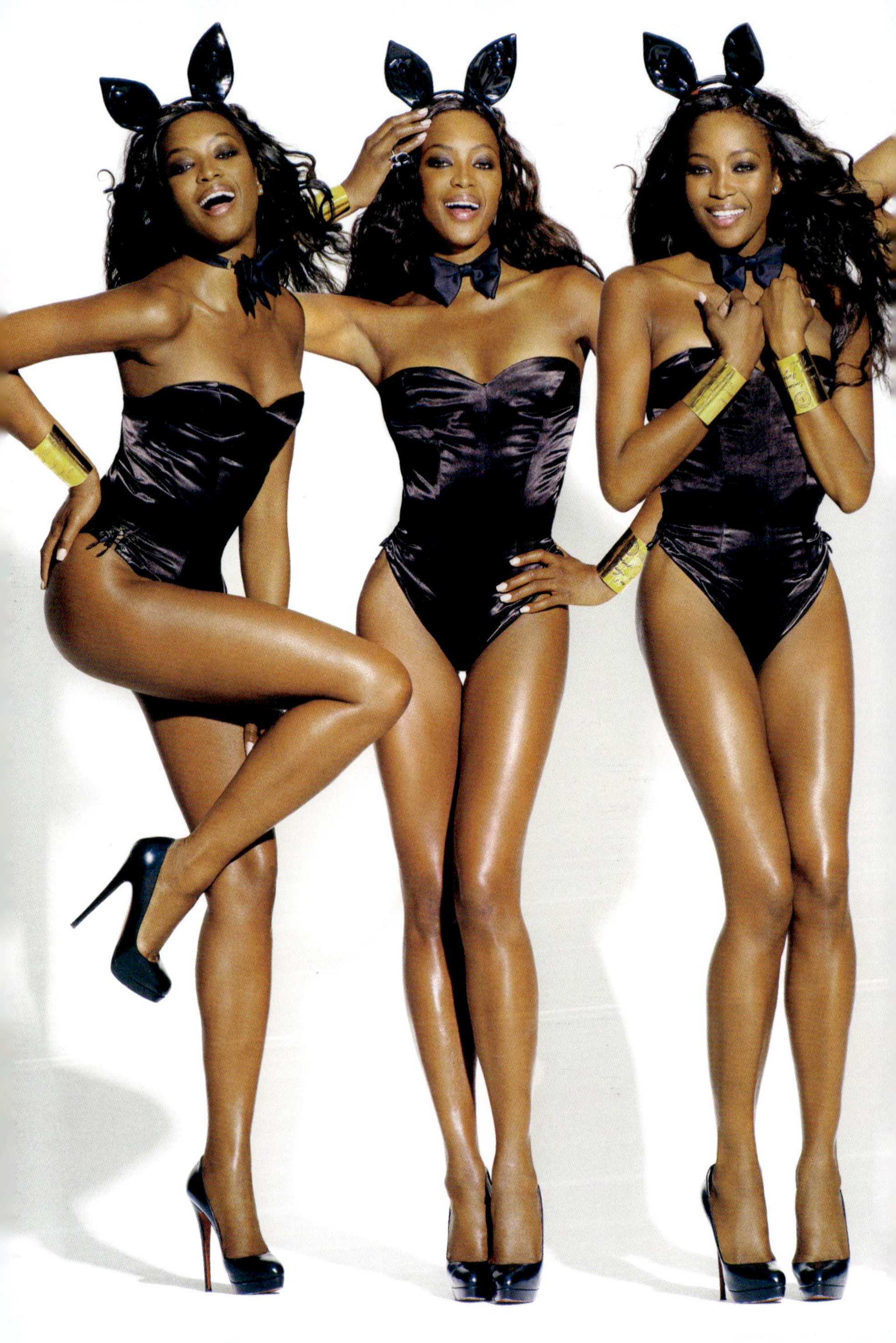

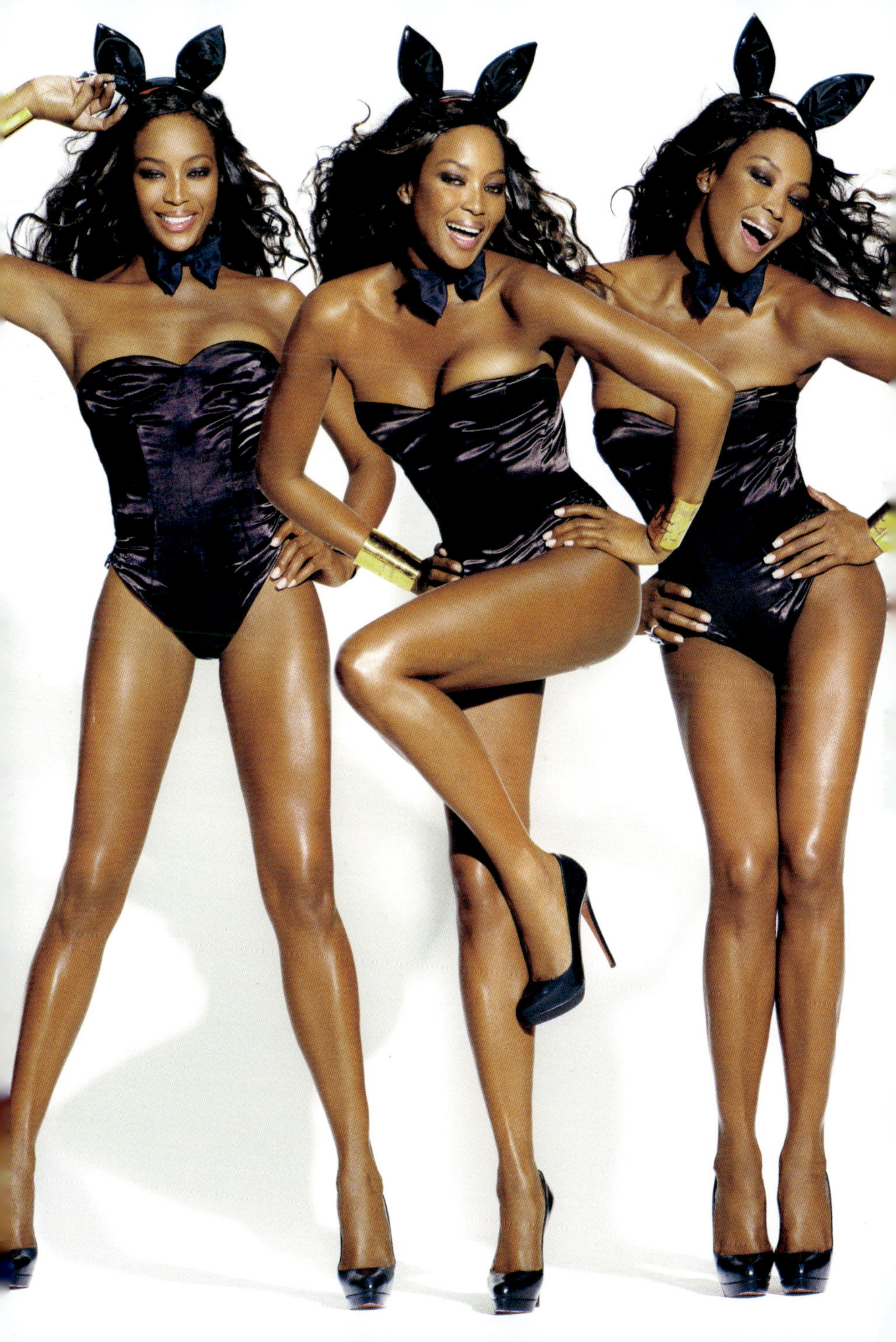

NAOMI REALLY TOOK ME
UNDER HER WING WHEN
I STARTED MODELLING.
IN THE YEARS SINCE WE MET
WE HAVE BECOME REALLY
CLOSE, SHE IS LIKE FAMILY
TO ME. SHE IS THE ULTIMATE
SUPERMODEL. . . . TALL,
STRONG AND BEAUTIFUL.

KATE MOSS

Mario Testino, 2009

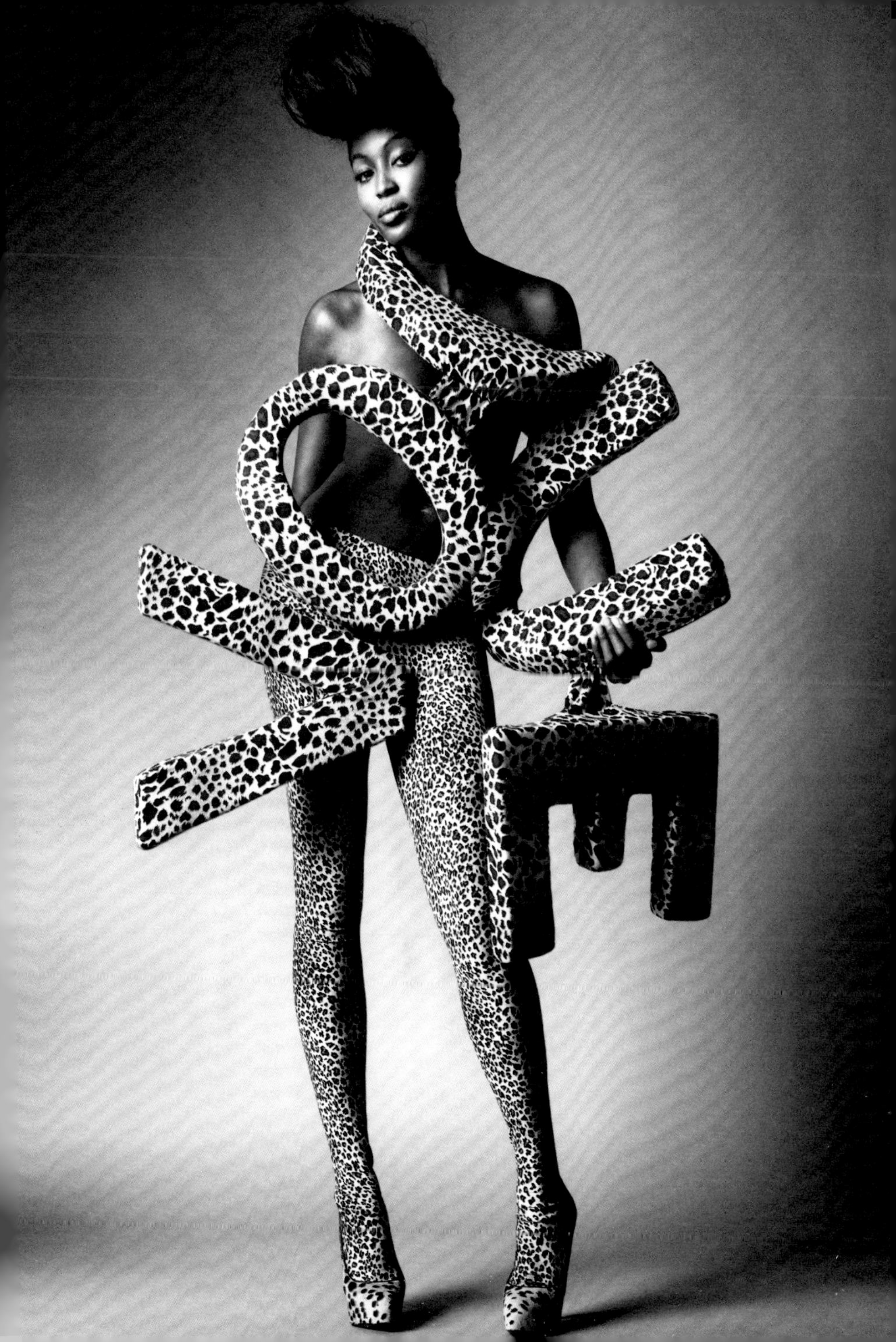

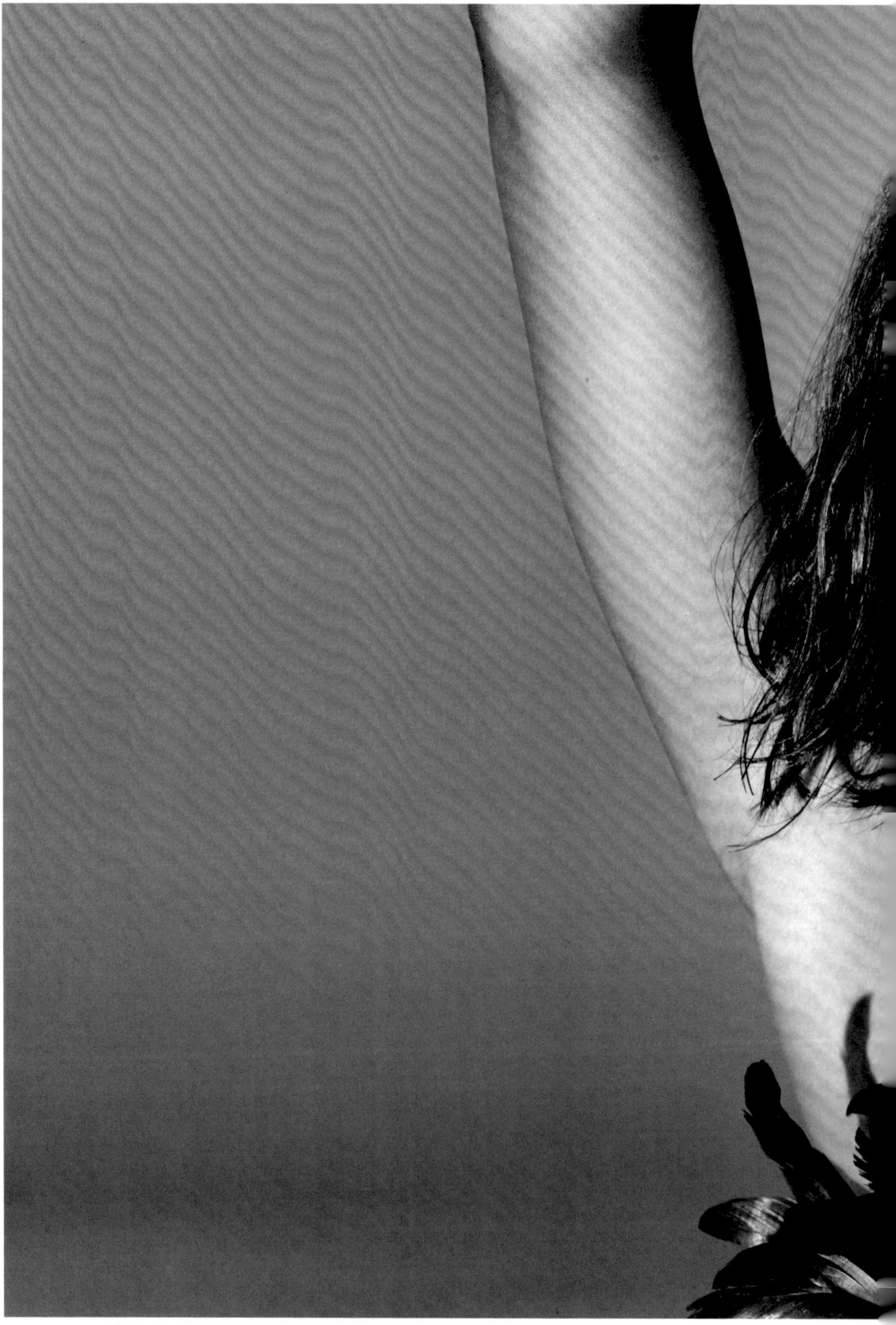

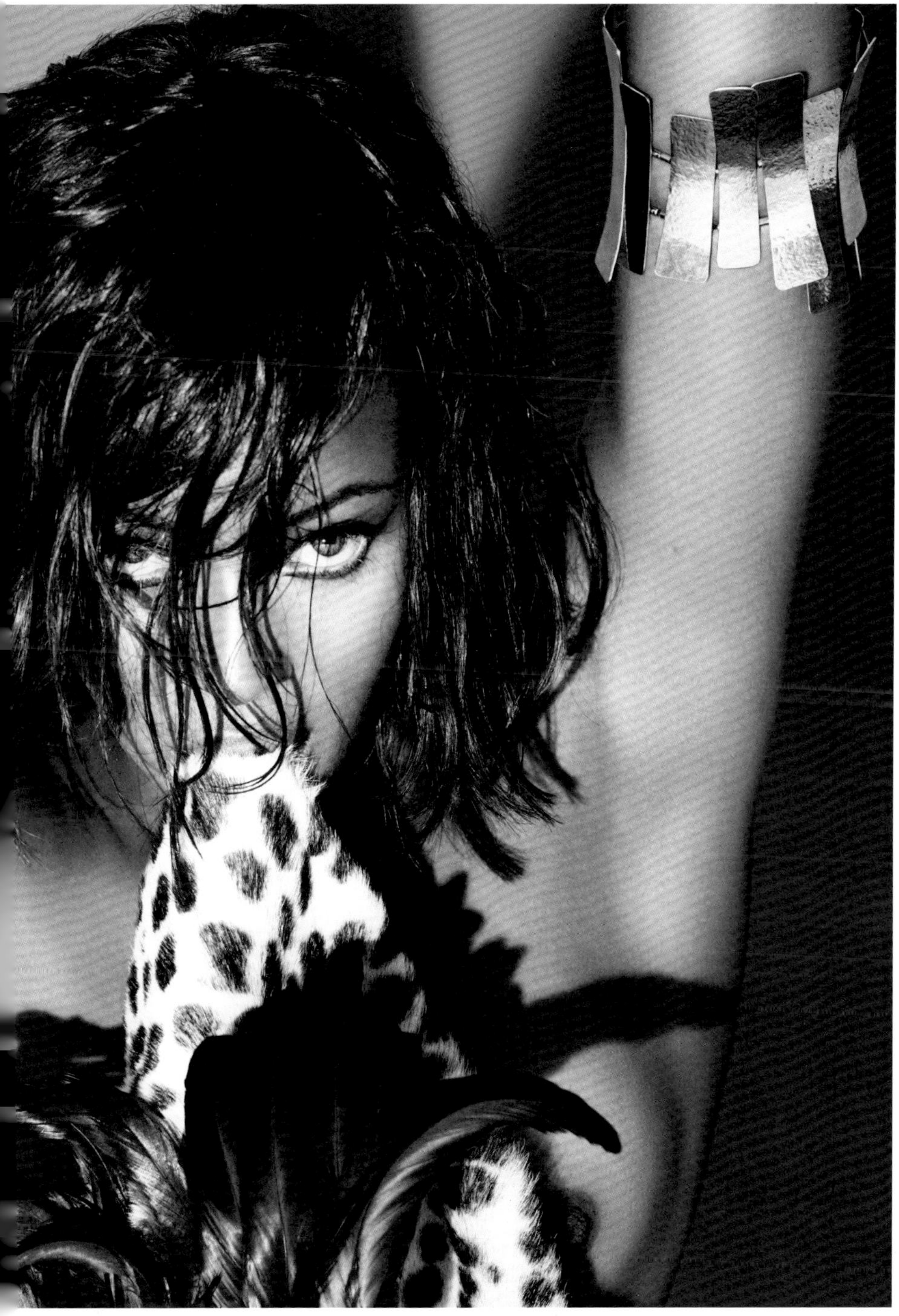

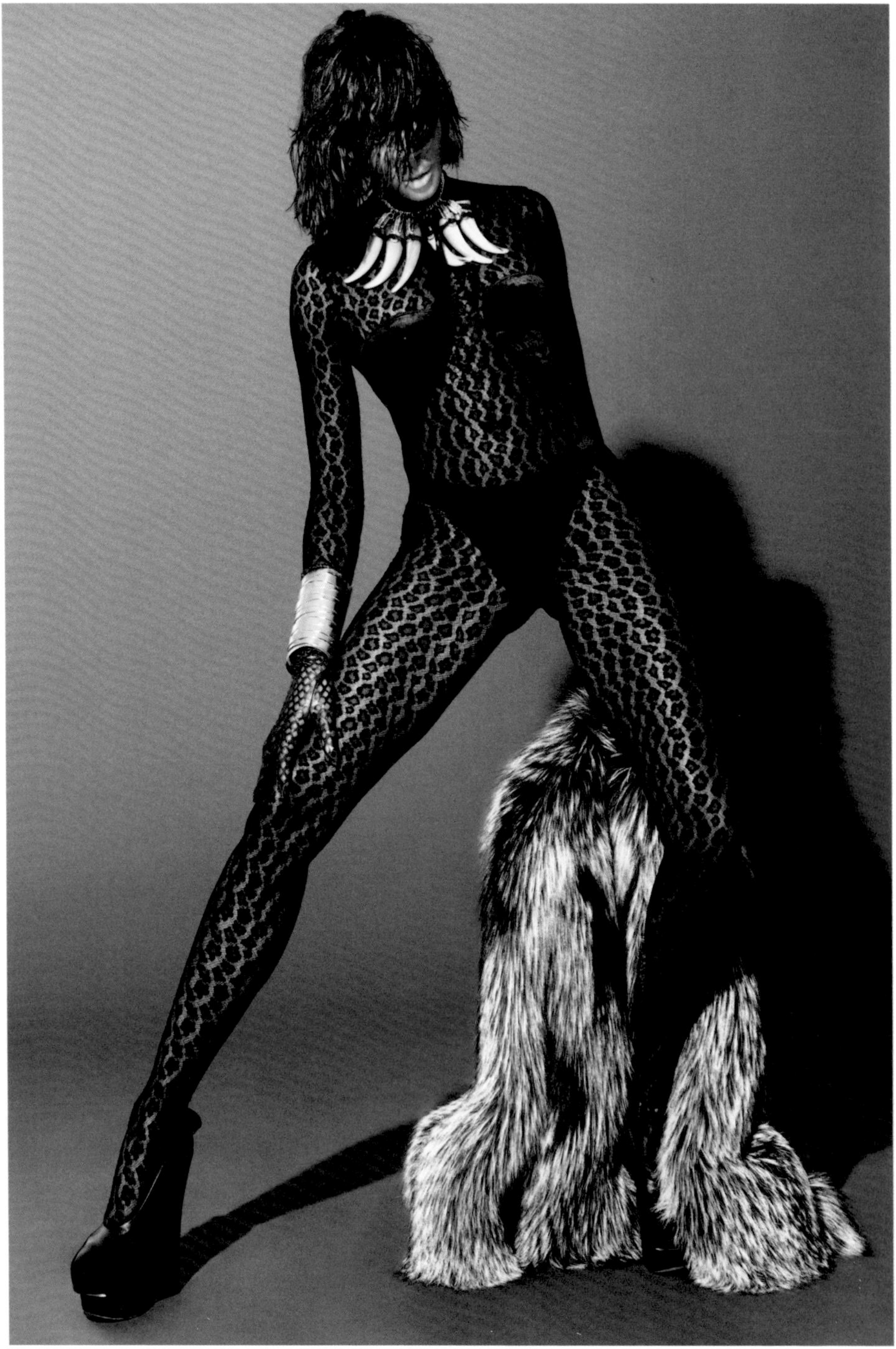

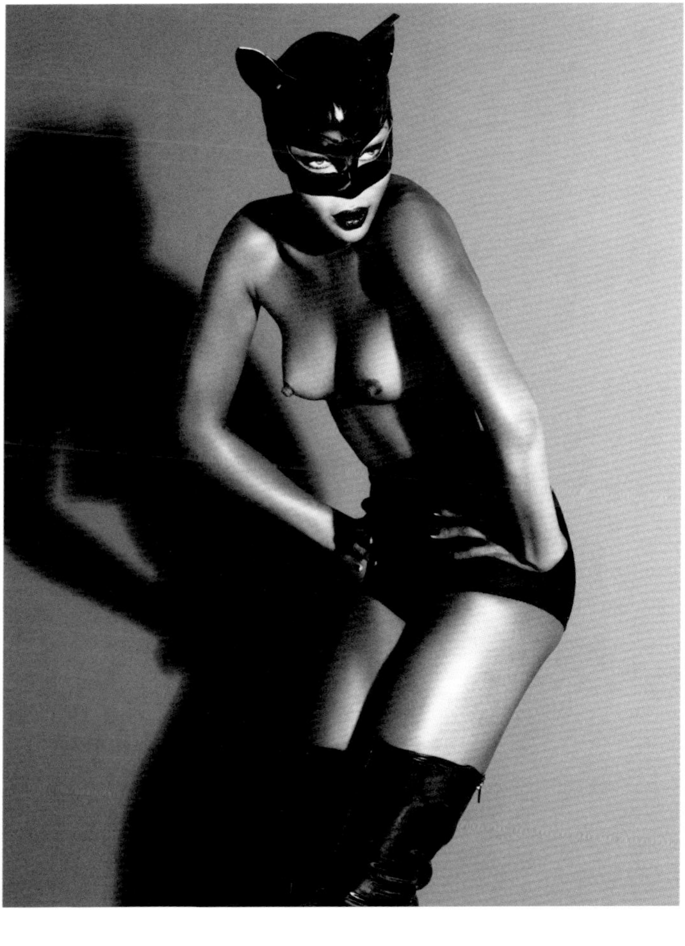

(Previous & This Spread) **Mert Alas & Marcus Piggott, 2008**

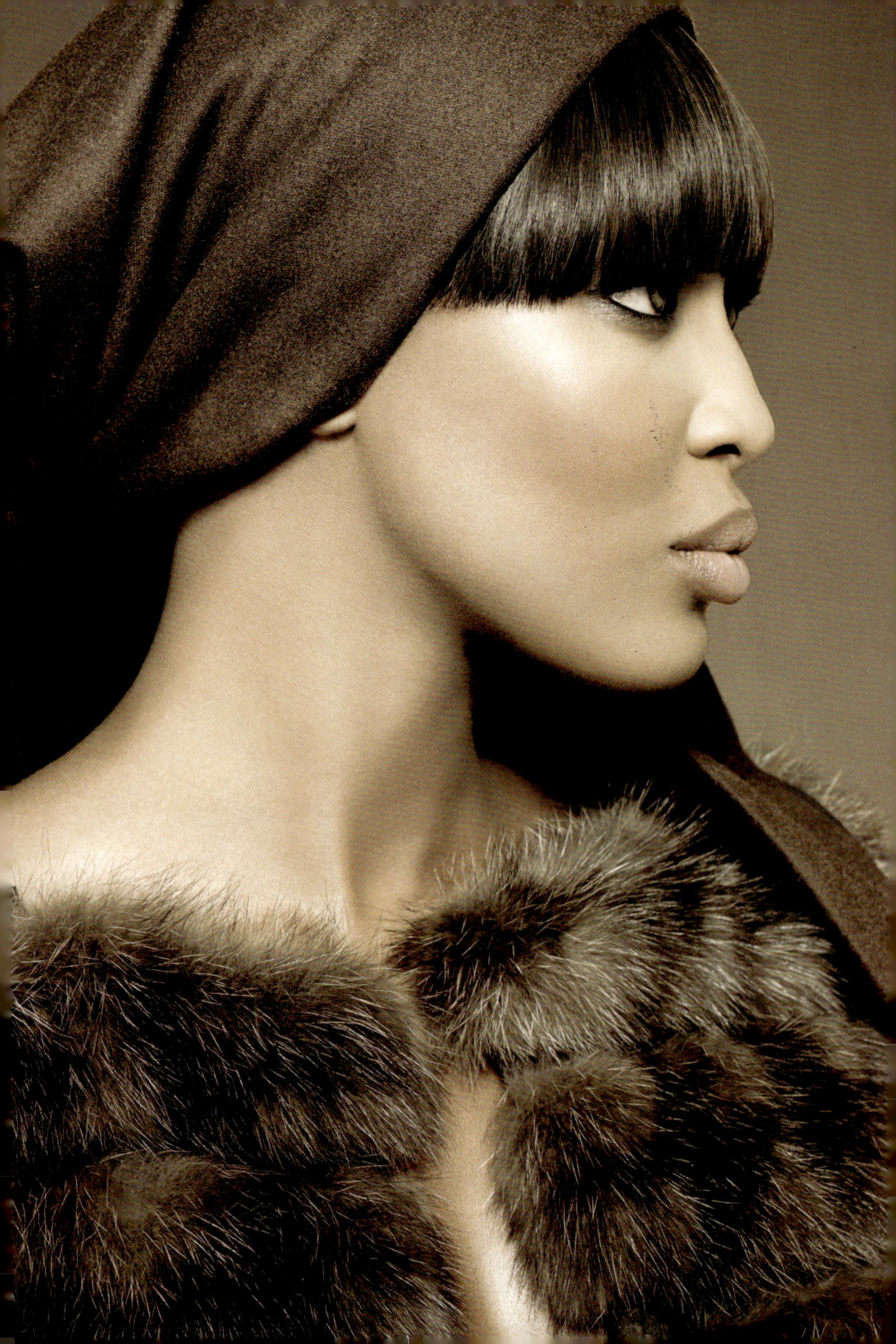

SHE IS TRUTHFUL
AND FAITHFUL!
LOVE THE WOMAN
AS MUCH AS
THE ICON!

CARINE ROITFELD

Tom Munro, 2009 • *(Following Spread)* **Jean-Paul Goude, 2009**

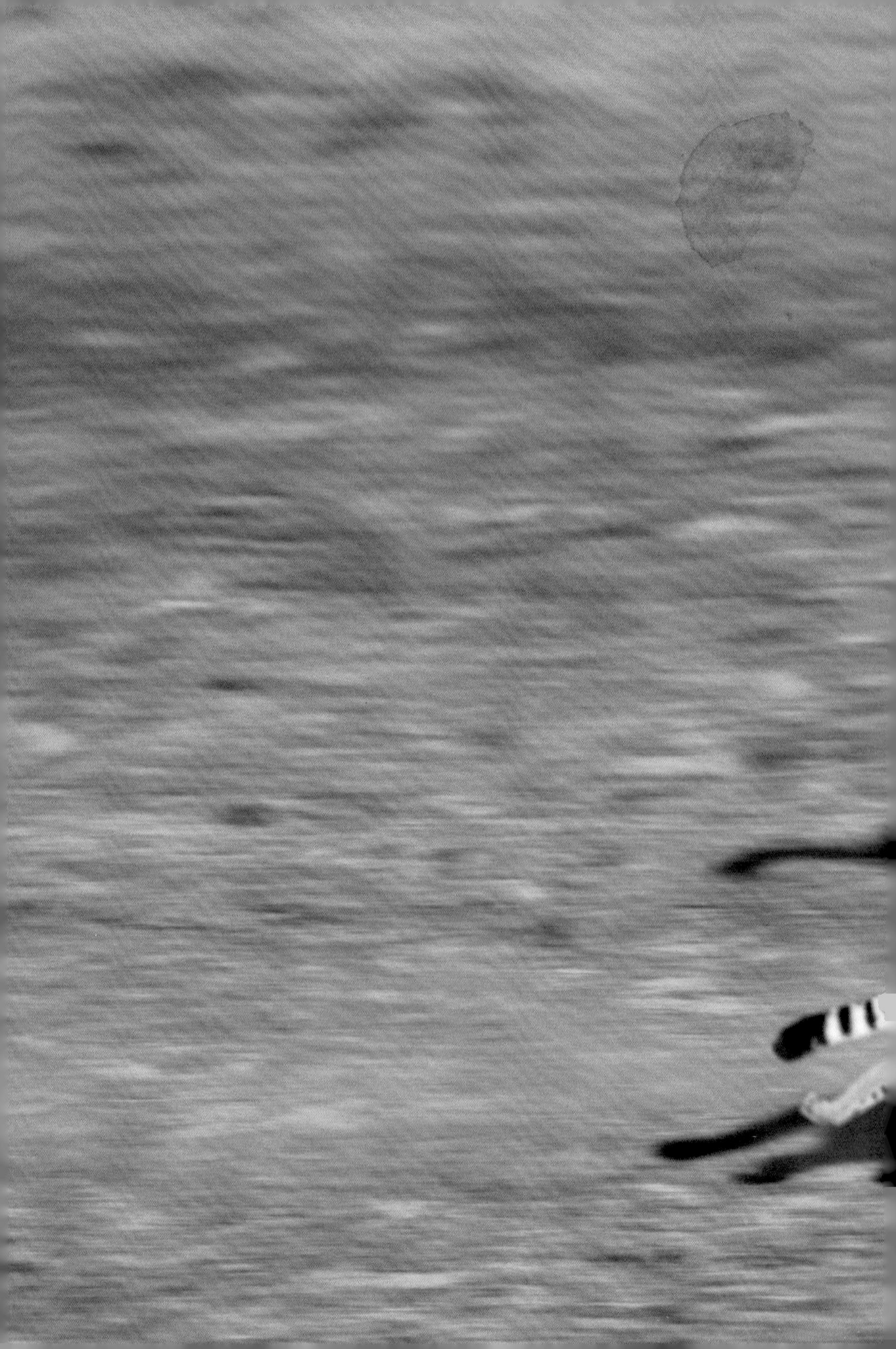

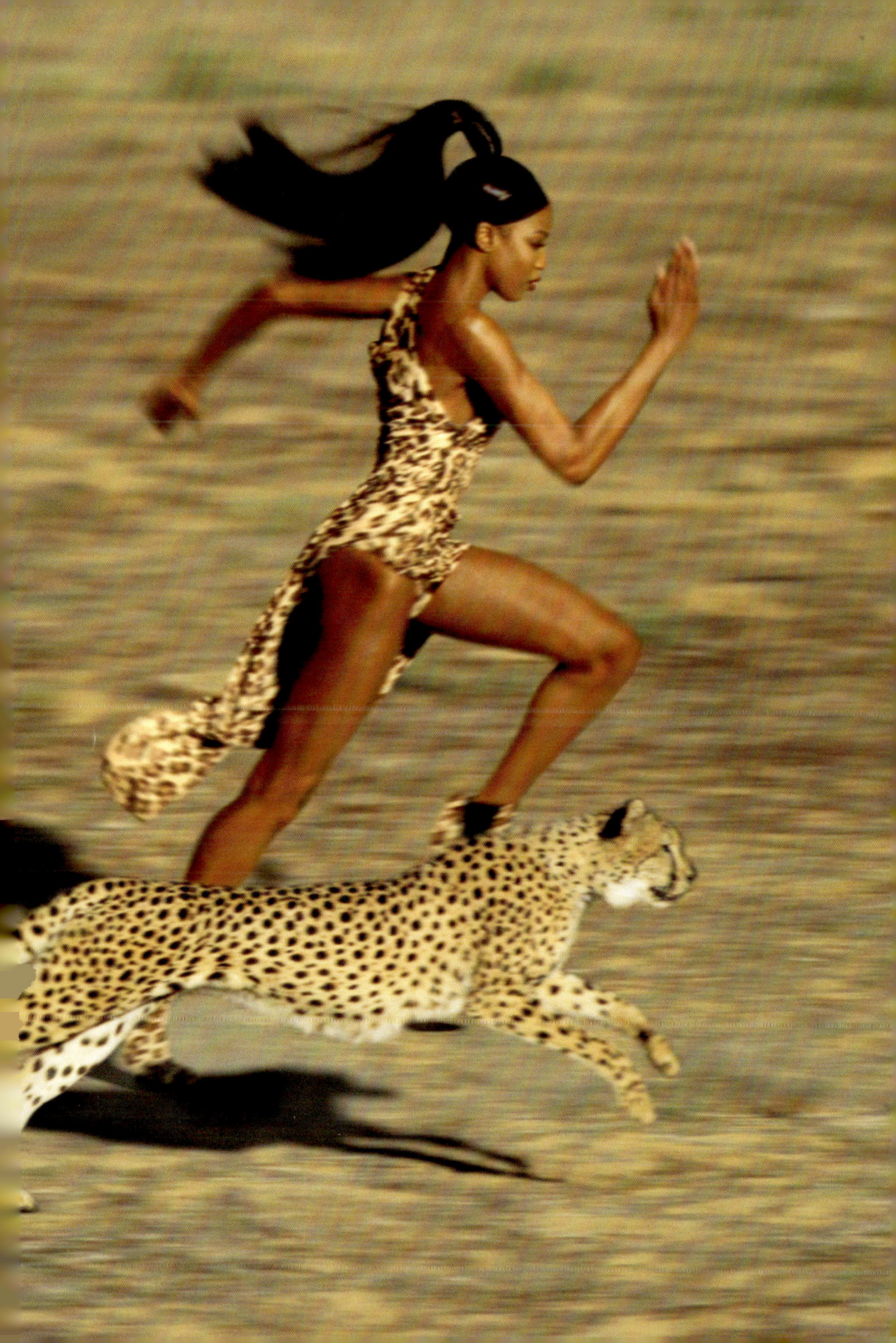

François Nars, 2009 • *(Following Spread)* **Ellen von Unwerth, 2010**

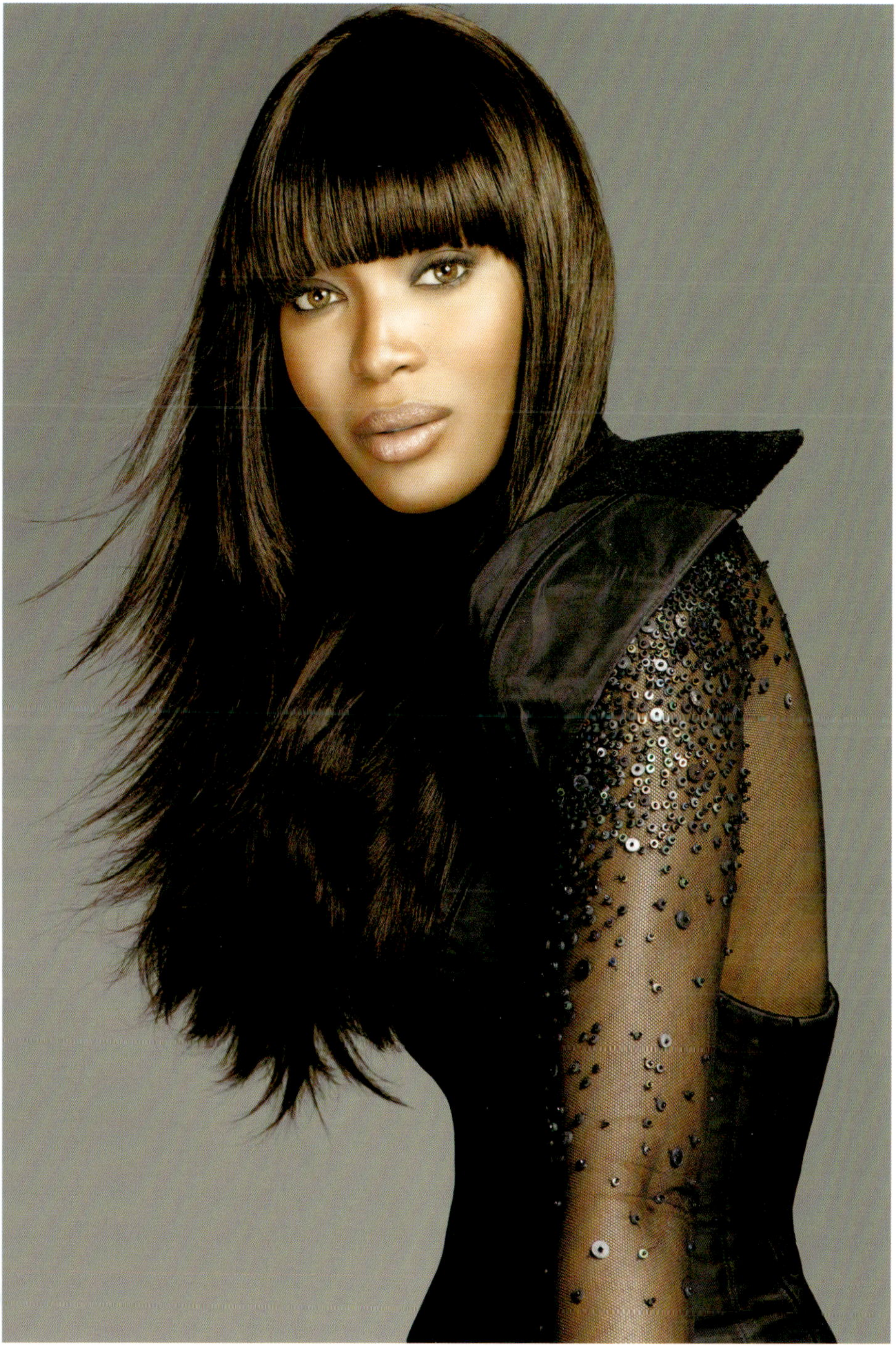

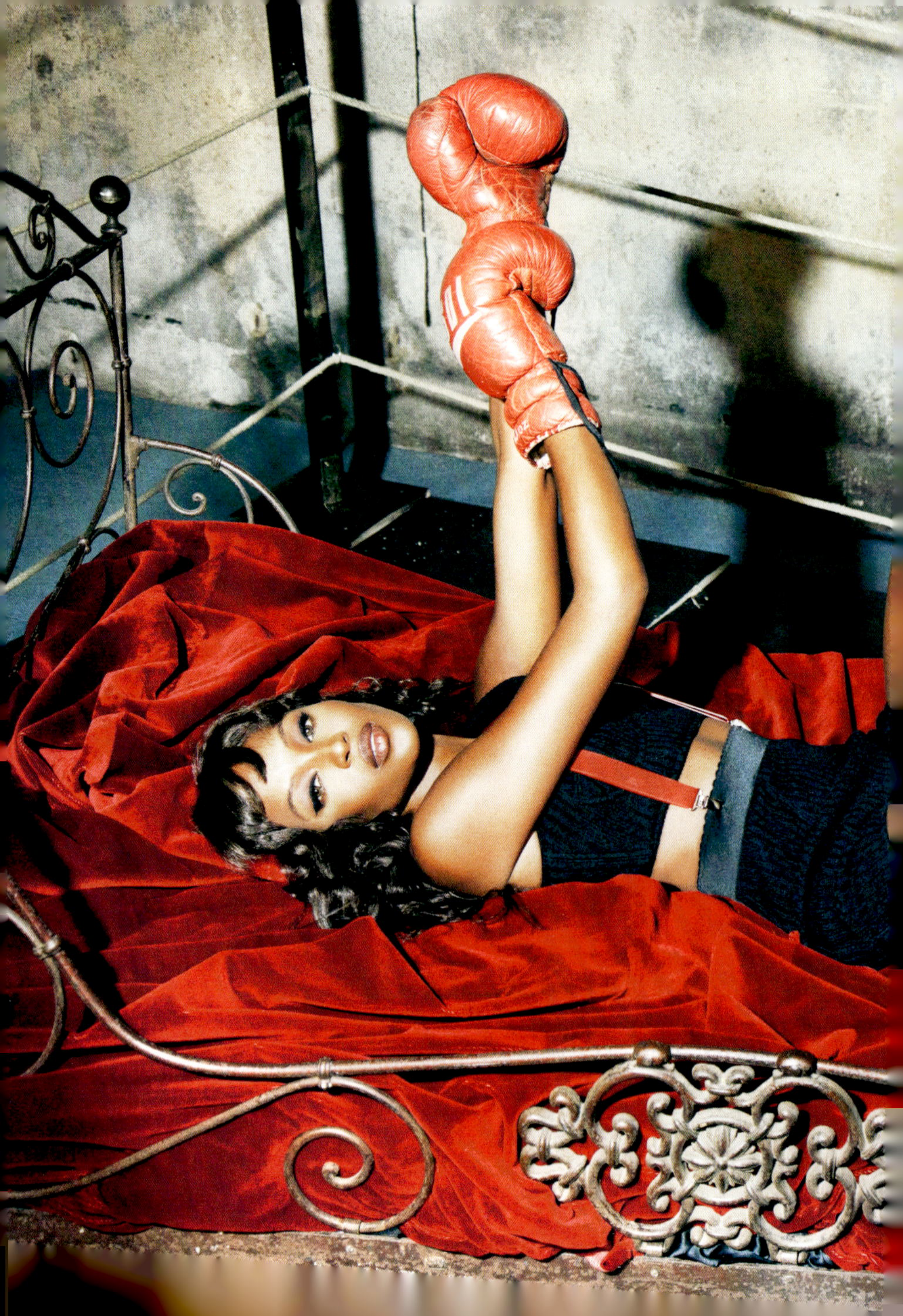

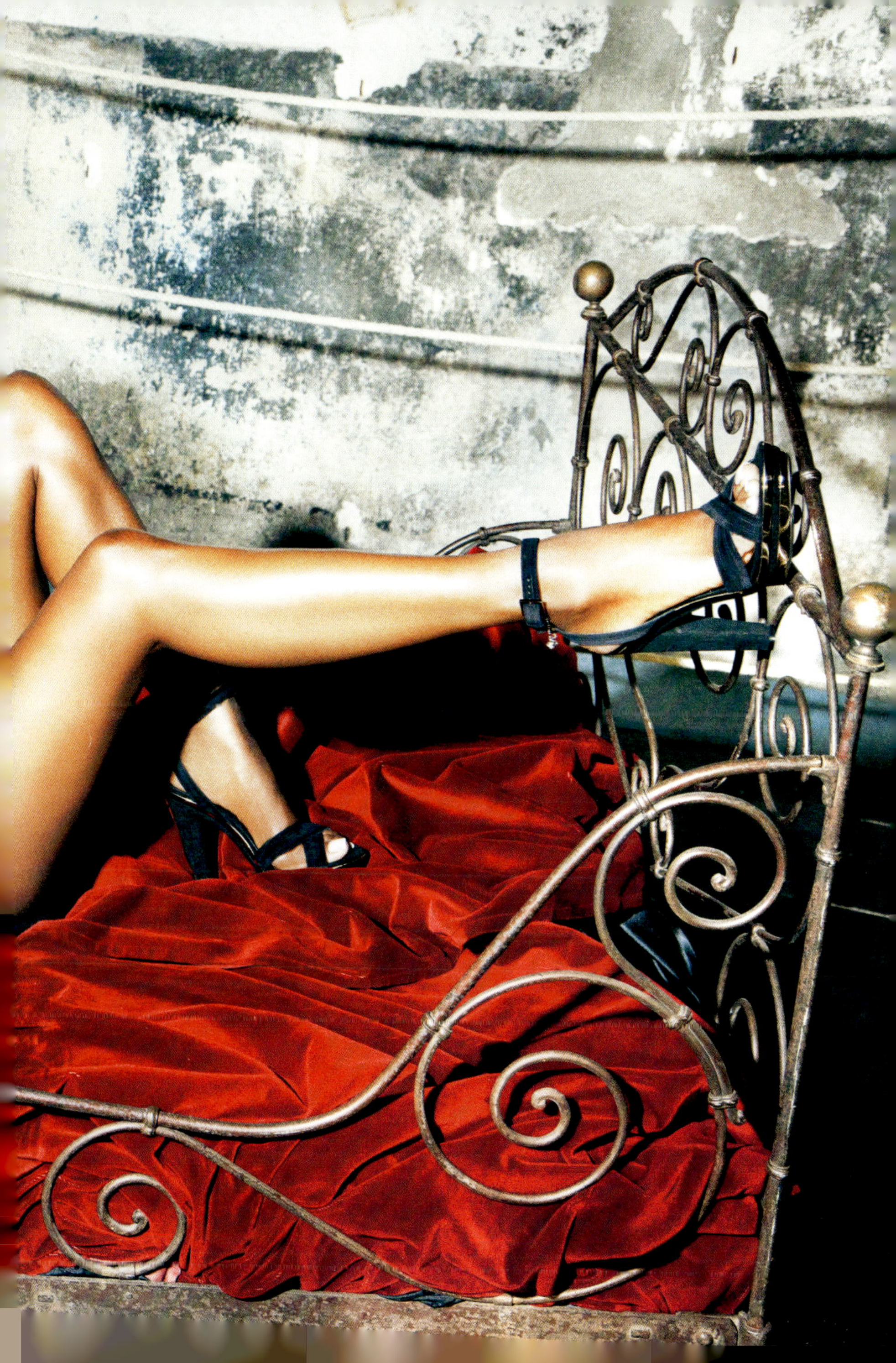

A RELENTLESS ENERGY, A BRITISH STYLE ICON AND A PIONEER – NAOMI, WE SALUTE YOU!

CHRISTOPHER BAILEY

(Opposite & Following Spread) **Mert Alas & Marcus Piggott, 2010**

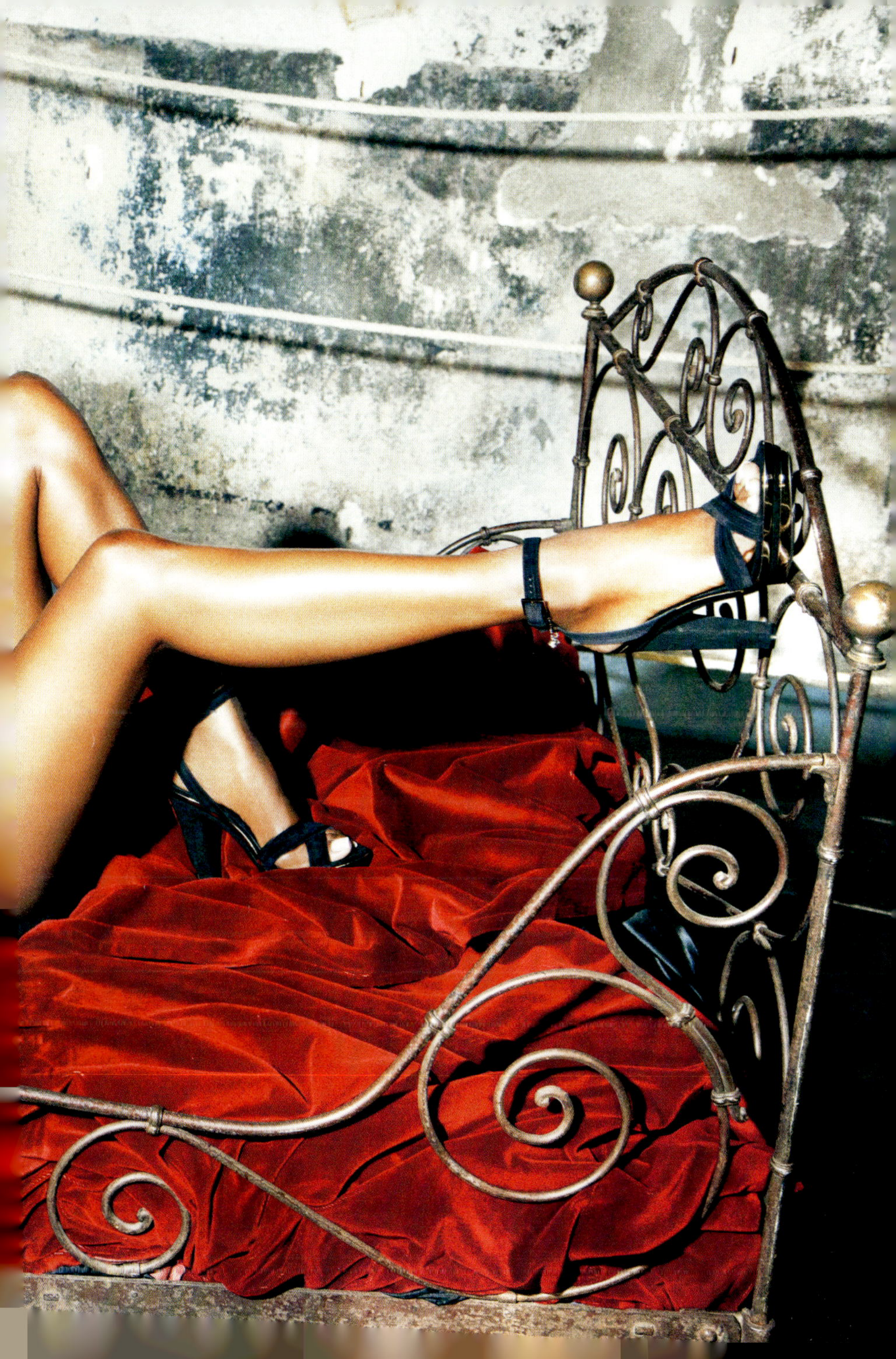

A RELENTLESS ENERGY, A BRITISH STYLE ICON AND A PIONEER – NAOMI, WE SALUTE YOU!

CHRISTOPHER BAILEY

(Opposite & Following Spread) **Mert Alas & Marcus Piggott, 2010**

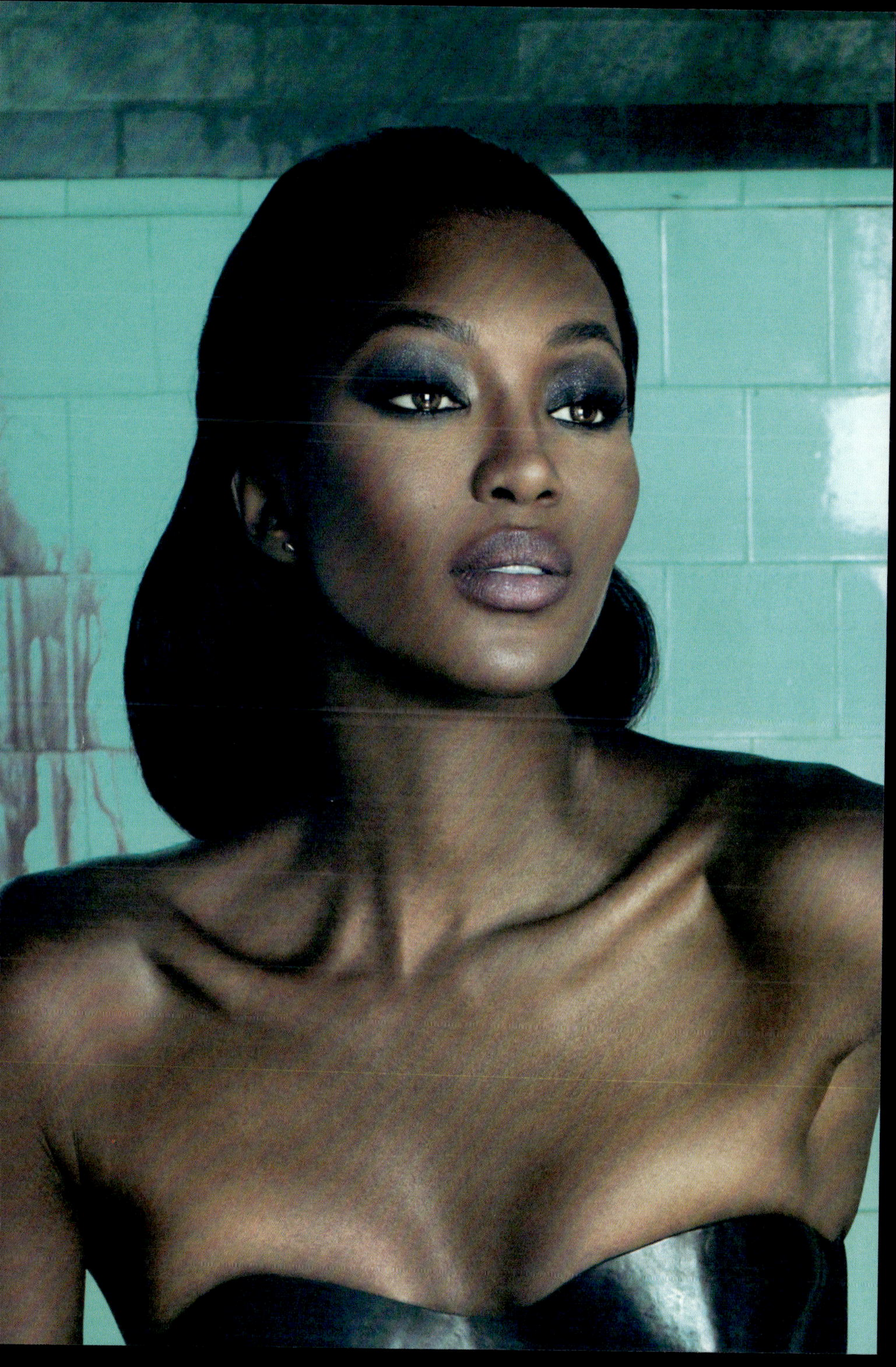

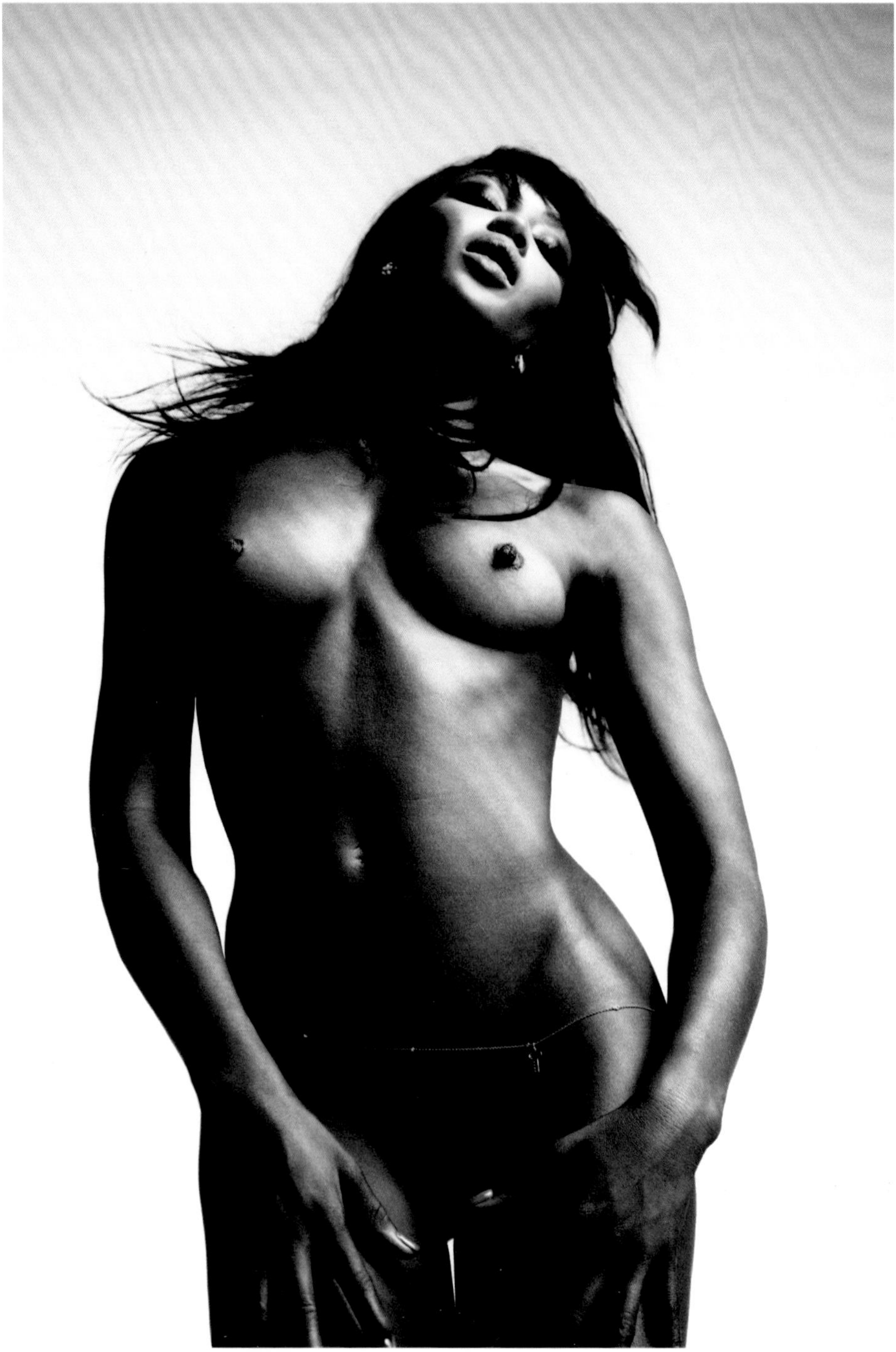

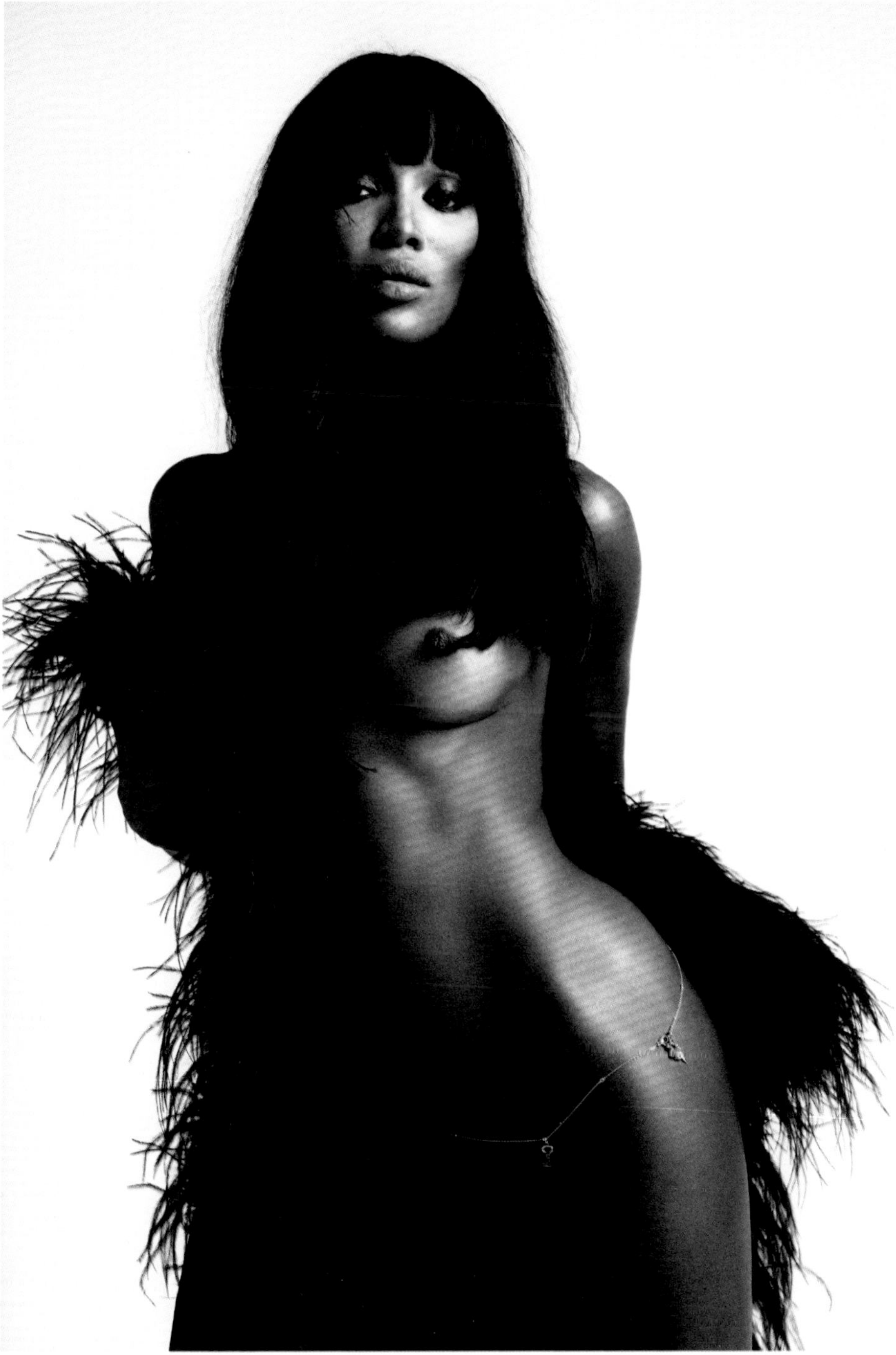

NAOMI IS ONE OF THE
MOST INSPIRATIONAL WOMEN
I HAVE EVER MET. HER BEAUTY
IS TIMELESS AND HER WARMTH
AND LOYALTY IS BOUNDLESS.
NAOMI IS TRULY
AN ICON OF OUR TIME.

SARAH BURTON

Nick Knight, 2010

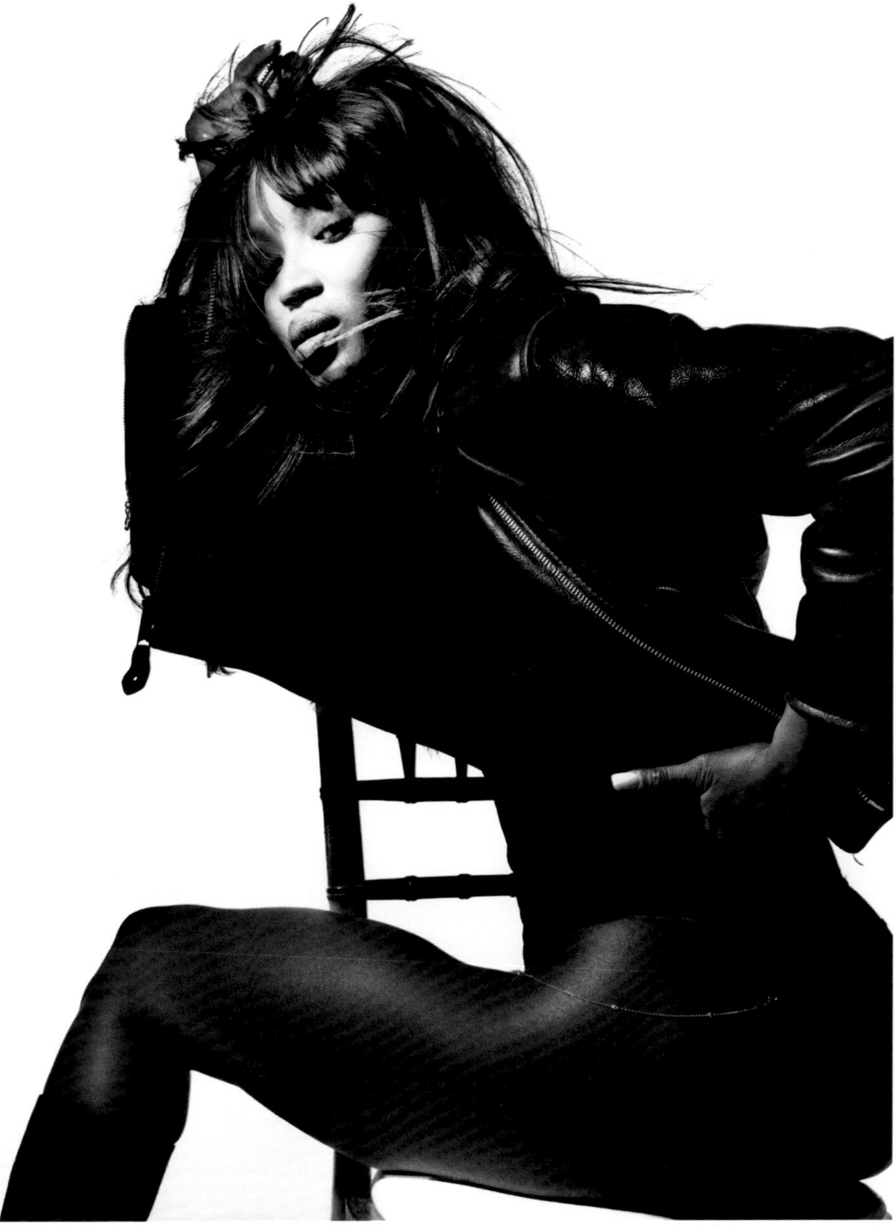

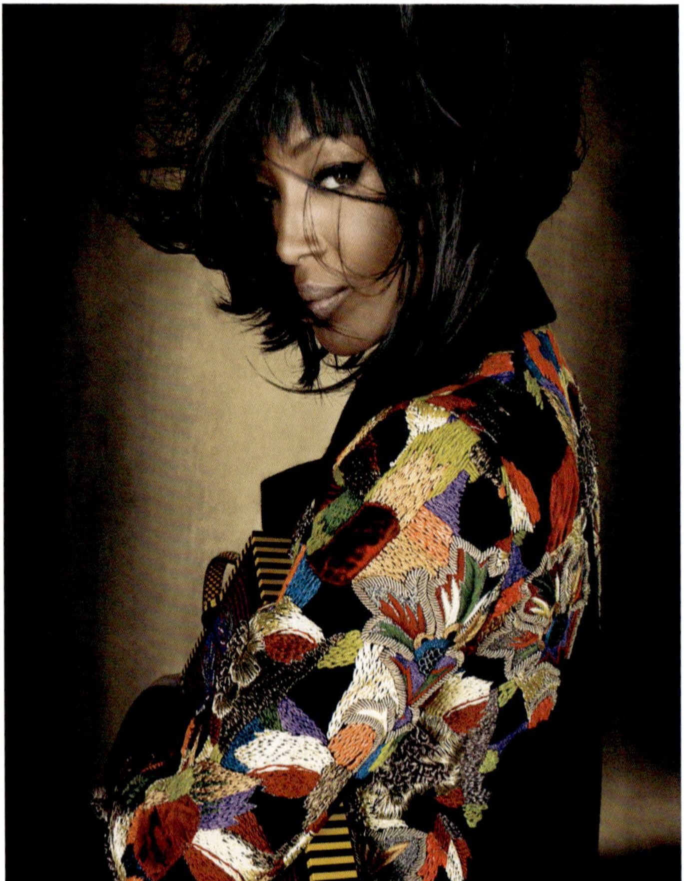

Emma Summerton, 2012
(Following Spread) **Mert Alas & Marcus Piggott, 2012**

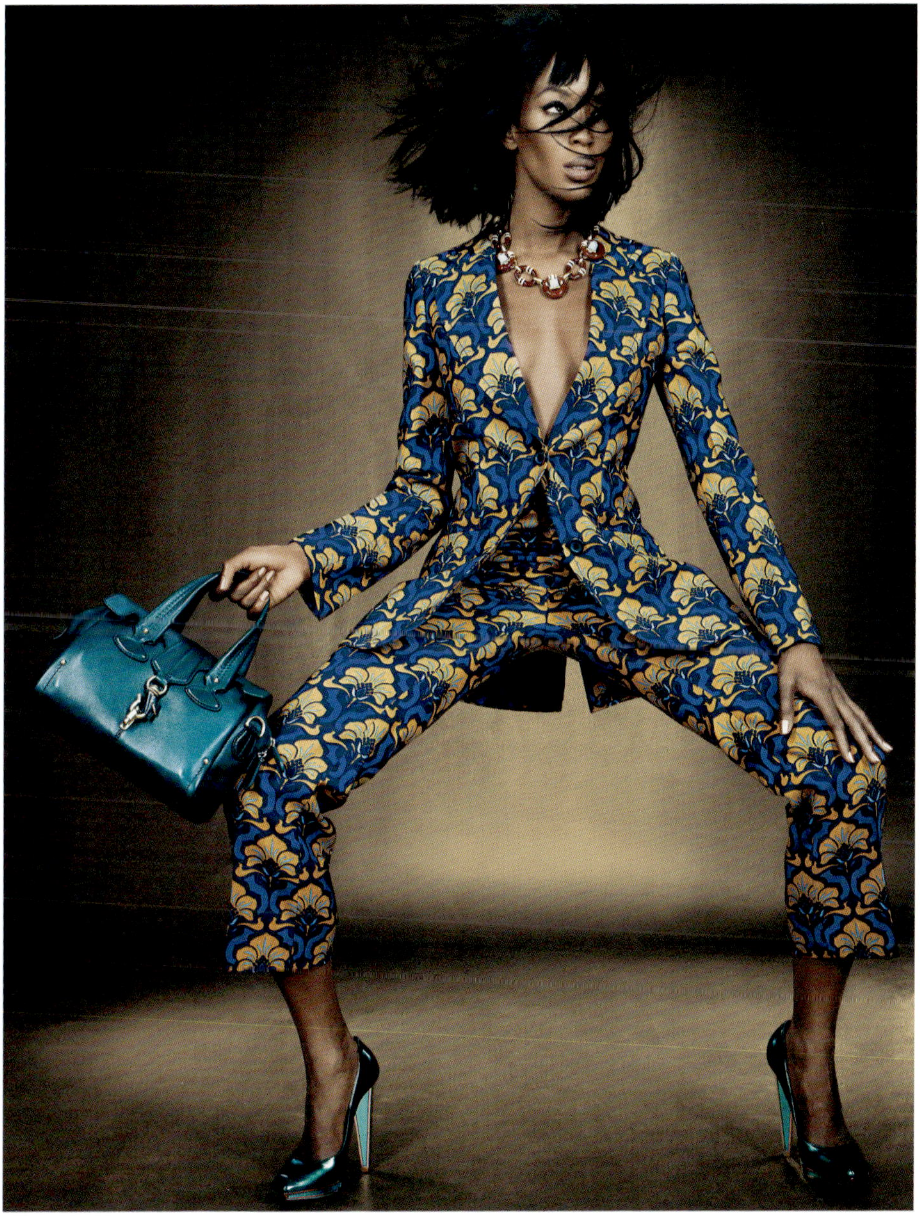

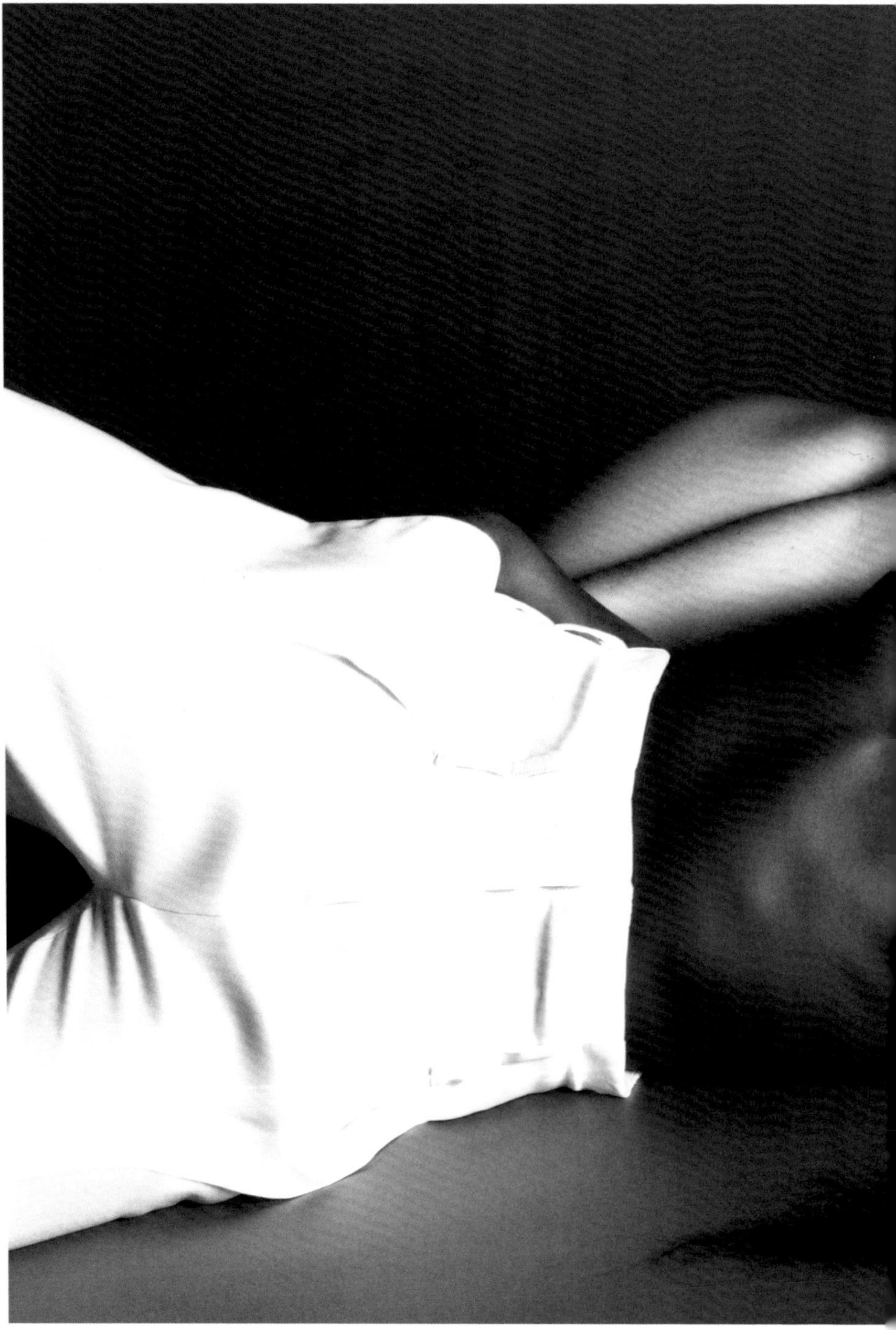

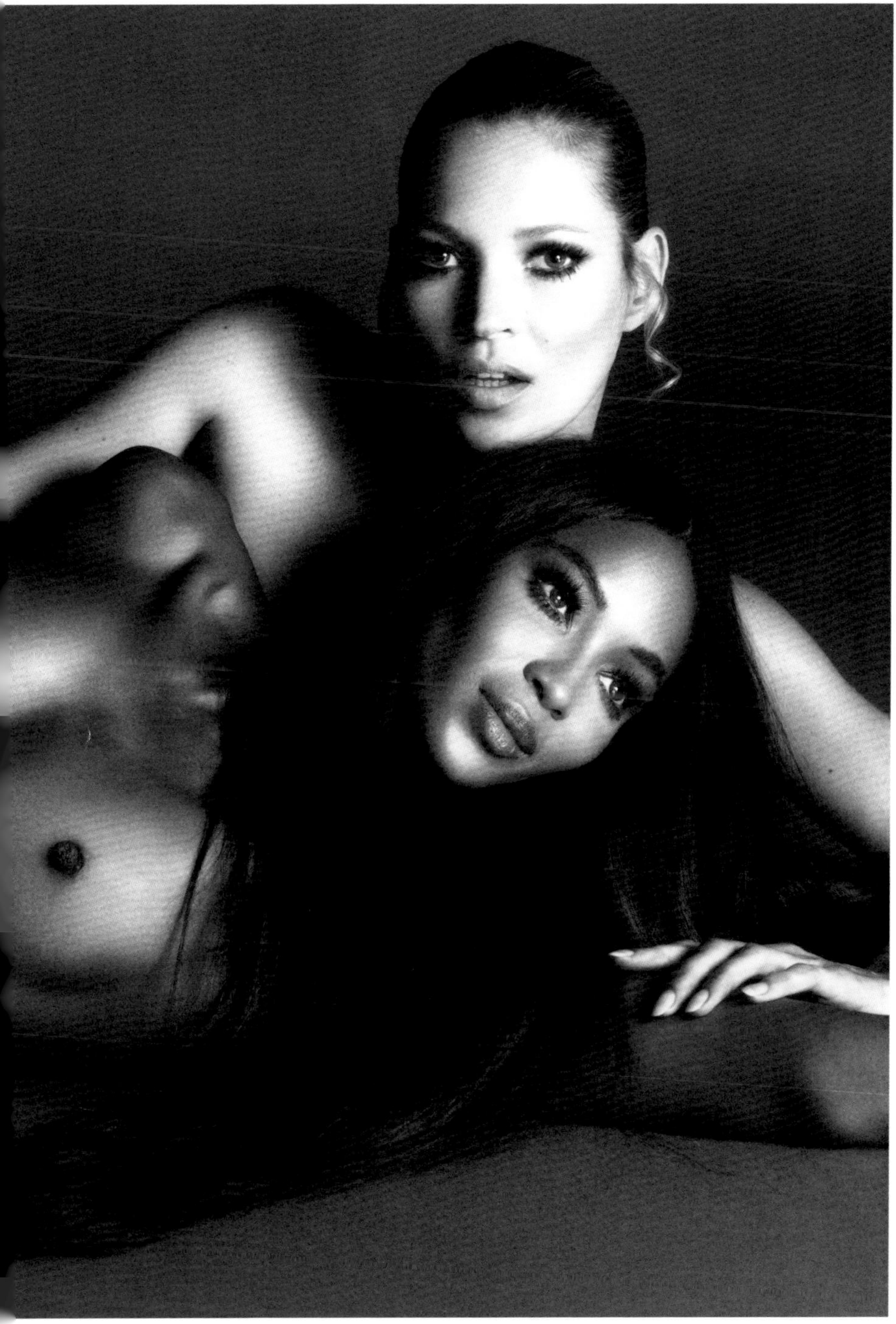

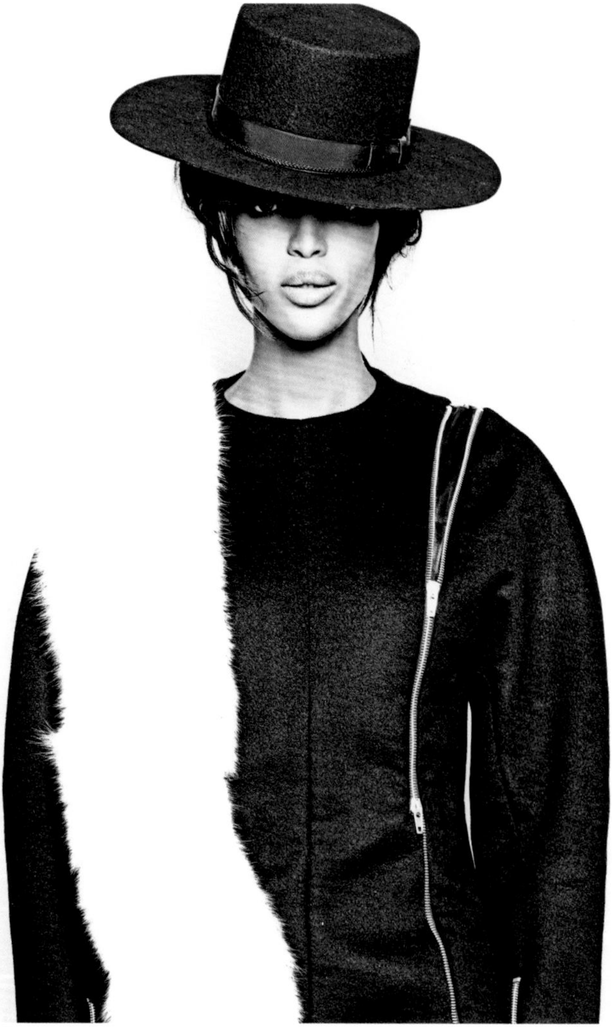

Natalia Alaverdian, 2012

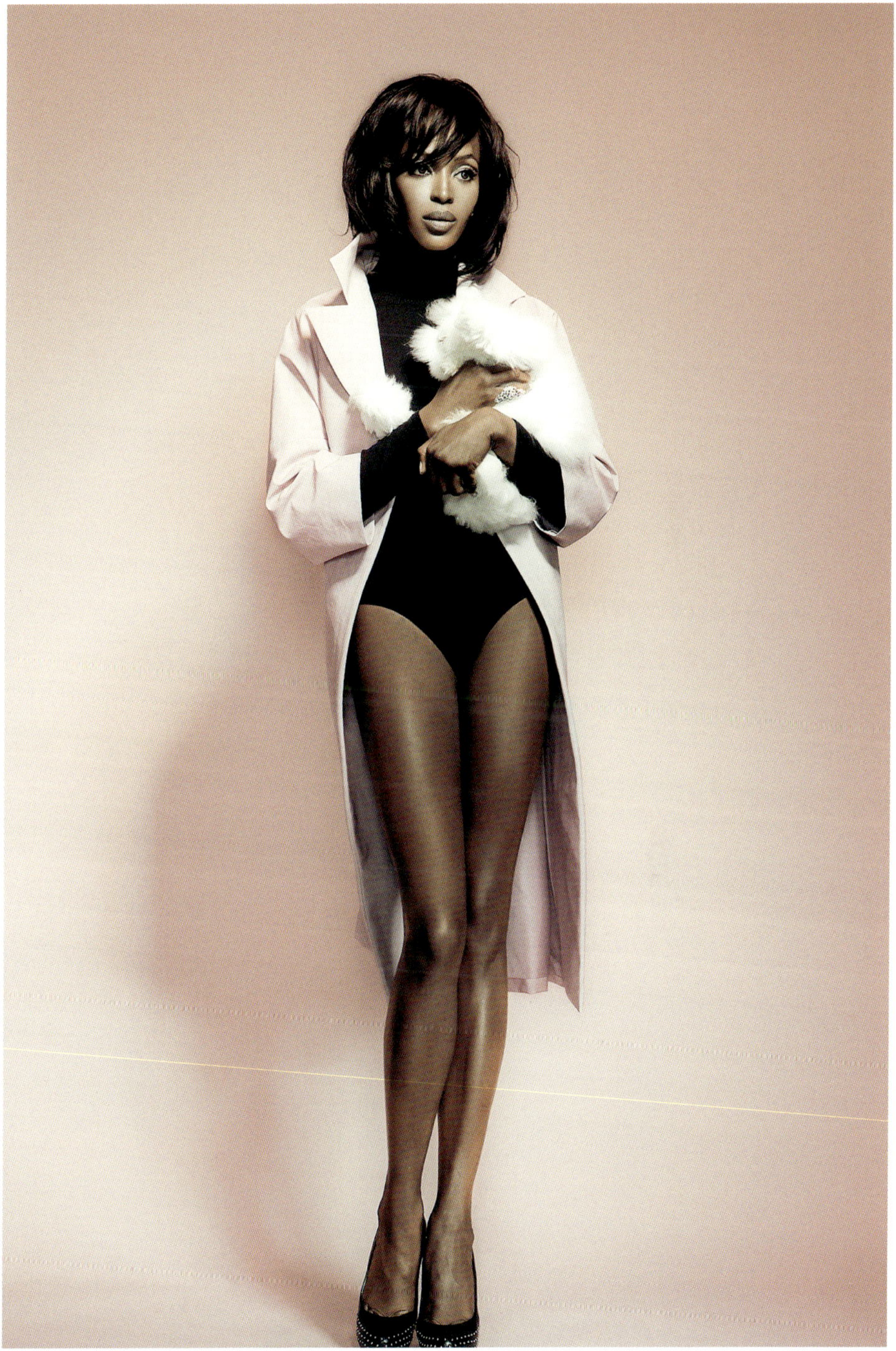

ALL THE CLICHÉS GENUINELY DO APPLY TO NAOMI – YOU COULD NOT MAKE HER UP . . . SHE REALLY IS LARGER THAN LIFE.

EDWARD ENNINFUL

Luigi & Iango, 2014

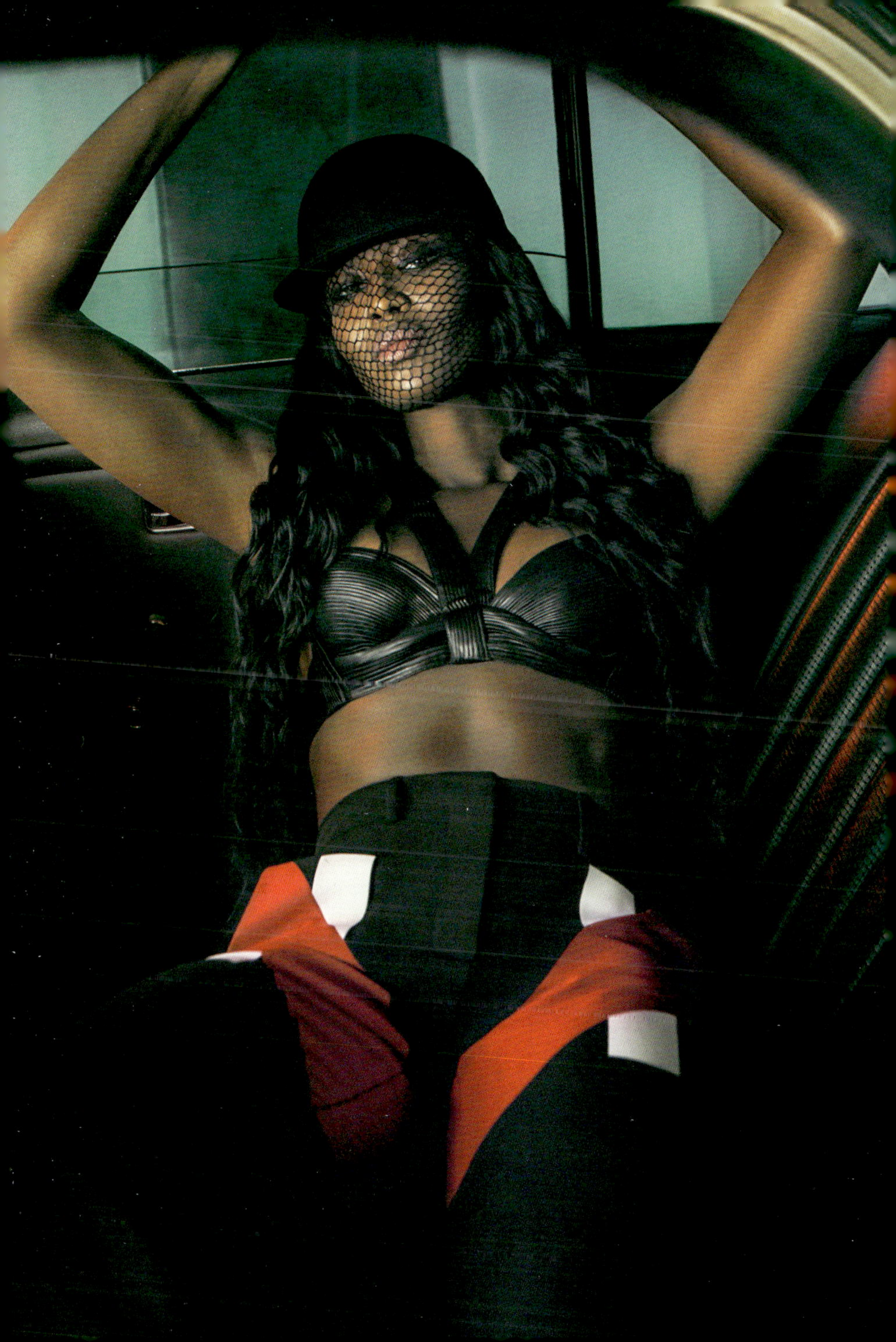

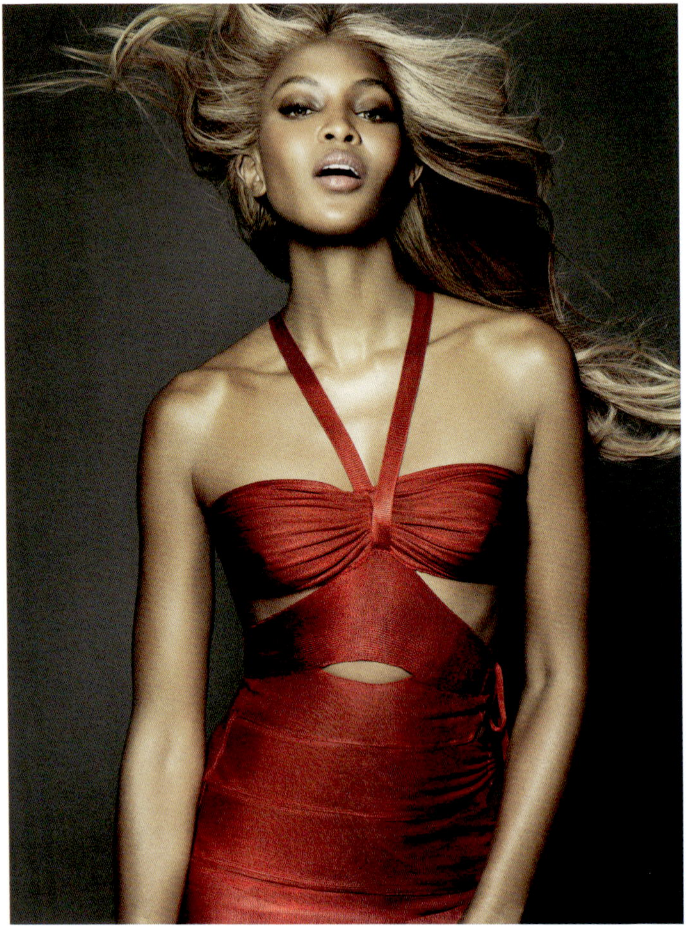

Tom Munro, 2013

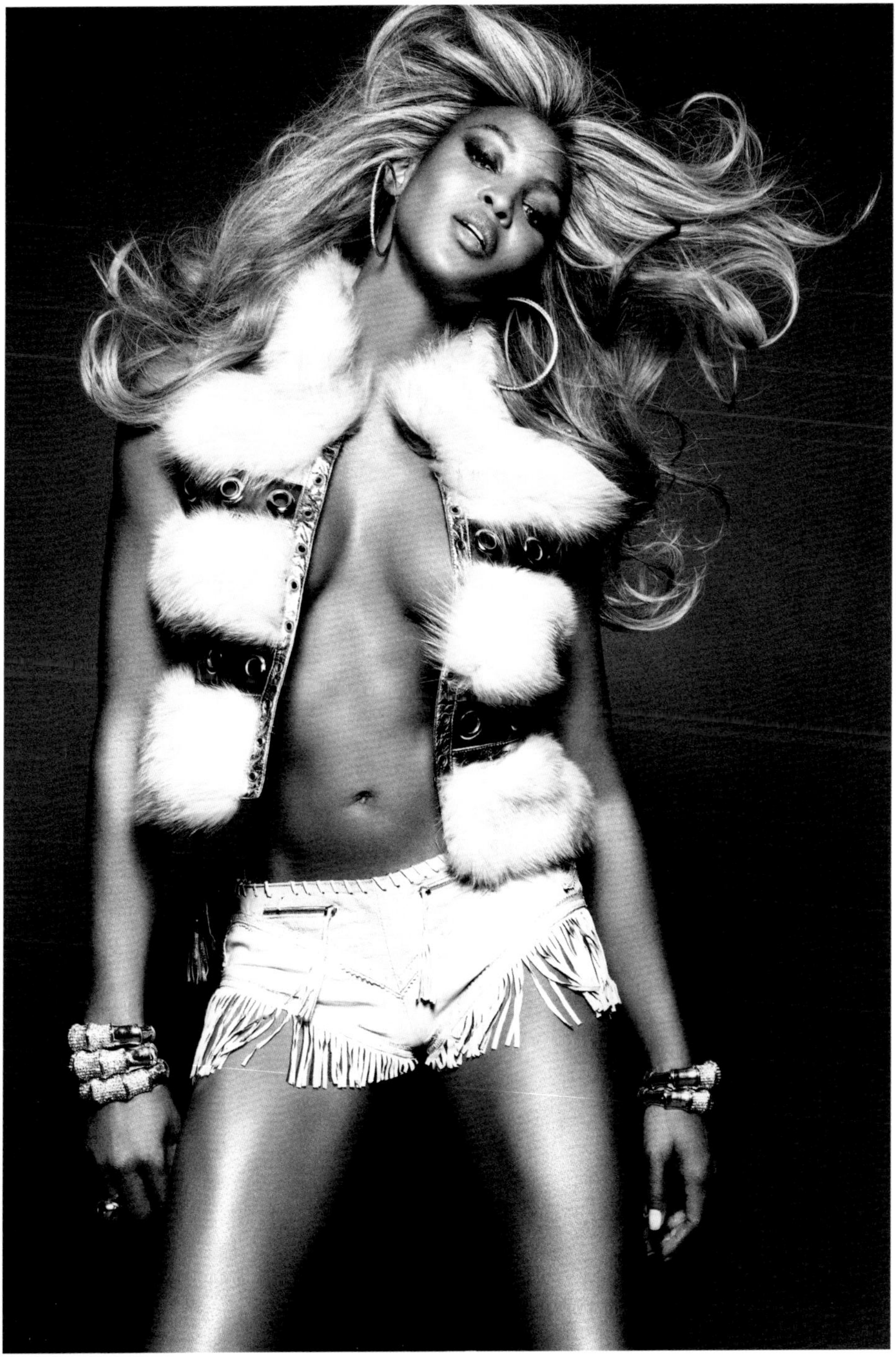

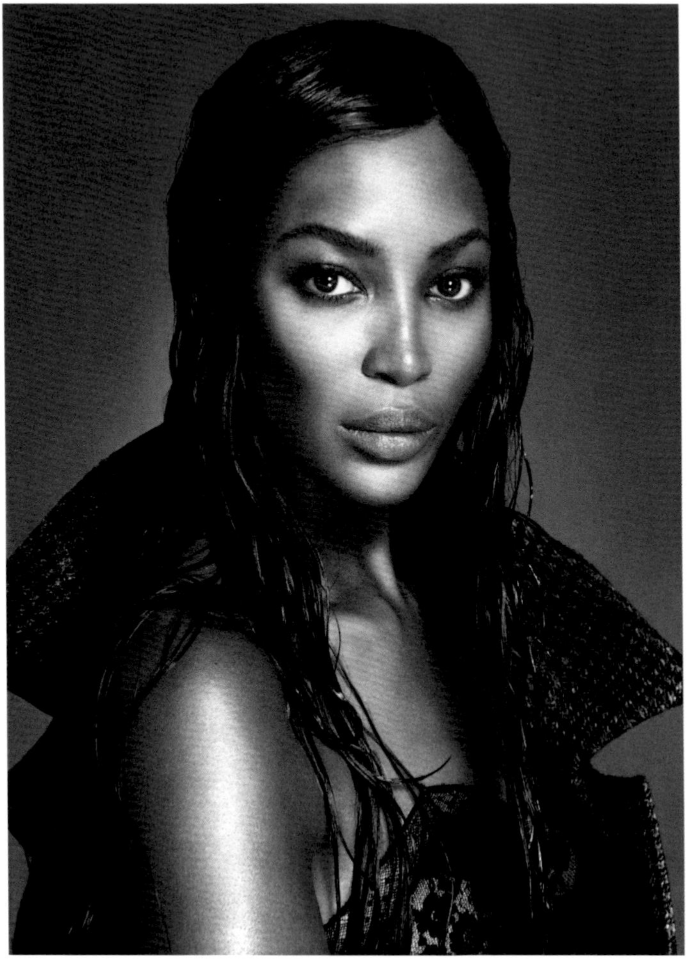

Mert Alas & Marcus Piggott, 2013 • *(Following Spread)* **Ellen von Unwerth, 2015**

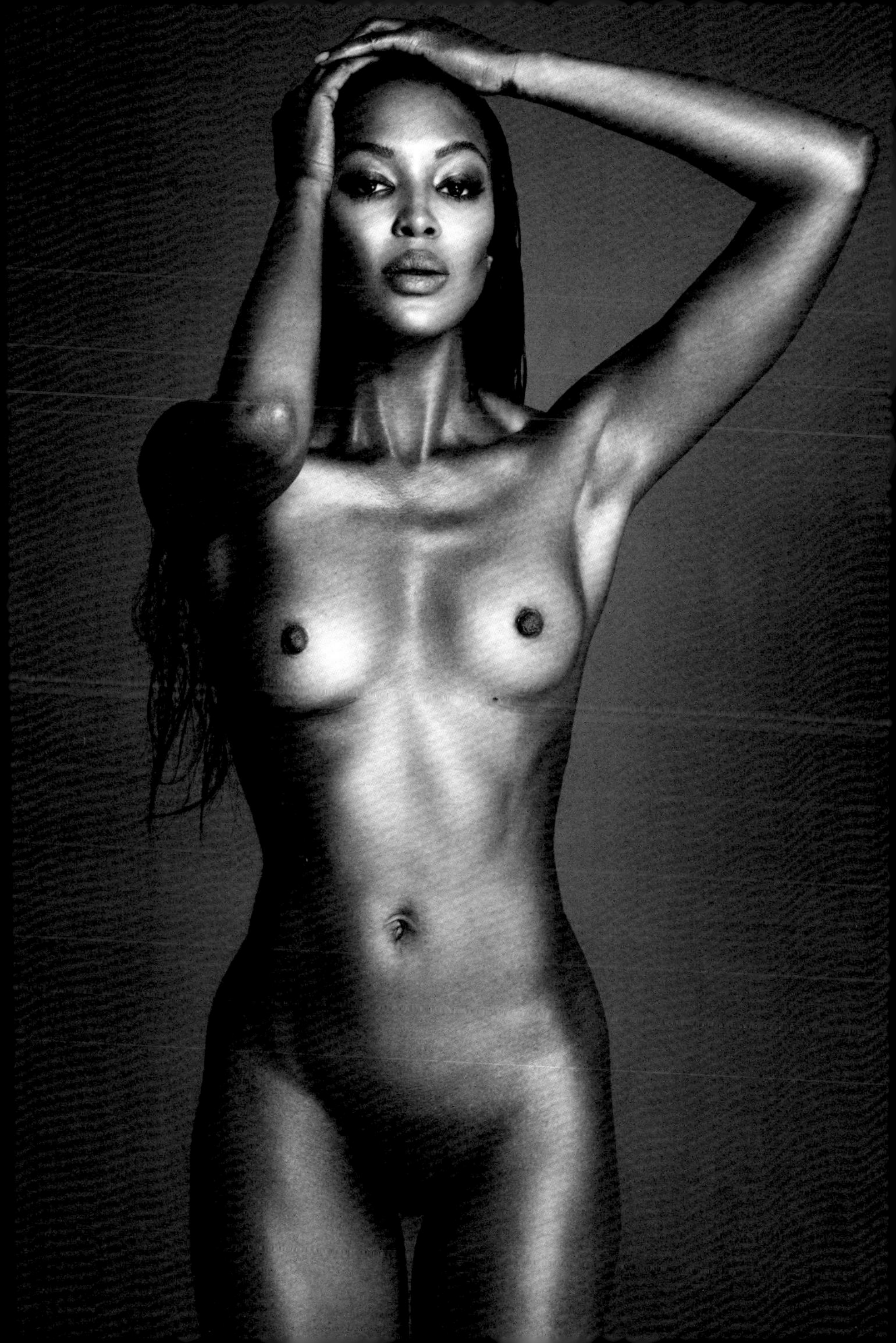

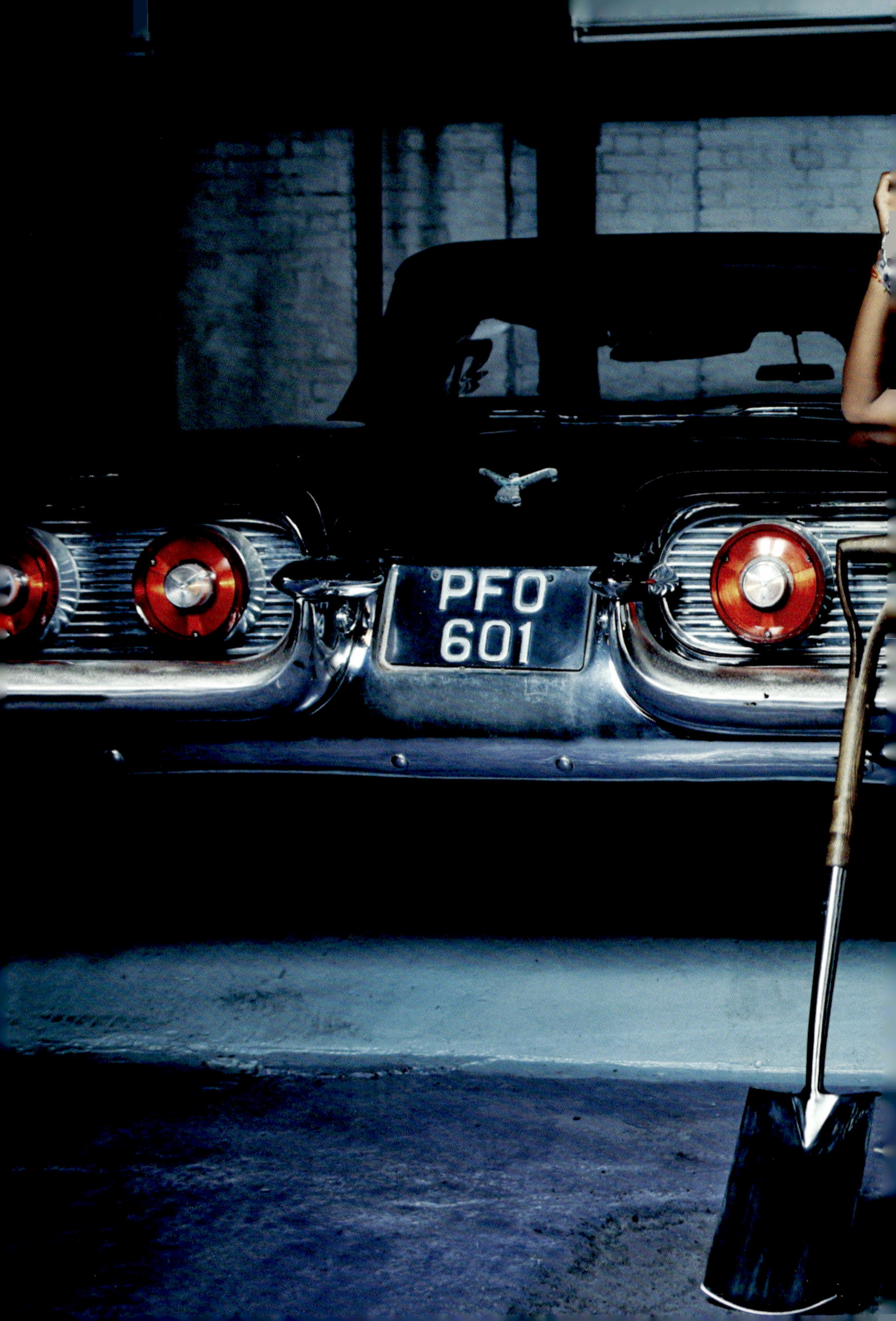
PFO
601

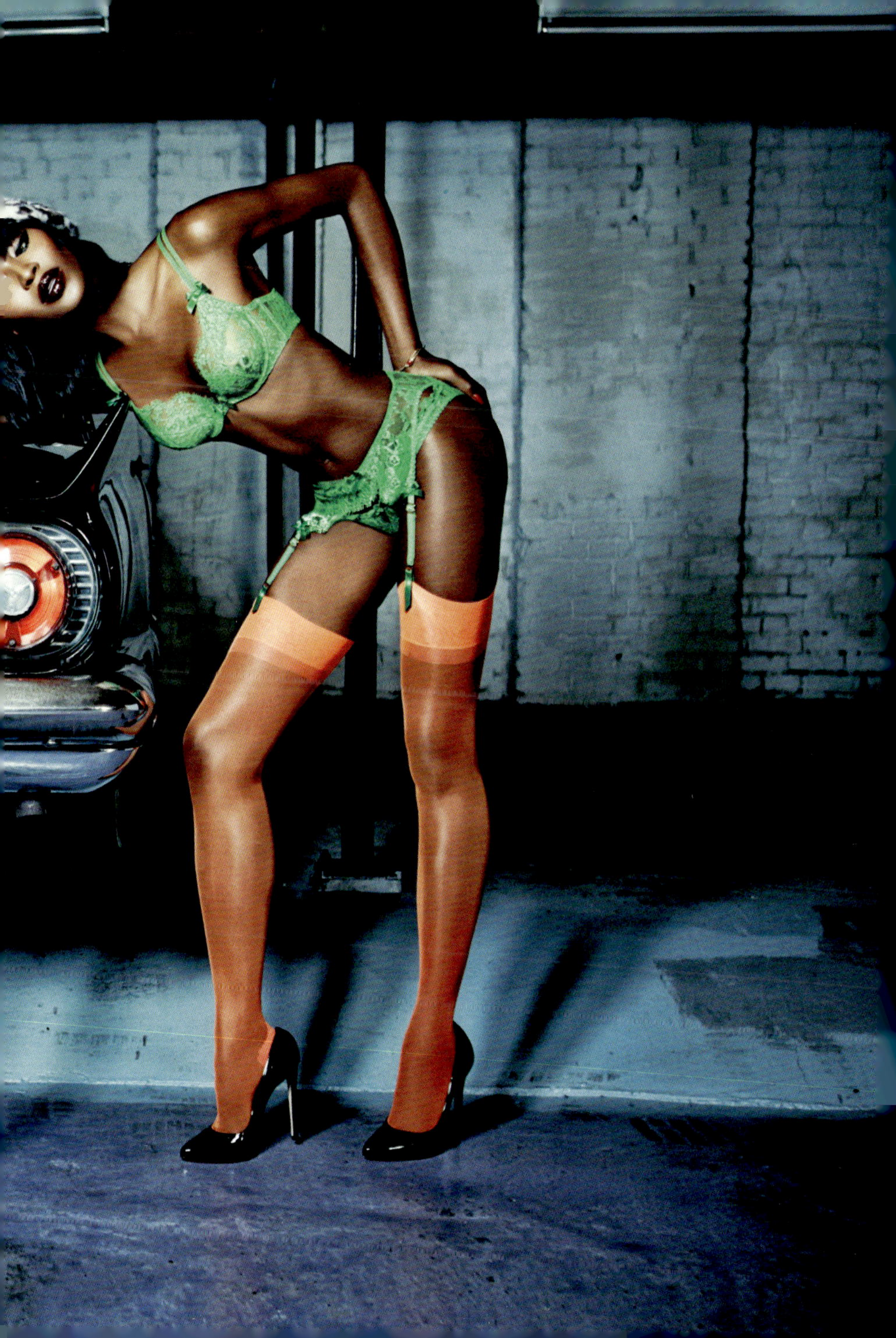

NAOMI IS AMONGST THAT RAREFIED GROUP OF PEOPLE THAT YOU SENSE WOULD BE THE BEST AT WHATEVER THEY CHOOSE TO DO IN LIFE.

JONY IVE

Gui Paganini, 2016

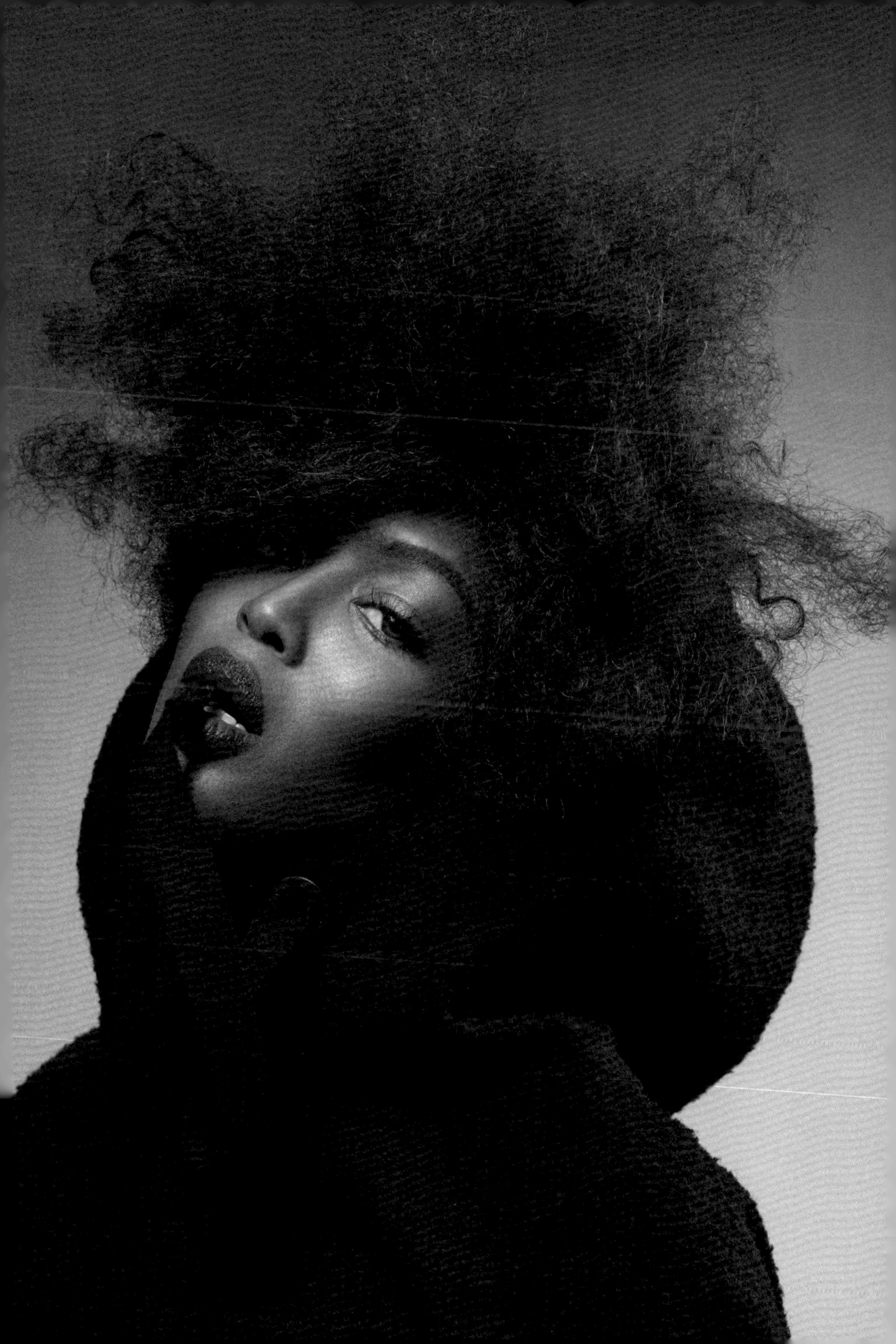

Cuneyt Akeroglu, 2017

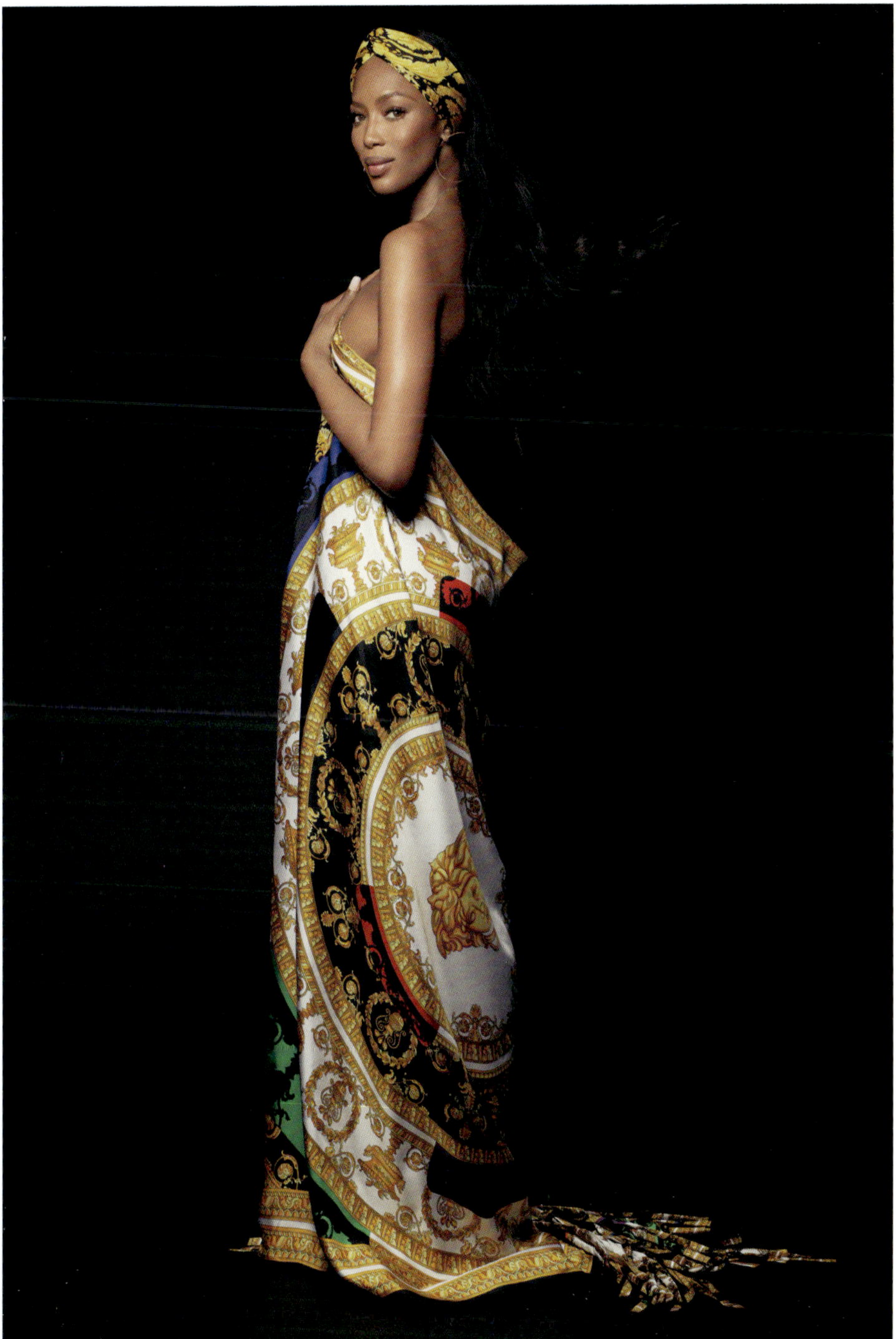

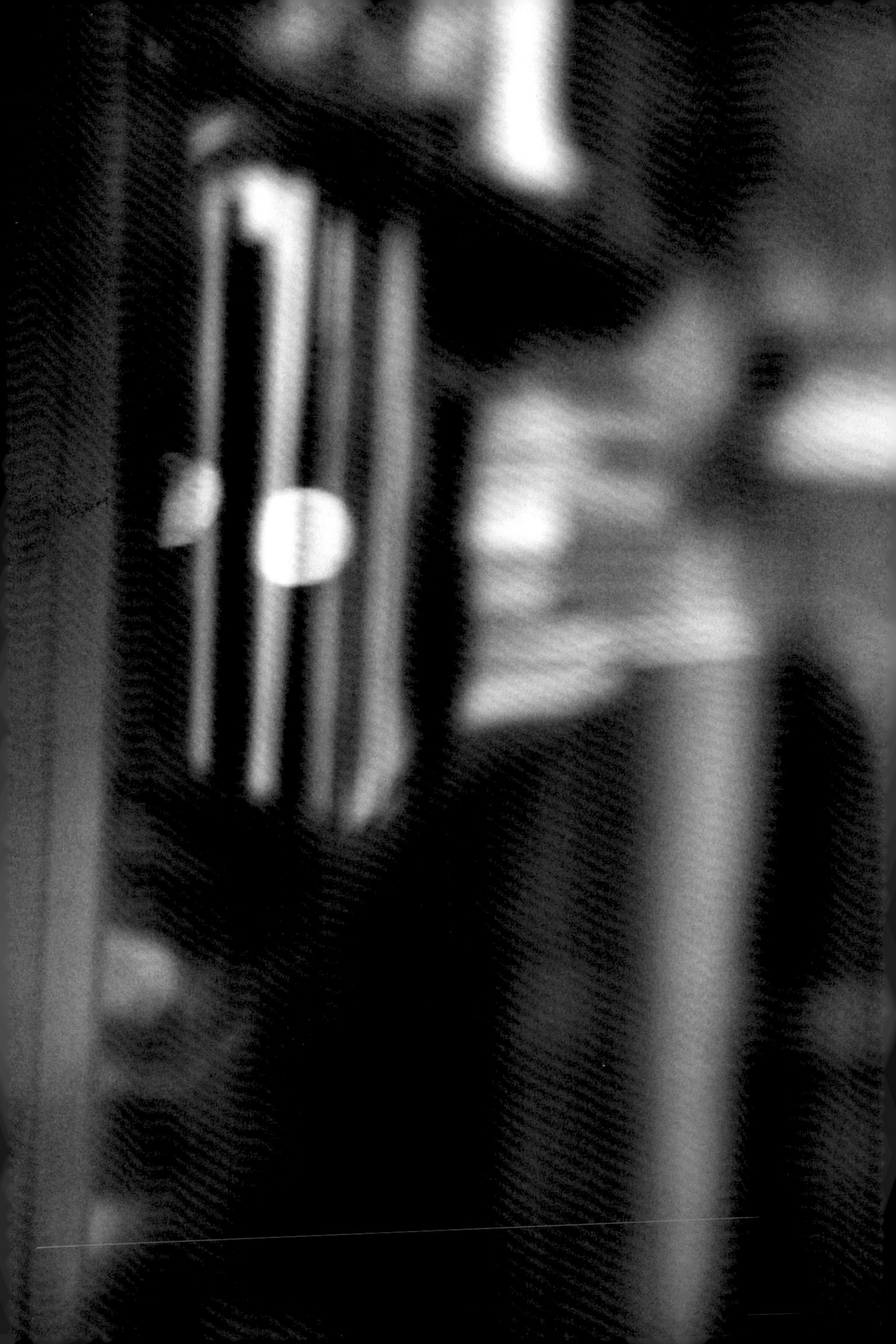

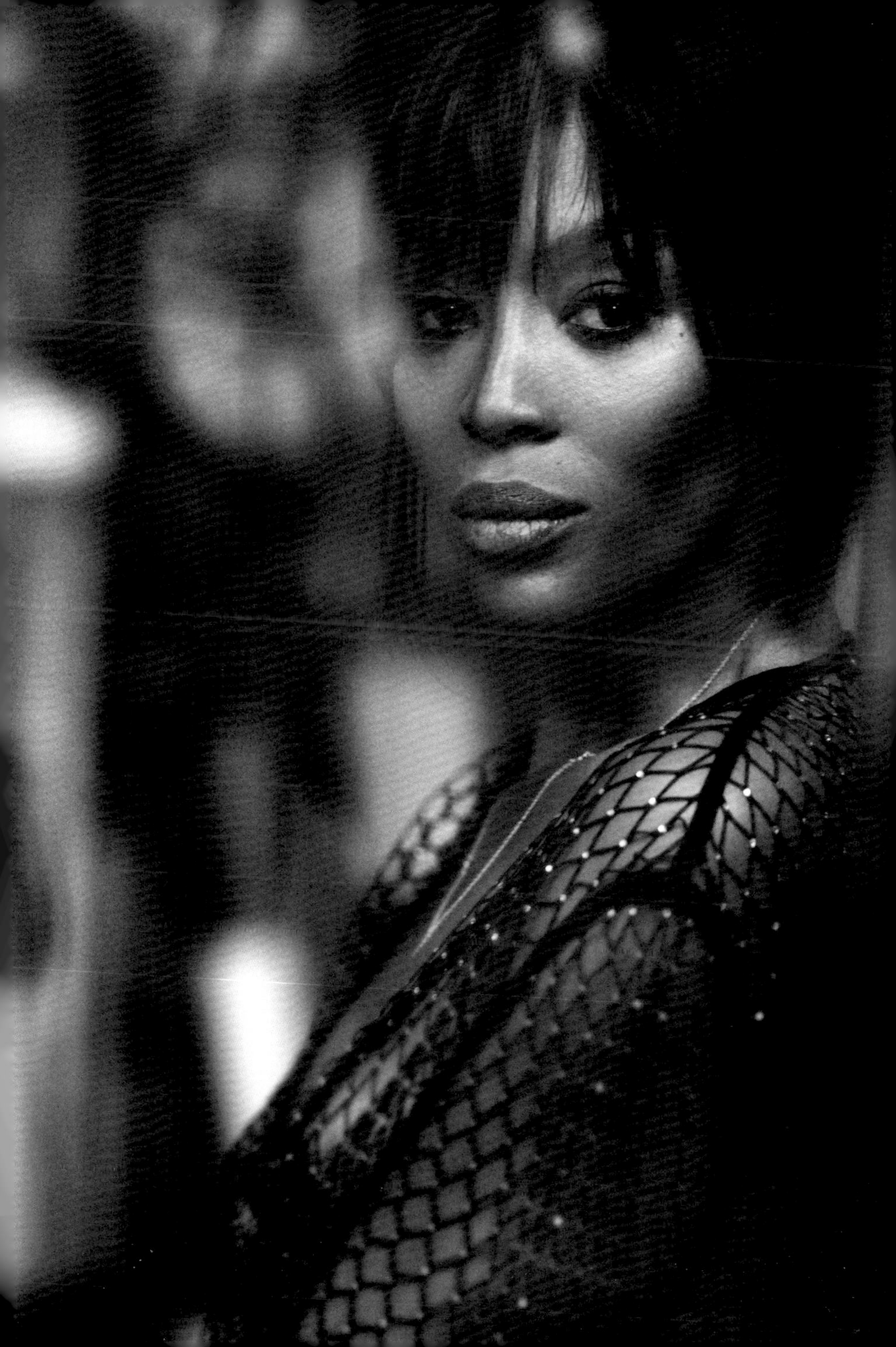

(Previous Spread & Opposite) **Peter Lindbergh, 2018**

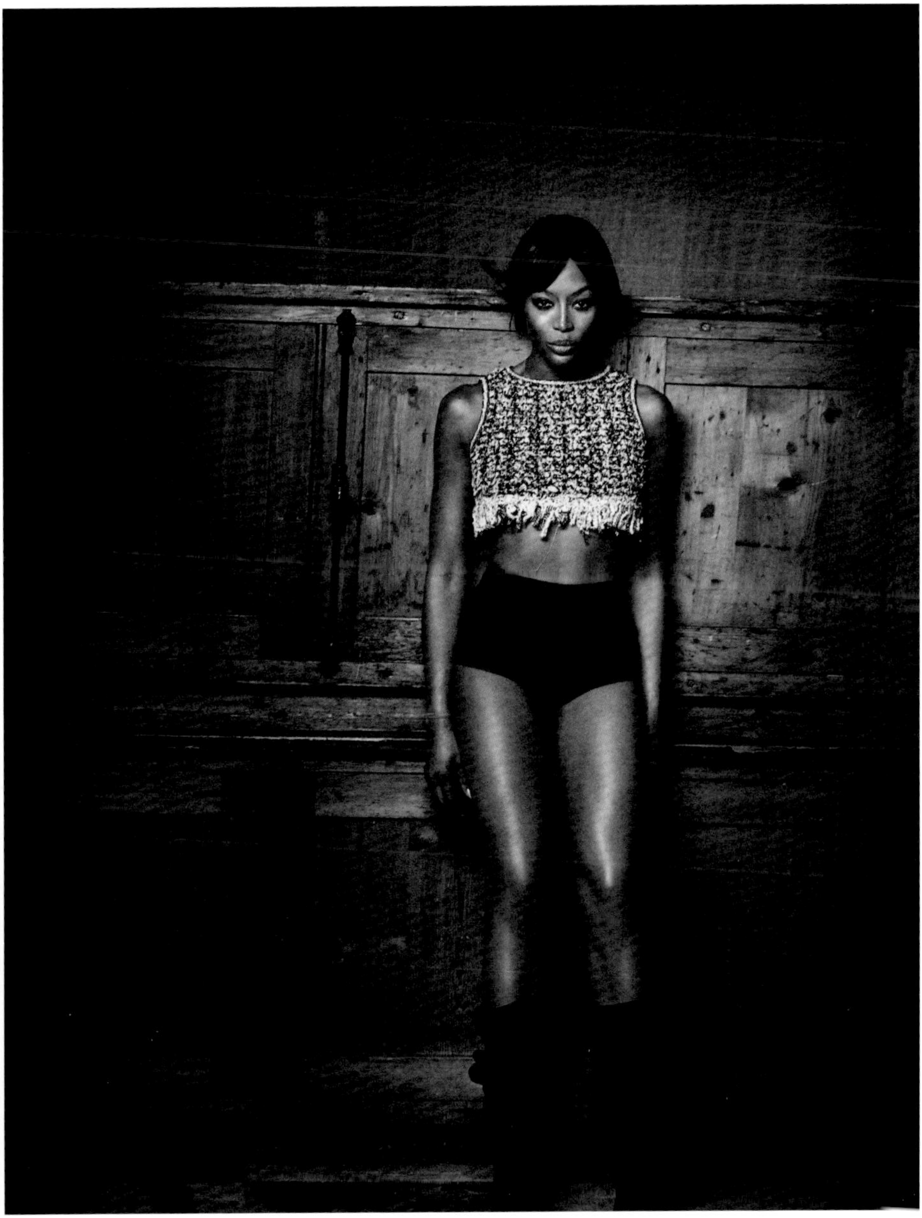

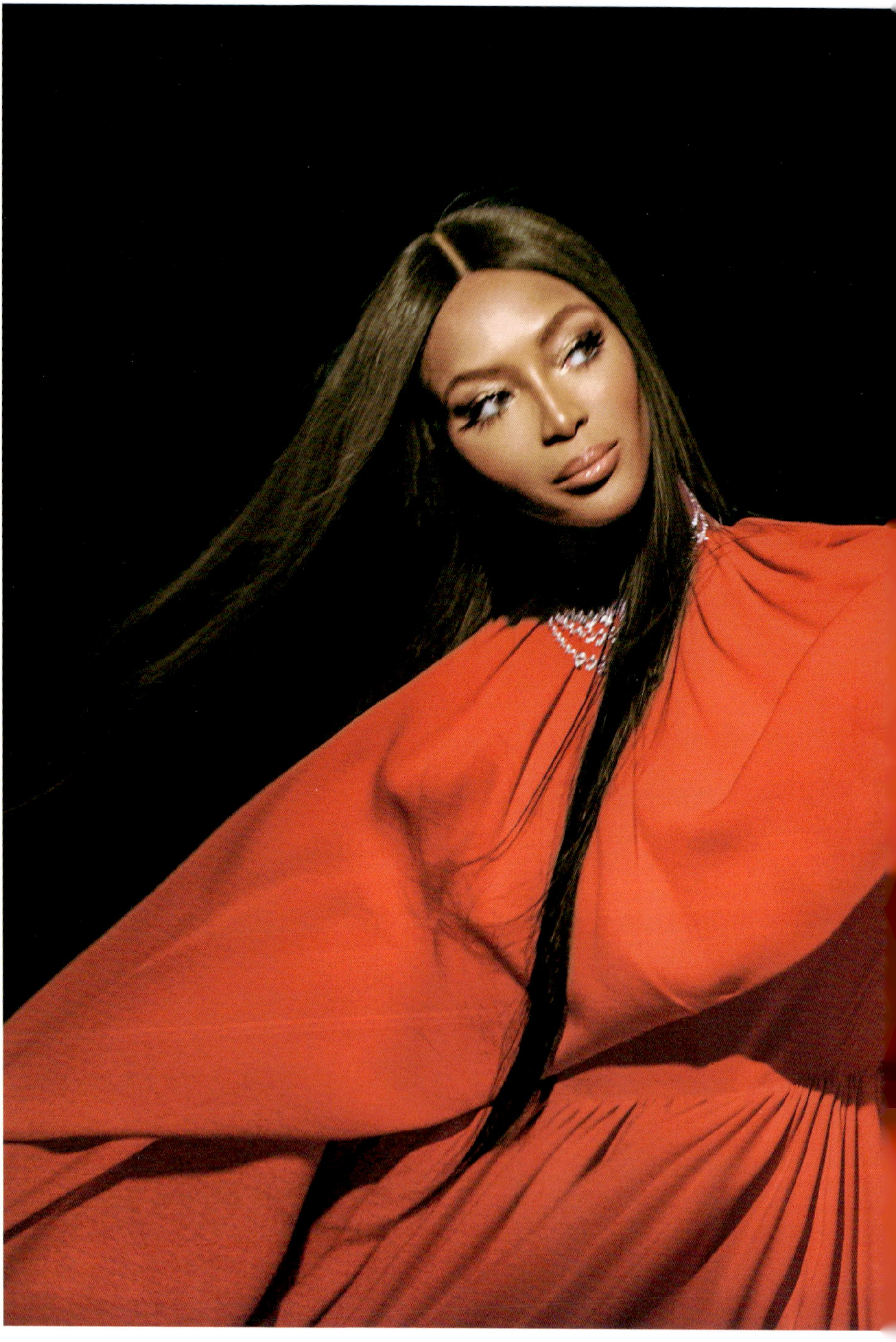

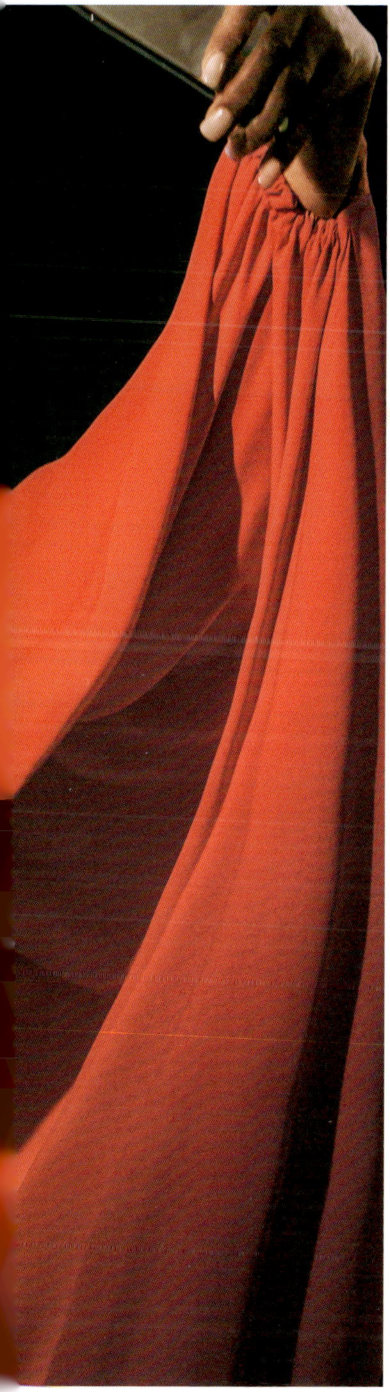

I HATE TO BE SEEN AS A FAILURE IN OTHER YOUNG BLACK GIRLS' EYES WHEN THEY READ SOME OF THE STUFF THAT'S BEEN WRITTEN ABOUT ME. ALL I CAN KEEP DOING IS TRY TO BREAK THE BARRIERS THAT ARE STILL THERE.

NAOMI CAMPBELL

(Previous Spread & Opposite) **Steven Meisel, 2019**

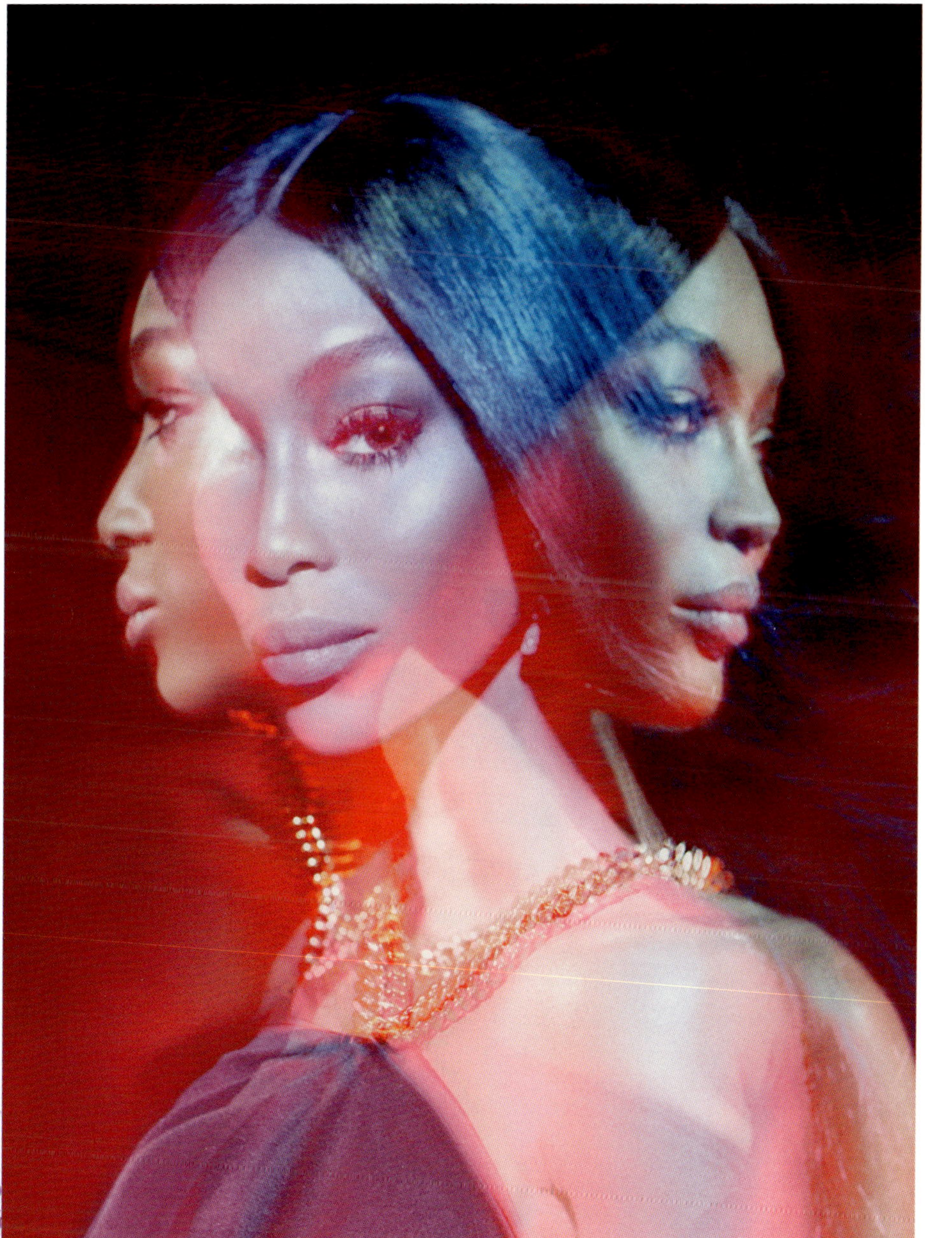

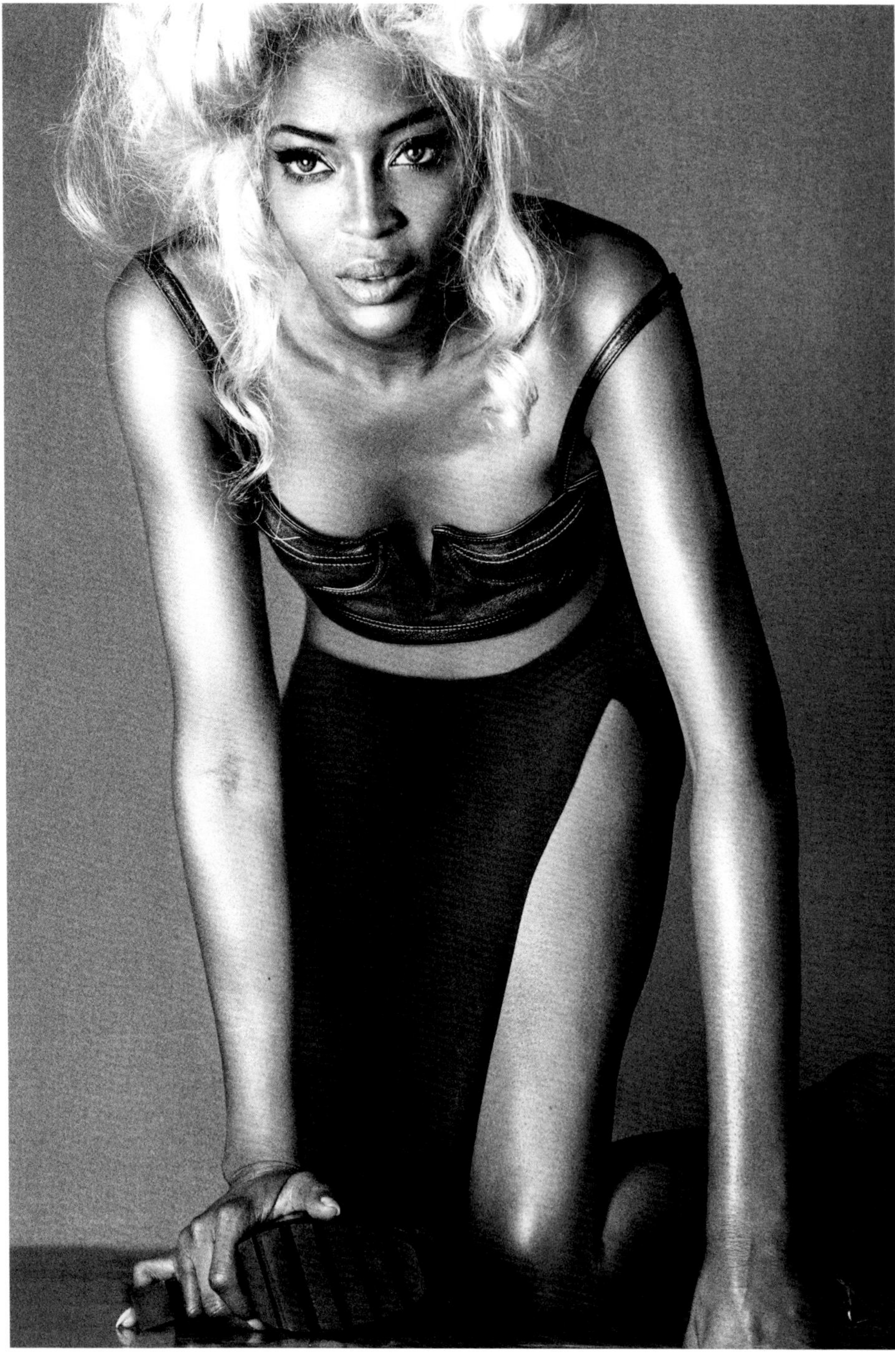

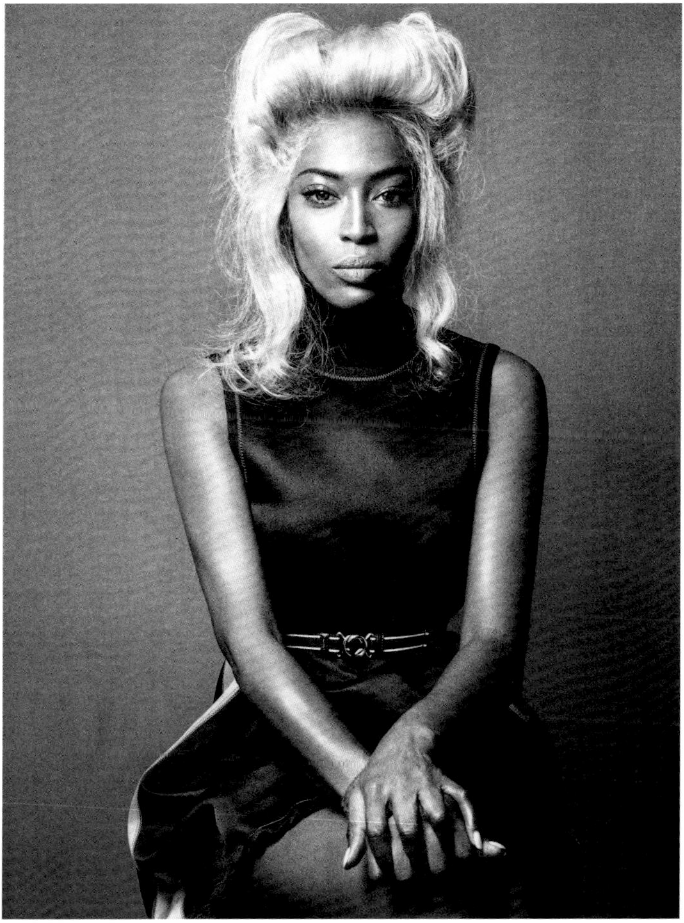

Steven Klein, 2016

(Opposite & Following Spread) **Steven Meisel, 2022**

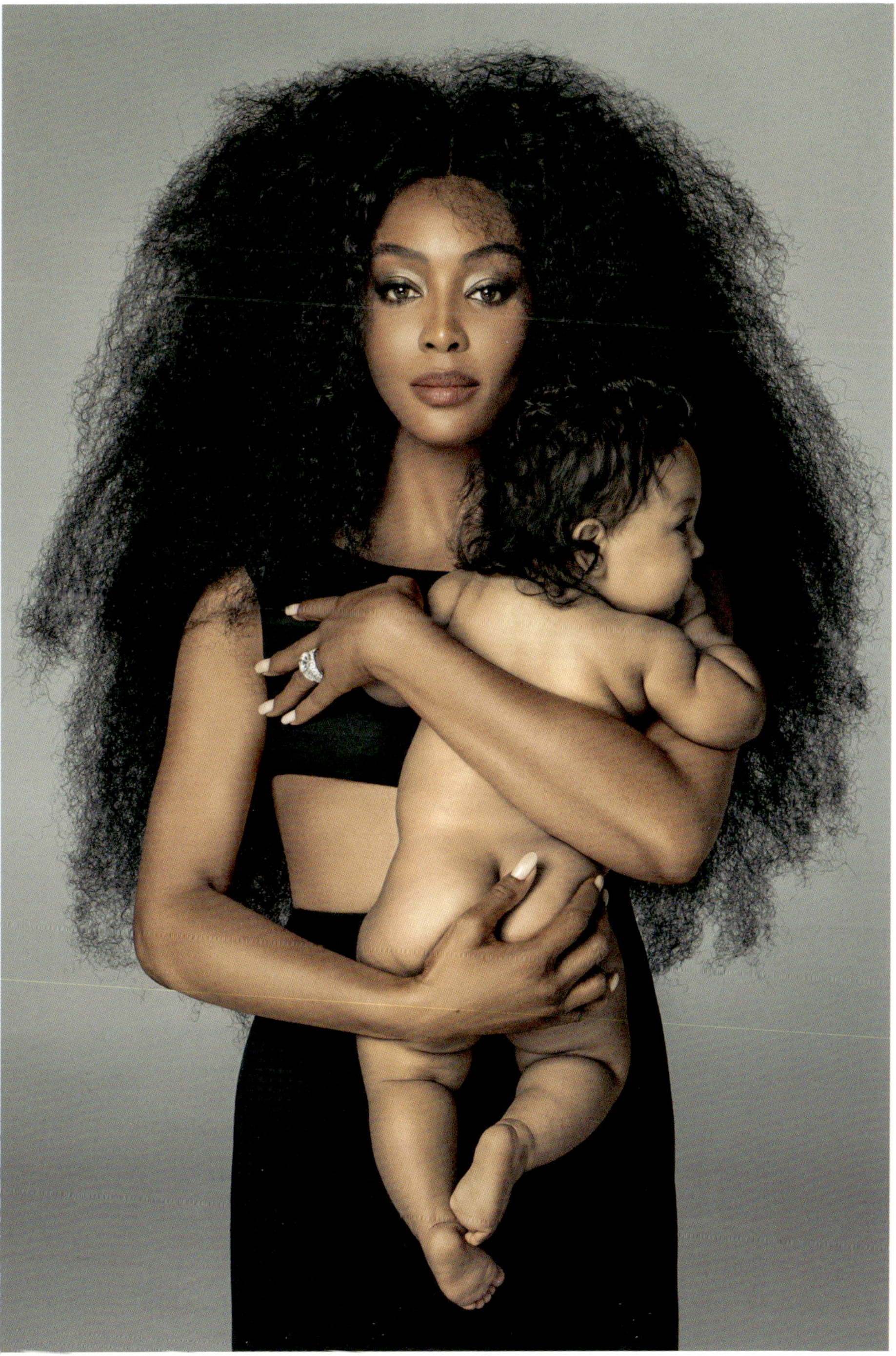

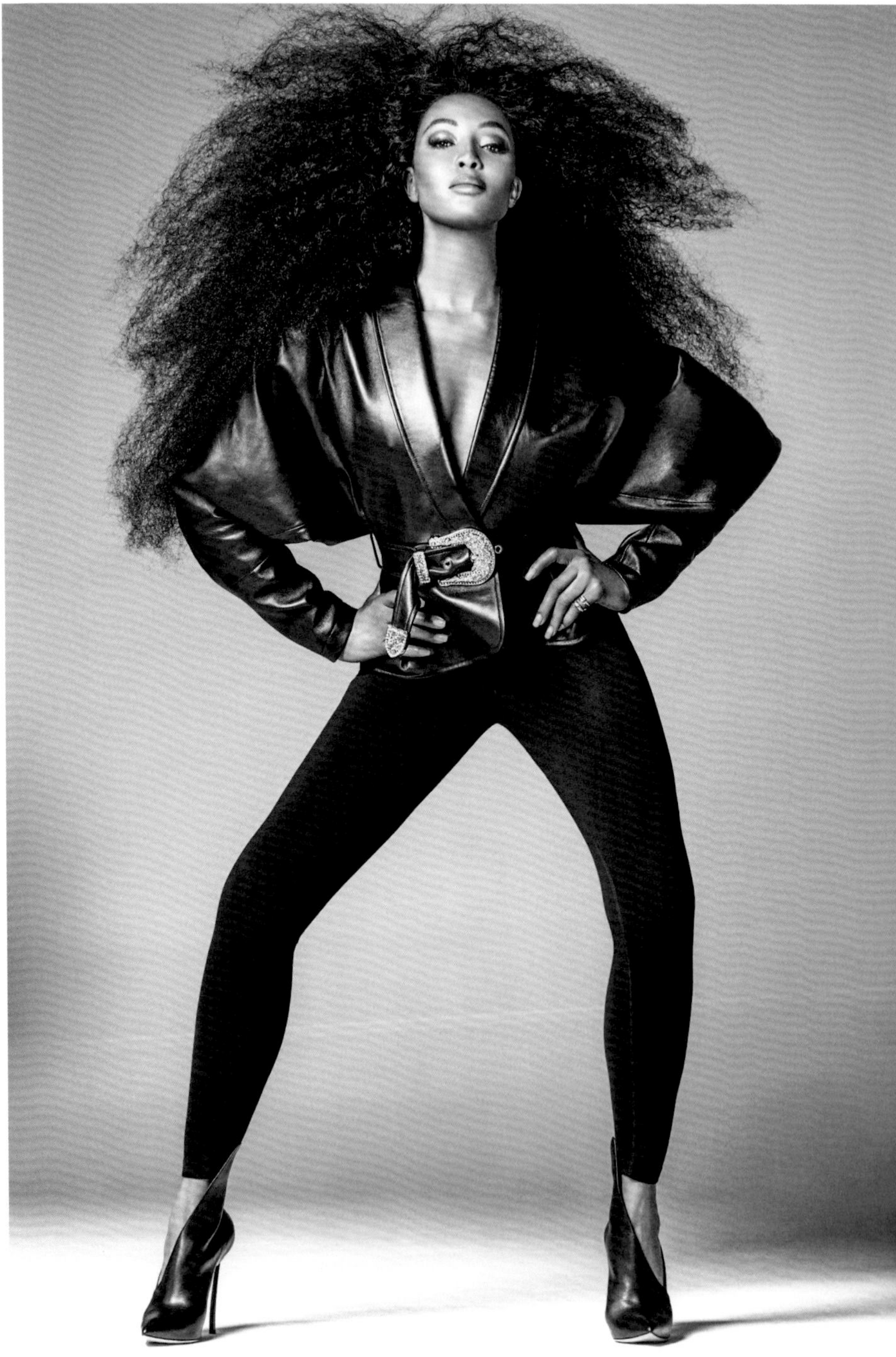

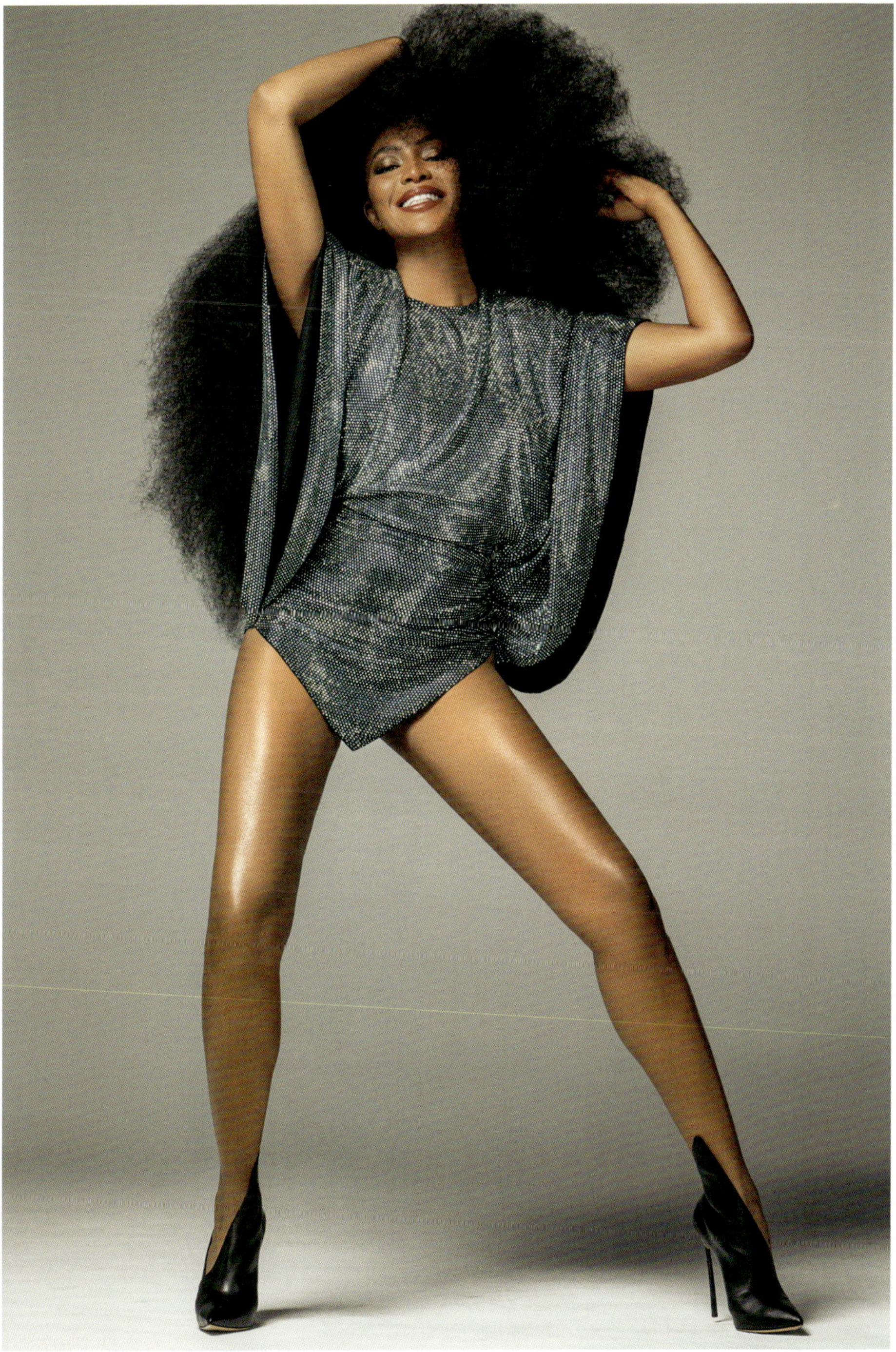

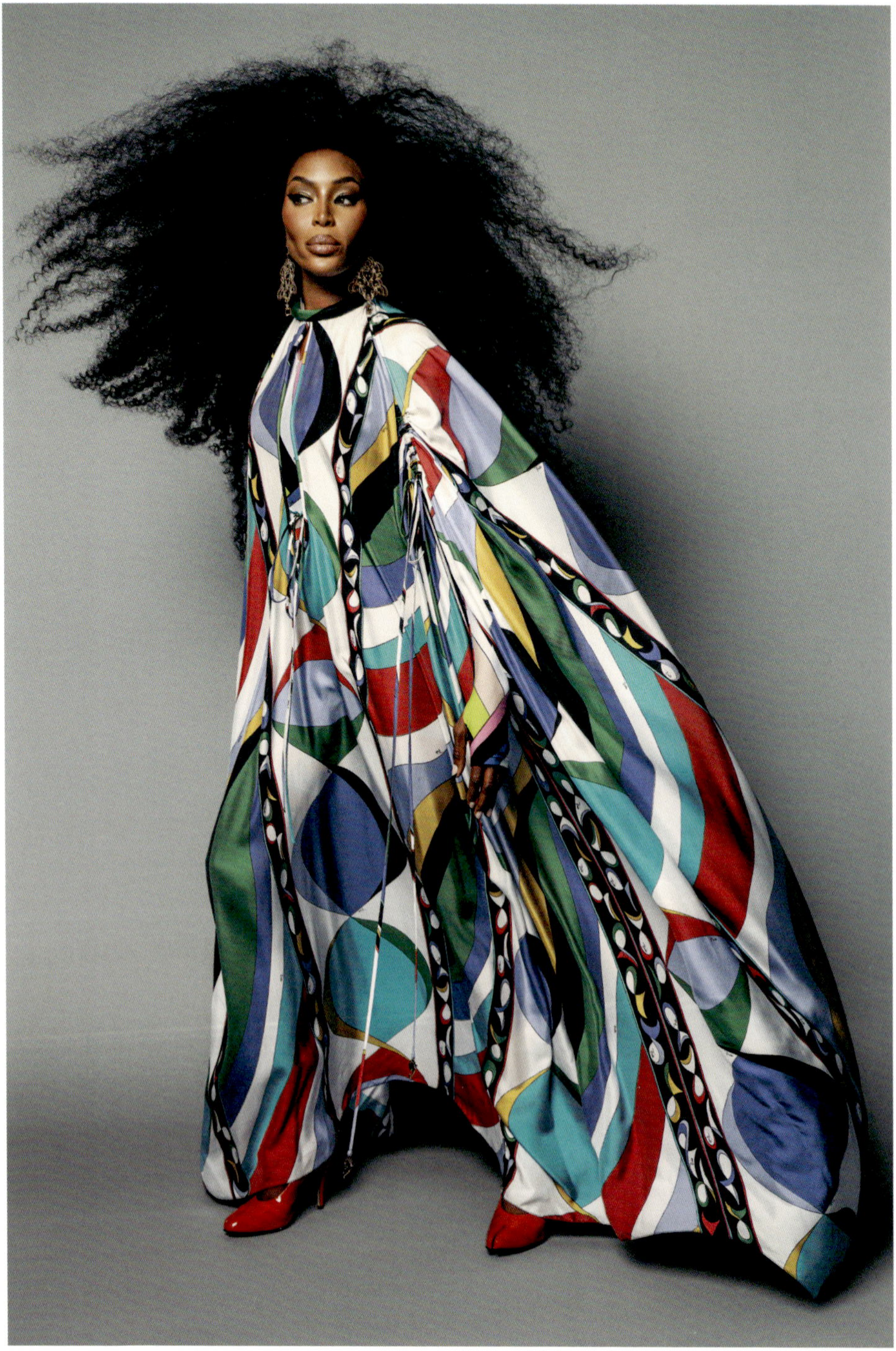

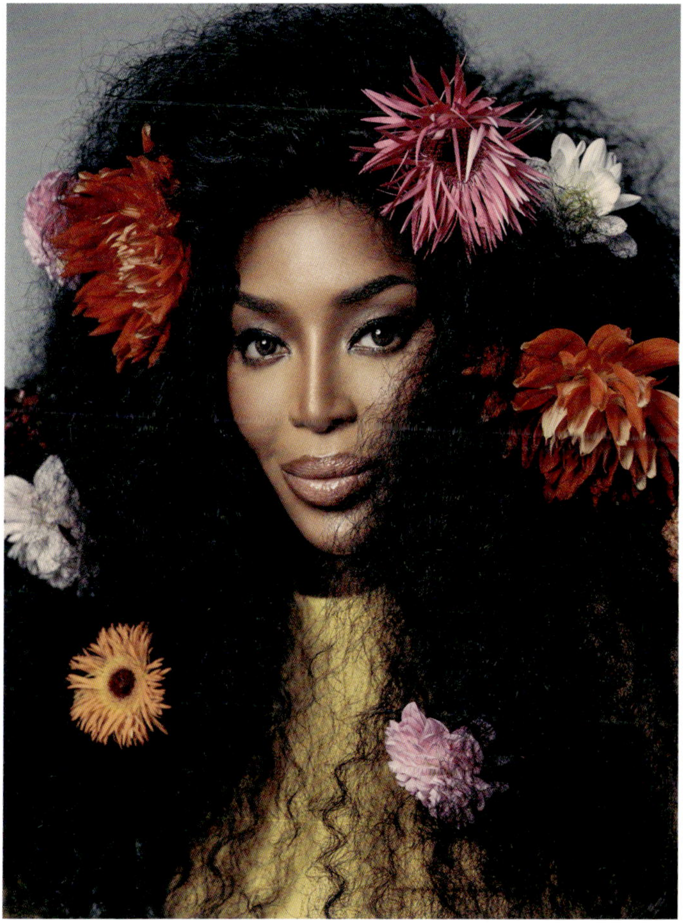

Leslie Zhang, 2023

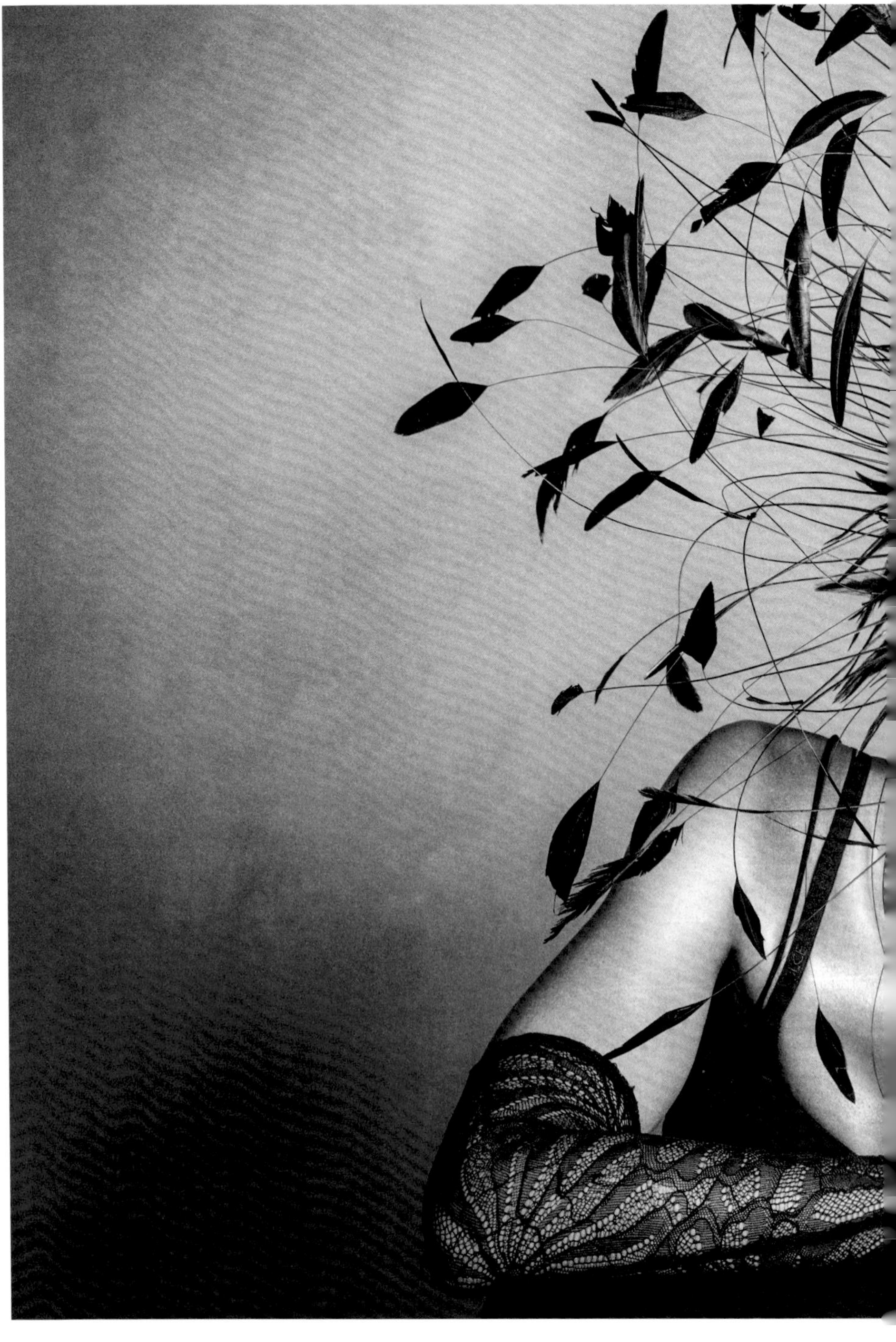

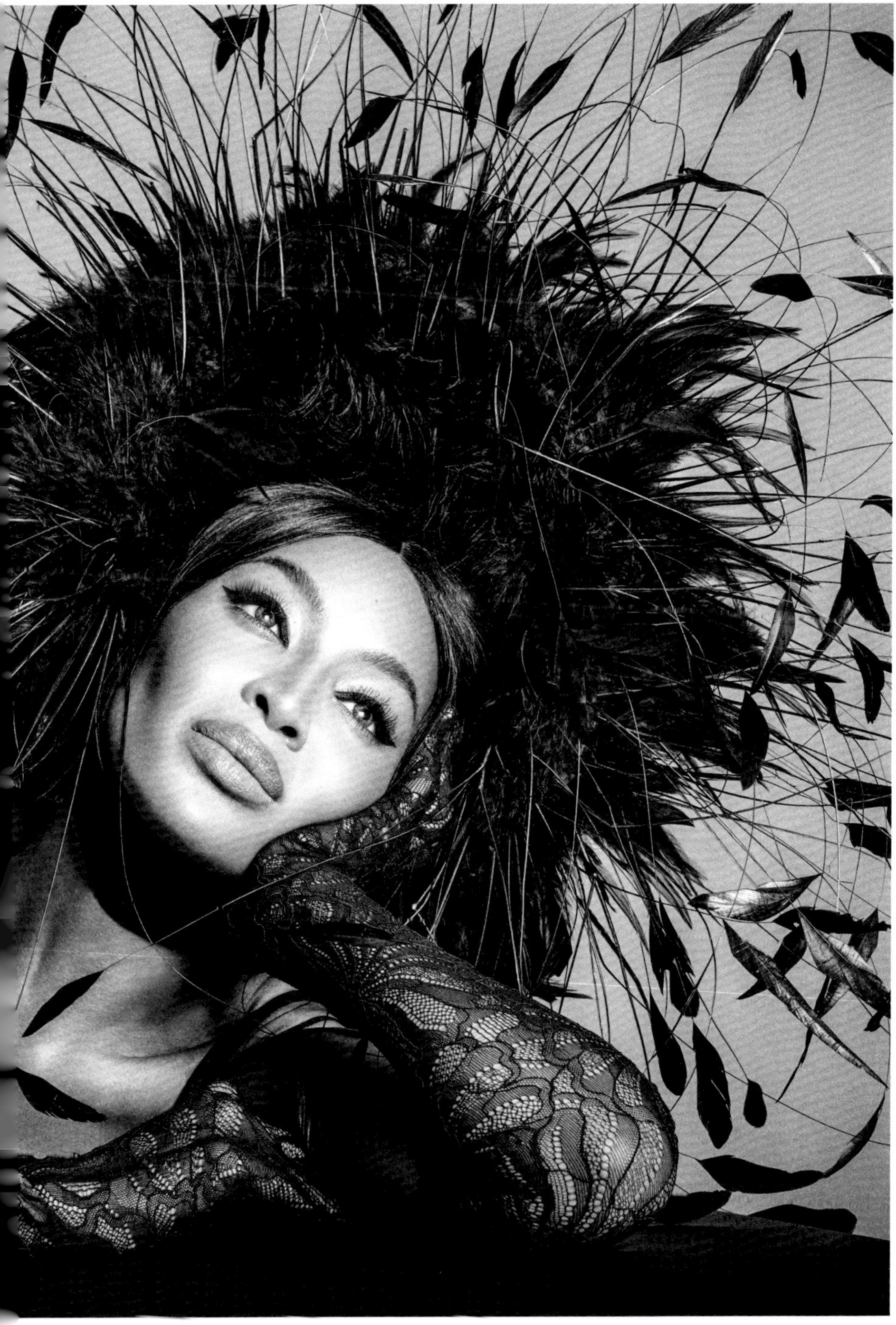

(Previous Spread & Opposite) **Luigi & Iango, 2023**

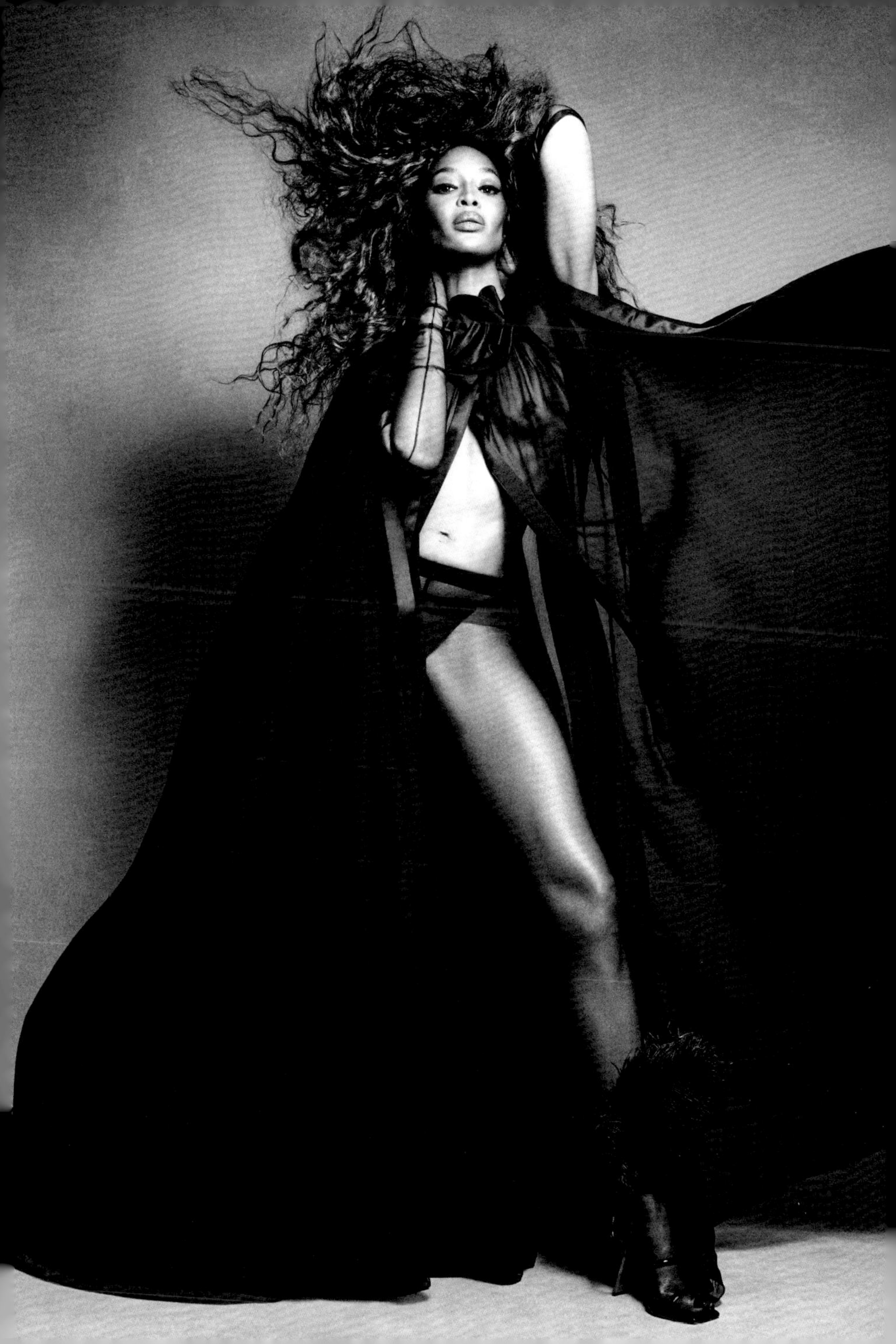

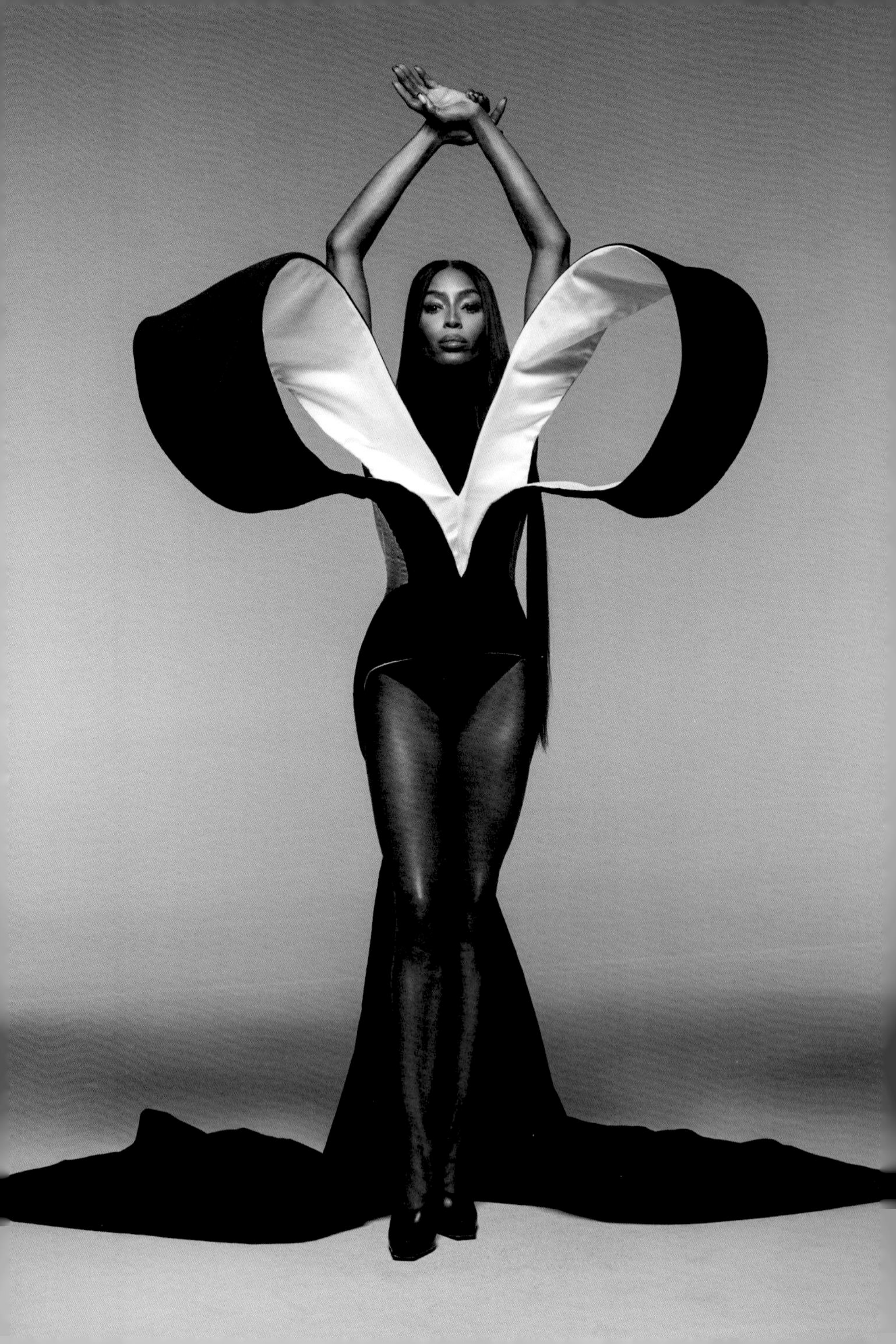

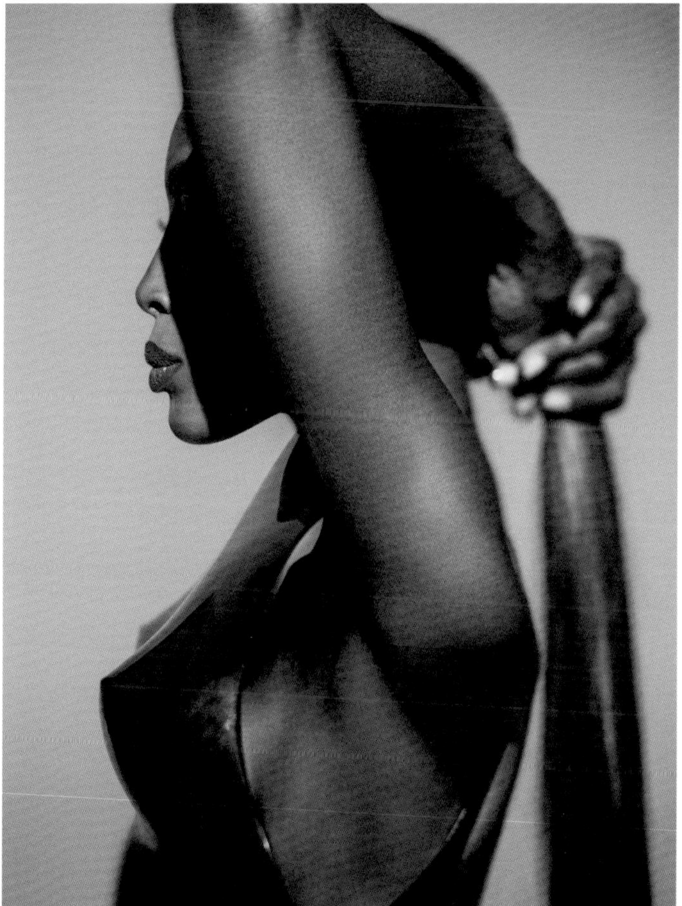

Nick Knight, 2024

Sølve Sundsbø, 2024

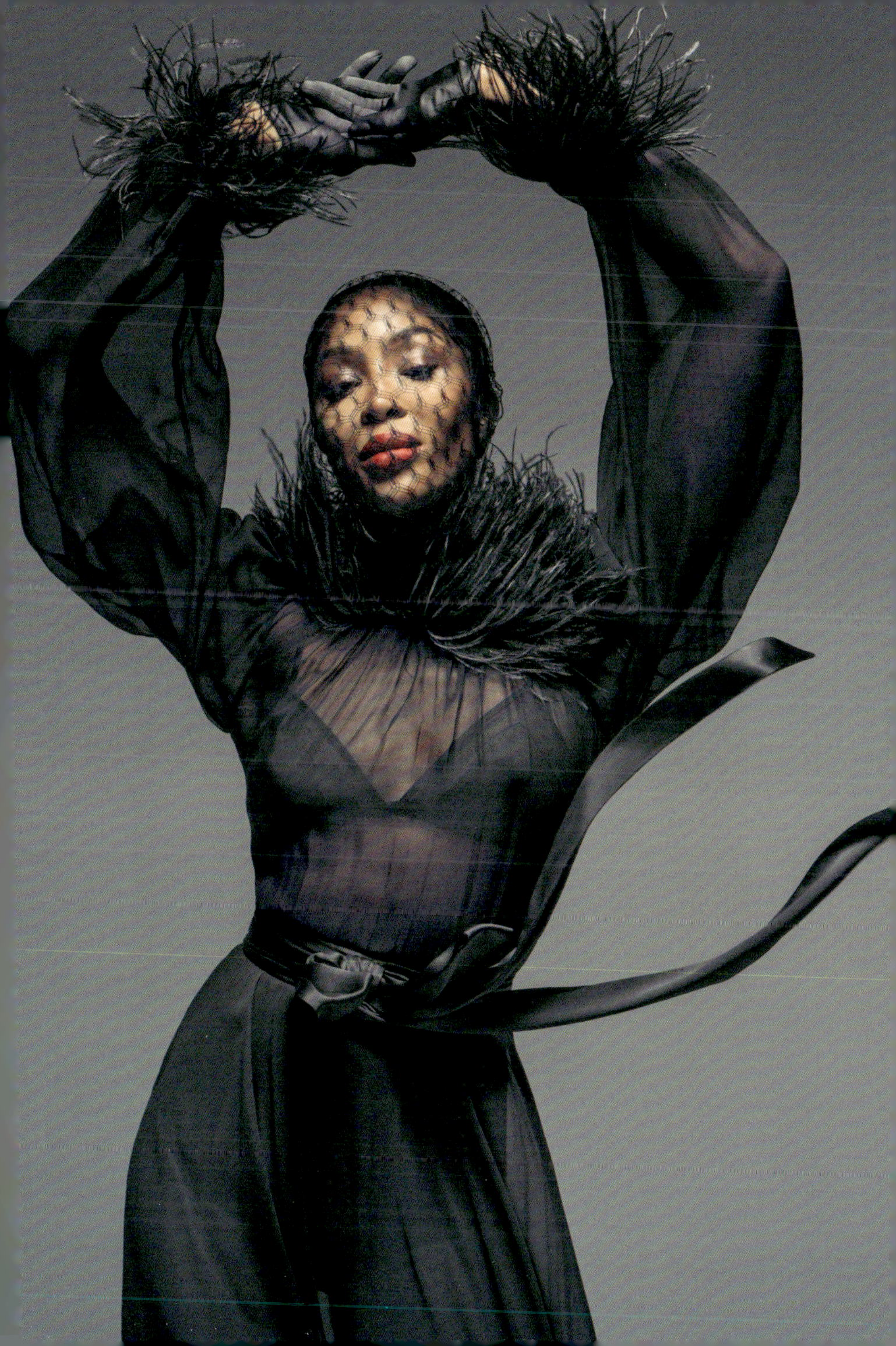

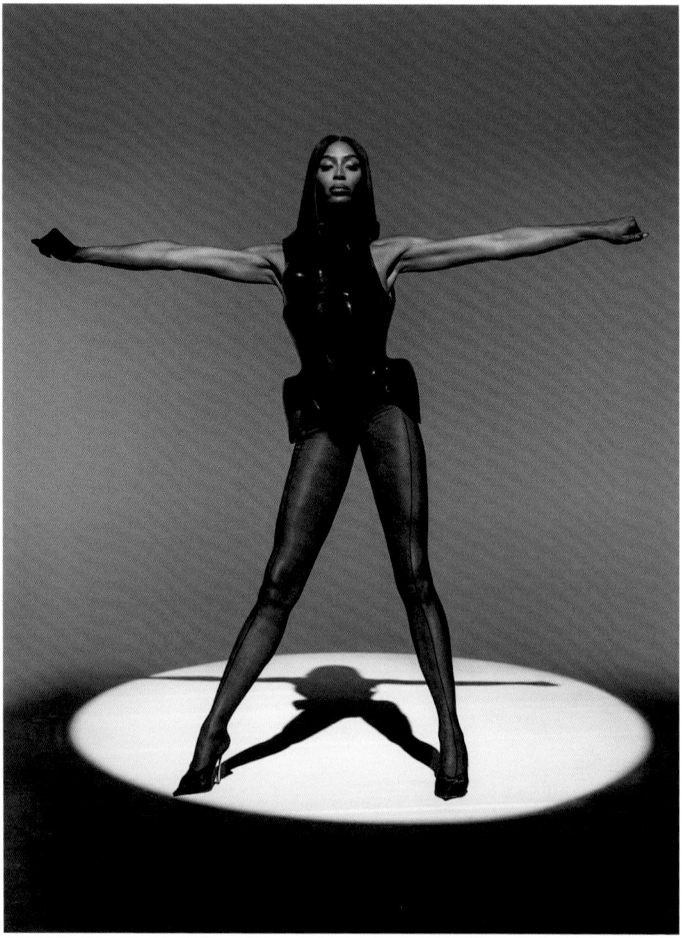

Nick Knight, 2024

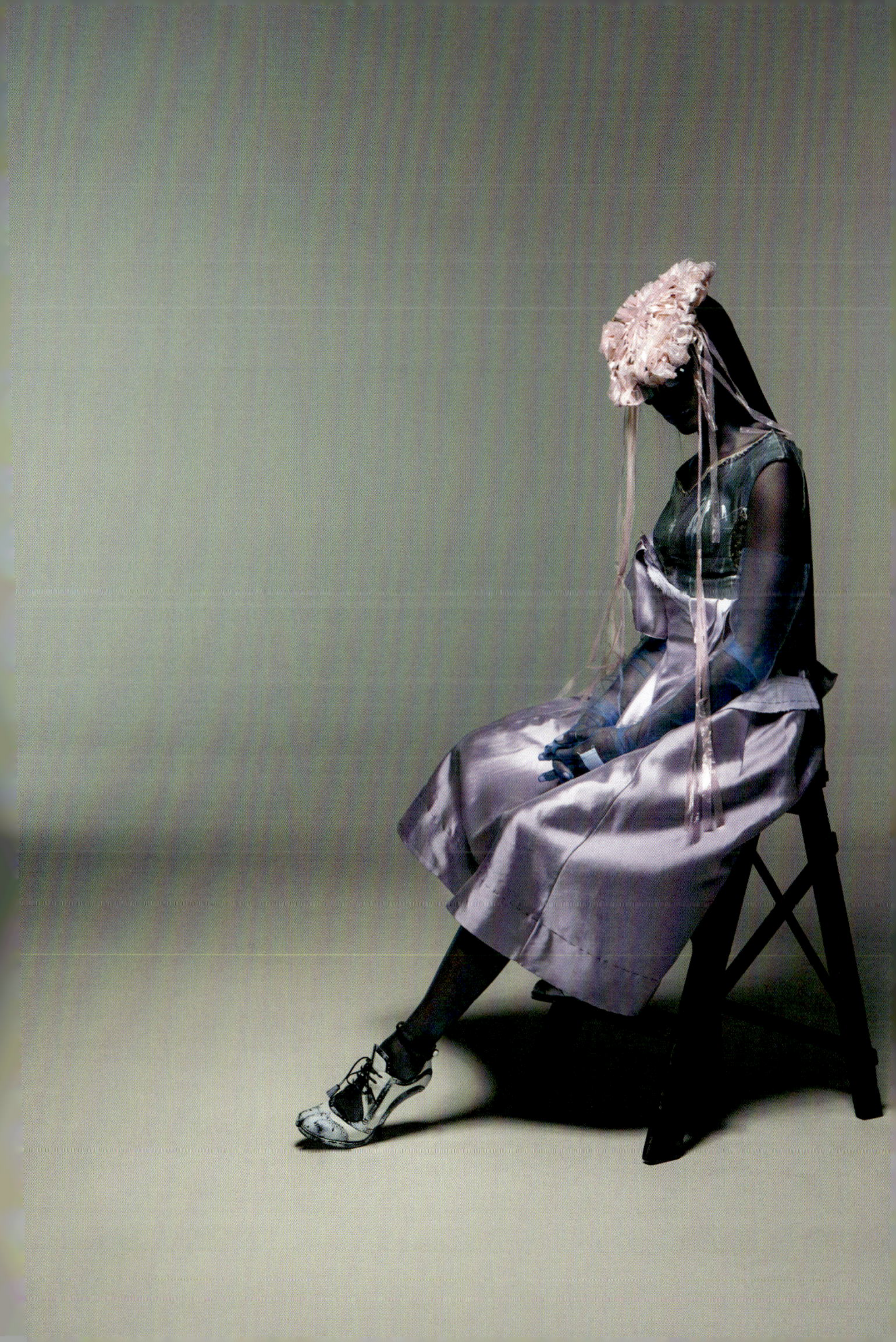

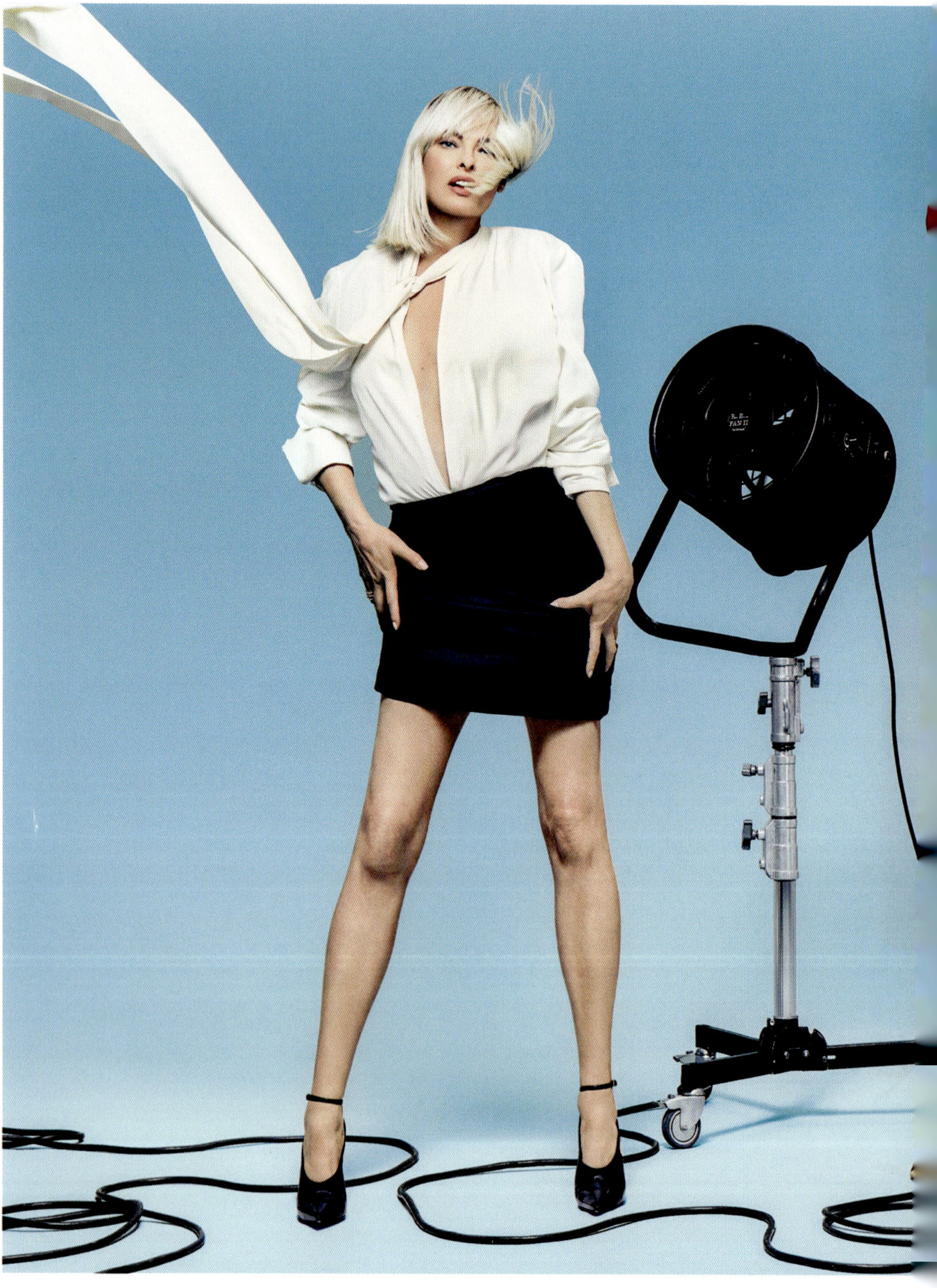

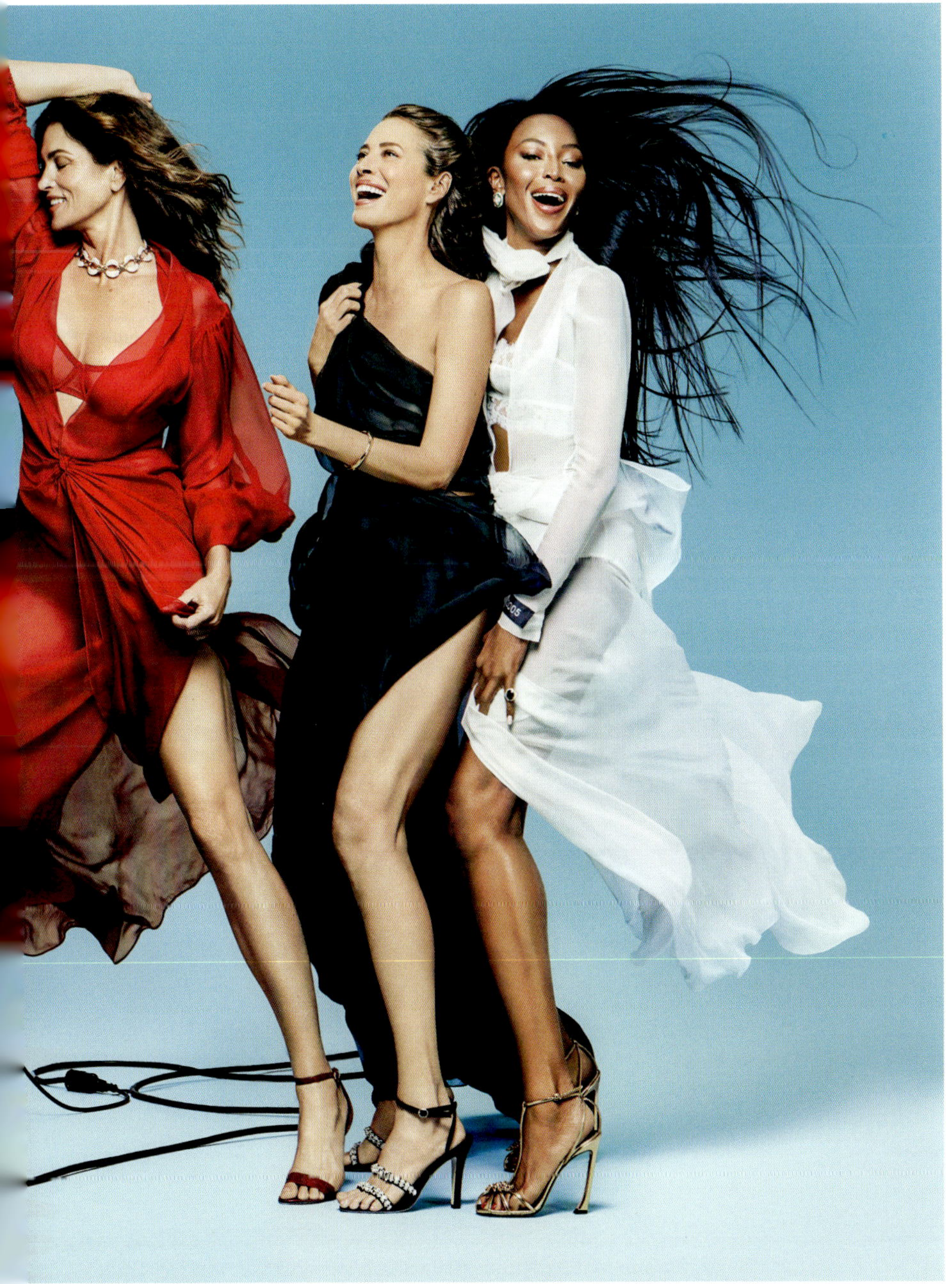

SHE IS CONNECTED TO EVERYBODY.

LINDA EVANGELISTA

(Previous Spread & Opposite) **Rafael Pavarotti, 2023**

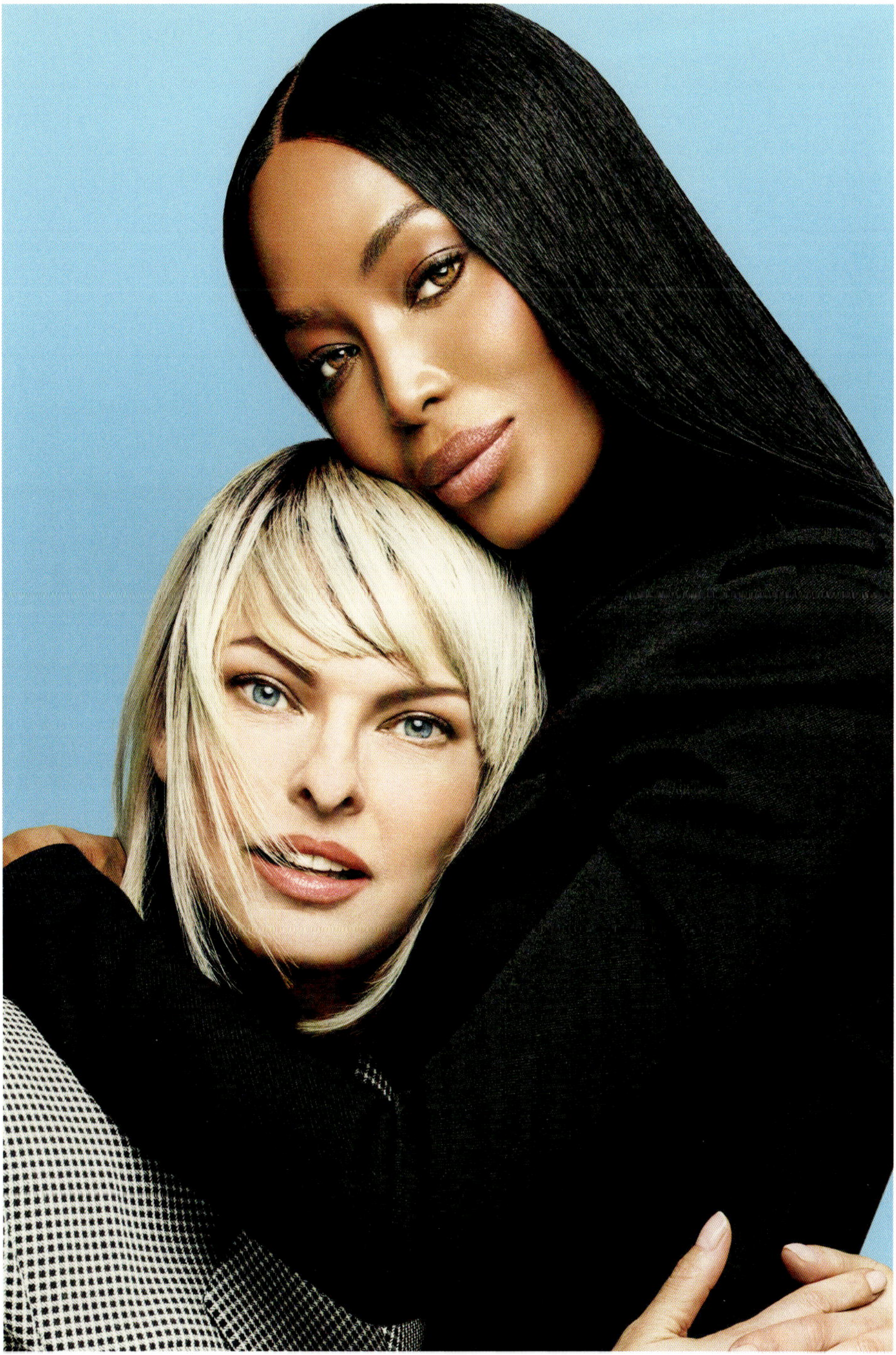

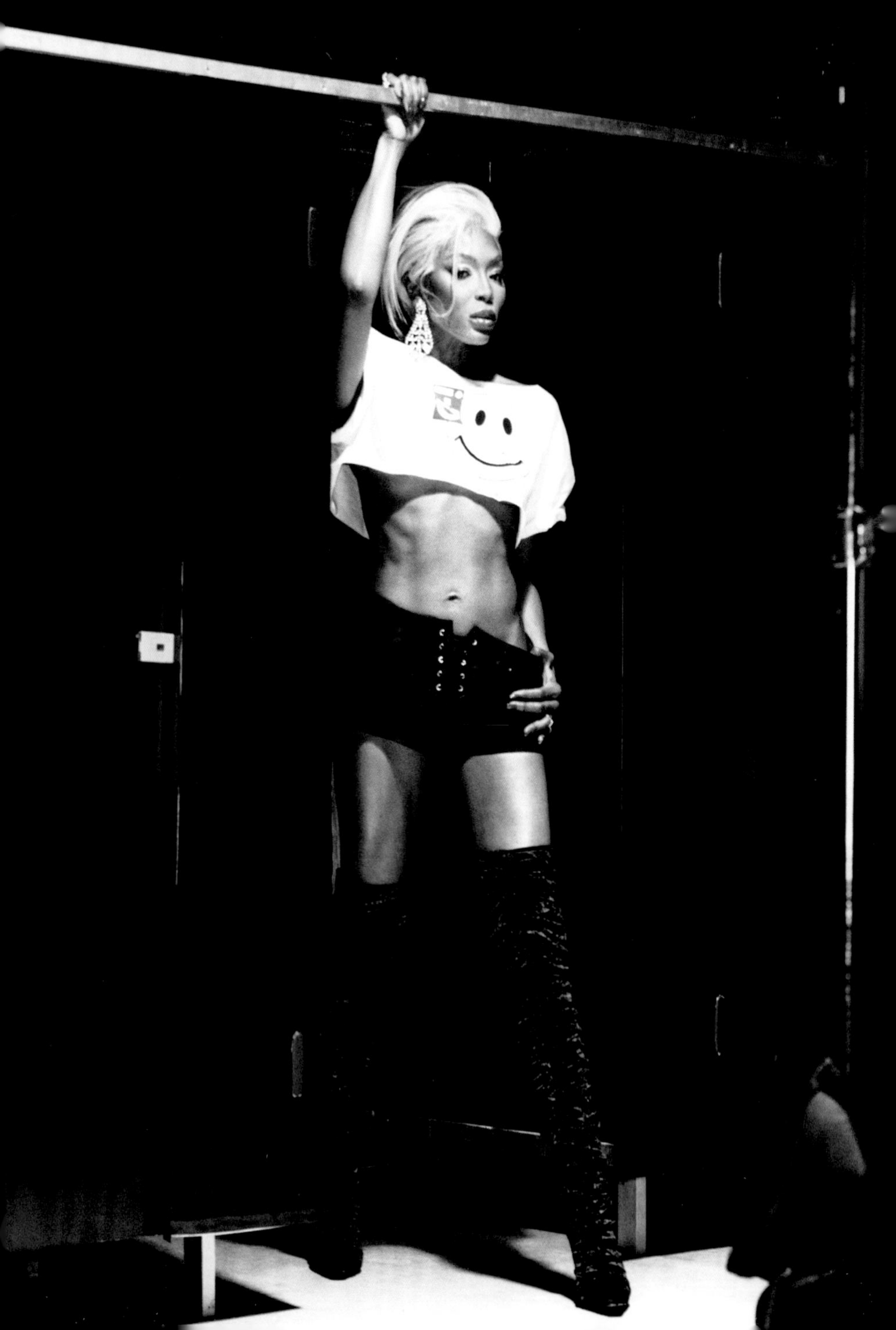

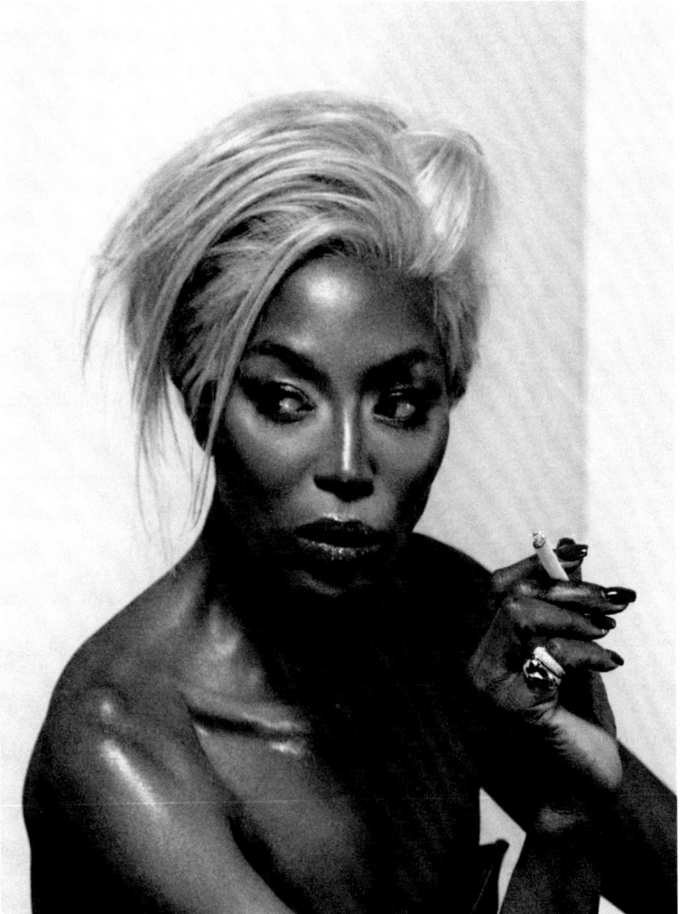

Thibaut Grevet, 2025

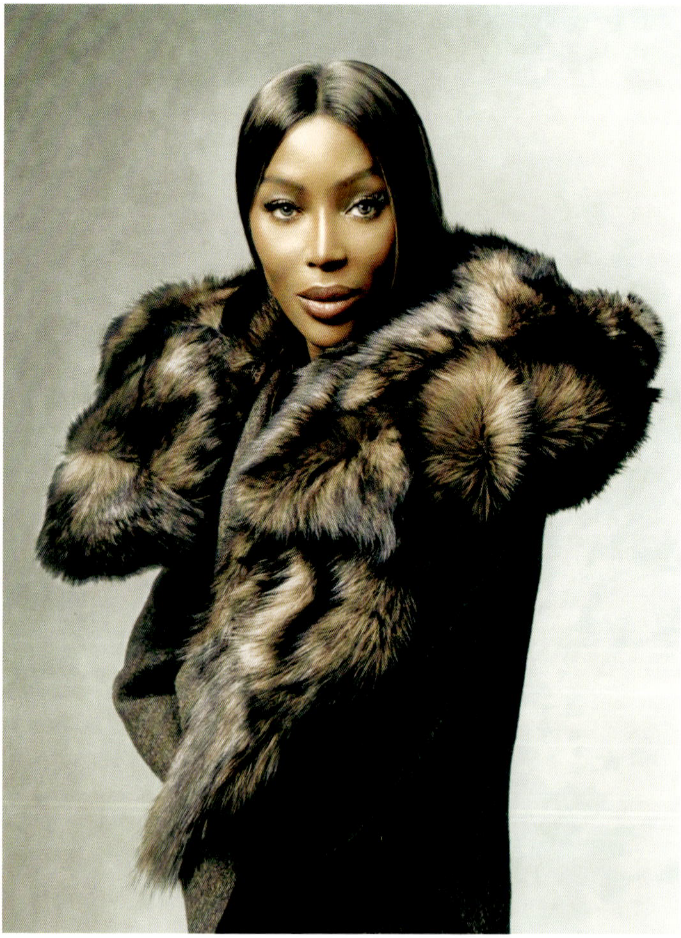

MAR + VIN, 2025

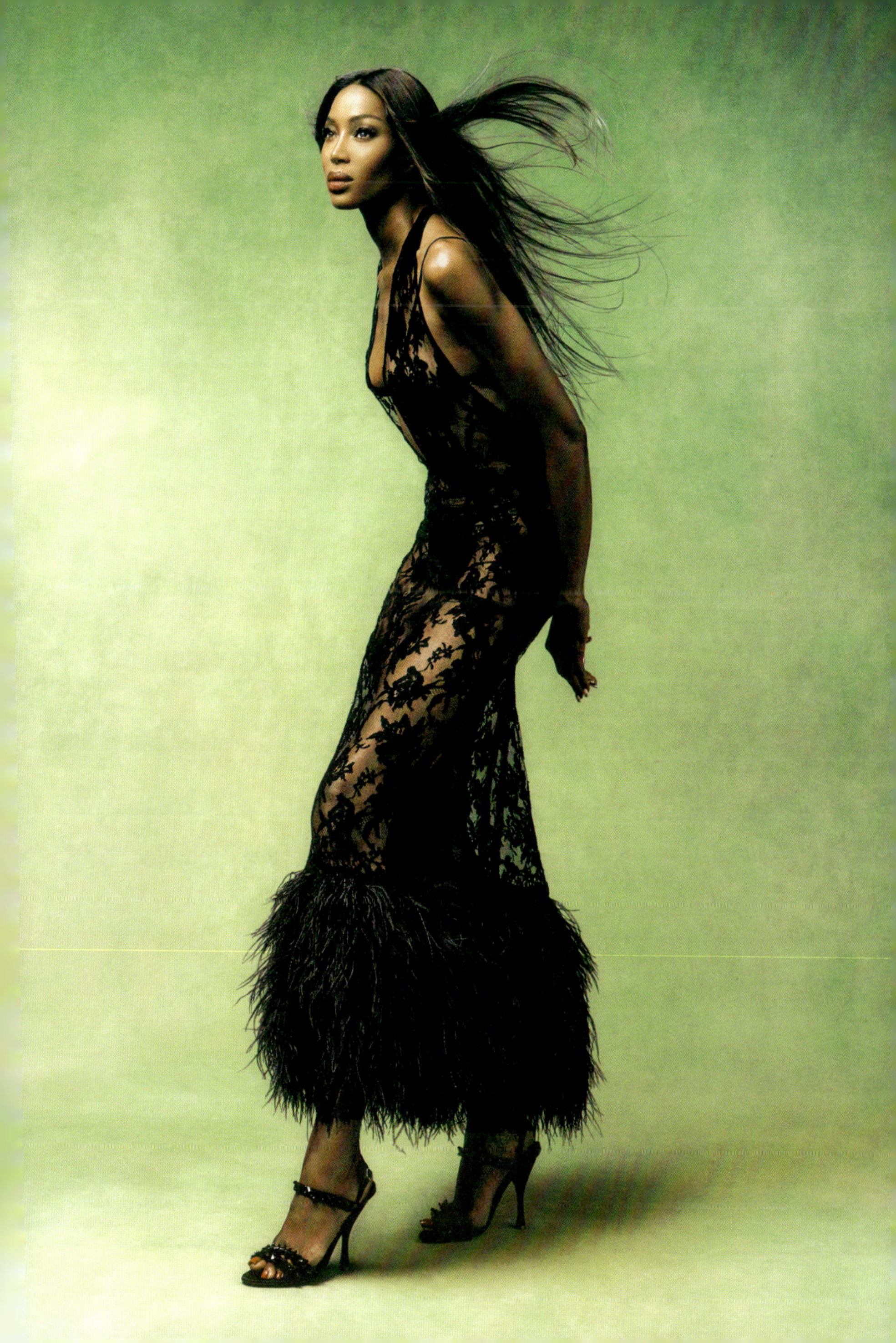

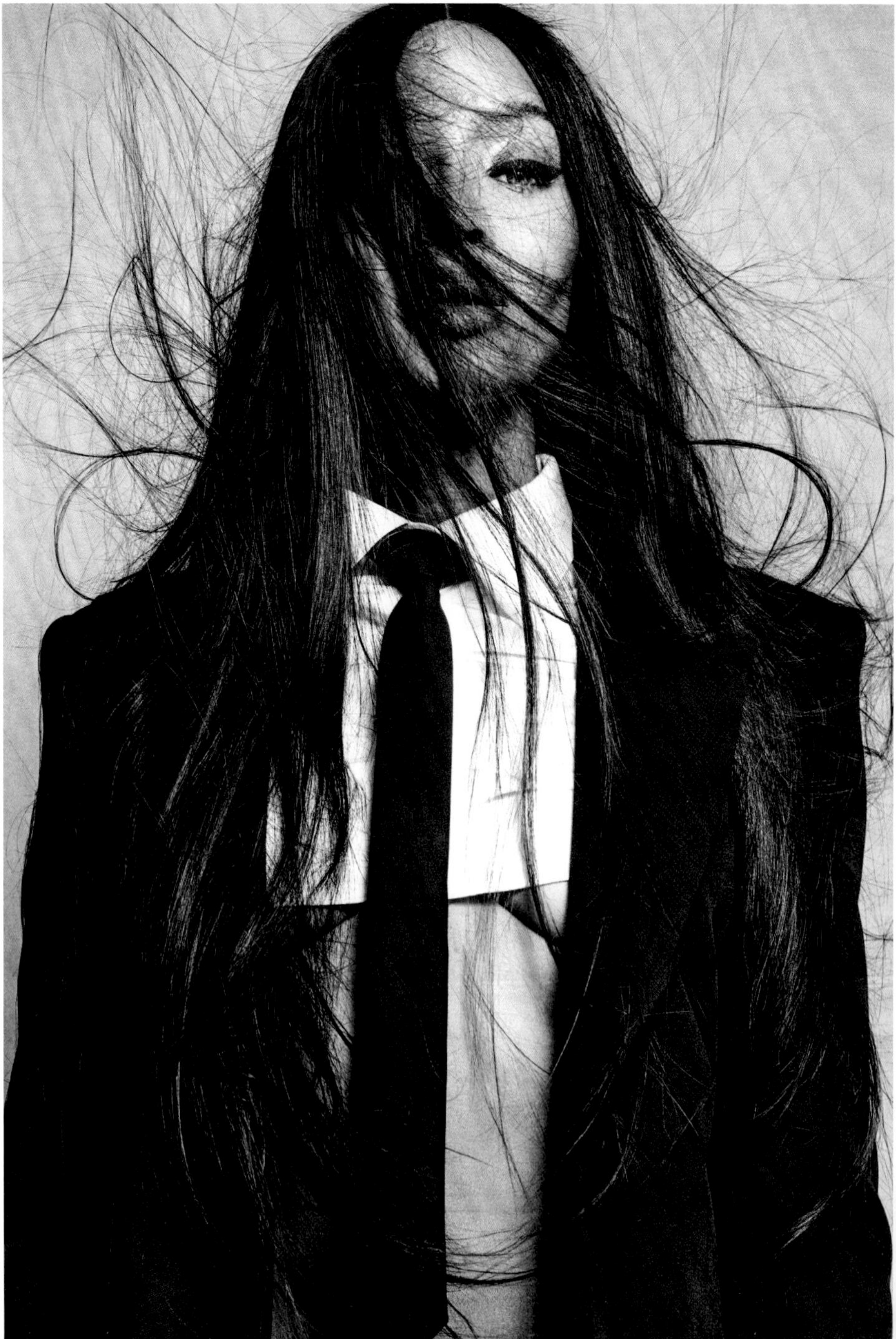

PHOTO CREDITS

@ Cuneyt Akeroglu: 155
© Natalia Alaverdian: 142, 143
© The Richard Avedon Foundation: 66
© Gilles Bensimon: 88, 89
© Martin Brading: 4, 5
© Anton Corbijn: 64, 65, 69
© Terence Donovan Archive: 2
© Arthur Elgort / Trunk Archive: 7
© Sebastian Faena: 115
© Jean-Paul Goude: 126/127
© Thibaut Grevet: 186, 187
© Simon Harris: 107
© Steven Klein / Trunk Archive: 164, 165
© Nick Knight / Trunk Archive: 137, 176, 177, 180, 181
© David LaChapelle: 84, 86/87
© Laspata DeCaro: 108, 109
© Thierry Le Gouès: 50, 51
© Peter Lindbergh Foundation: 11, 12, 14, 15, 16, 17, 32/33, 34, 44, 45, 52, 55, 56, 57, 58/59, 74/75, 94/95, 106, 156/157, 159
© Luigi & Iango: 145, 172/173, 175, 190
© Edward (Maxey) Mapplethorpe: 30
© MAR+VIN: 188, 189
© Steven Meisel / Art + Commerce: 20/21, 22, 23, 61, 112/113, 160/161, 163, 167, 168, 169
© Mert Alas and Marcus Piggott / Courtesy art partner: front cover, 92/93, 99, 100, 101, 102, 103, 120/121, 122, 123, 133, 134, 135, 140/141, 148, 149, back cover
© Tom Munro: 124
© Tom Munro / Trunk Archive: 146, 147
© François Nars: 129
© Helmut Newton Foundation / Trunk Archive: 78/79, 81
© Gui Paganini: 153
© Rafael Pavarotti / Art + Commerce: 182/183, 185
© Pierre et Gilles: 73
© Herb Ritts / Trunk Archive: 28, 31, 38, 39, 40, 49
© Paolo Roversi / Art + Commerce: 70, 71
© Mario Sorrenti / Courtesy art partner: 105, 111
© Emma Summerton / Trunk Archive: 138, 139
© Sølve Sundsbø / Art + Commerce: 179
© Mario Testino / Courtesy art partner: 77, 90, 91, 116/117, 119
© Ellen von Unwerth / Trunk Archive: 37, 46, 47, 62, 82/83, 96, 130/131, 150/151
© Max Vadukul: 43
© Albert Watson: 8
© Bruce Weber: 18, 25, 26, 27
© Leslie Zhang: 170, 171

Luigi & Iango, 2023

EACH AND EVERY
TASCHEN BOOK PLANTS A SEED!

Each year, we offset our annual carbon emissions with carbon credits at the Instituto Terra, a reforestation program in Minas Gerais, Brazil, founded by Lélia and Sebastião Salgado. To find out more about this ecological partnership, please check: www.taschen.com/institutoterra.
Inspiration: unlimited. Carbon footprint: (almost) zero.

Hohenzollernring 53, 50672 Köln, Germany
www.taschen.com

Original edition published in 2016
Edited by Naomi Campbell, London/New York, and Bethann Hardison, New York

Cover Mert Alas & Marcus Piggott, 2013

ISBN 978-3-7544-0023-4
Printed in Italy